Mysteries from
Baseball's Past

ALSO EDITED BY DAVID CICOTELLO
AND ANGELO J. LOUISA

*Forbes Field: Essays and Memories of the
Pirates' Historic Ballpark, 1909–1971*
(McFarland, 2007)

Mysteries from Baseball's Past

Investigations of Nine Unsettled Questions

EDITED BY ANGELO J. LOUISA
AND DAVID CICOTELLO

Foreword by Troy Soos

McFarland & Company, Inc., Publishers
Jefferson, North Carolina, and London

LIBRARY OF CONGRESS CATALOGUING-IN-PUBLICATION DATA

Mysteries from baseball's past : investigations of nine unsettled questions / edited by Angelo J. Louisa and David Cicotello ; foreword by Troy Soos.
    p.   cm.
Includes bibliographical references and index.

ISBN 978-0-7864-4554-7
softcover : 50# alkaline paper ∞

1. Baseball — United States — History.   I. Louisa, Angelo Joseph.   II. Cicotello, David, 1953–
GV863.A1M97   2010
796.357 — dc22   2010022440

British Library cataloguing data are available

© 2010 Angelo J. Louisa and David Cicotello. All rights reserved

No part of this book may be reproduced or transmitted in any form or by any means, electronic or mechanical, including photocopying or recording, or by any information storage and retrieval system, without permission in writing from the publisher.

Front cover: Eddie Cicotte (Library of Congress); Leroy Robert "Satchel" Paige and Charles Sylvester "Chick" Stahl (both National Baseball Hall of Fame Library, Cooperstown, New York); background image ©2010 Shutterstock

Manufactured in the United States of America

McFarland & Company, Inc., Publishers
  Box 611, Jefferson, North Carolina 28640
  www.mcfarlandpub.com

In memory of my mother-in-law,
Mary Faye Field Acre,
who couldn't have cared less about baseball,
but who loved a good mystery.
Angelo J. Louisa

To my daughter, Camille,
whose passion for sports
is both a delight and a mystery to me.
David Cicotello

Contents

Acknowledgments	ix
Foreword by Troy Soos	1
Introduction: When the National Pastime Meets a Good Mystery	
ANGELO J. LOUISA AND DAVID CICOTELLO	5
1. Delahanty's Disappearance: Where Is the King of Swatsville?	
JERROLD CASWAY	13
2. The Suicide of Chick Stahl	
DENNIS H. AUGER	29
3. The Strange Death of Harry C. Pulliam	
ANGELO J. LOUISA AND FLOYD SULLIVAN	44
4. In Search of Wilbur Cooper and Pete Alexander's 1–0 Game	
DAVID CICOTELLO	76
5. The Mysterious Mr. Cicotte	
GENE CARNEY	90
6. The O'Connell-Dolan Affair: Scandal or Hoax?	
DANIEL E. GINSBURG	108
7. Unraveling the Cobb-Speaker Scandal	
TIMOTHY M. GAY	120
8. Satch vs. Josh: The Showdown in Shadow Ball	
DAVID C. OGDEN	136

Contents

9. The Brooklyn Dodgers, the Move to Los Angeles,
   and the Search for Villains: Was Walter O'Malley
   a Bum, a Victim, or Something Else?
   ROBERT TRUMPBOUR   149

Editors and Contributors   185
Index   187

Acknowledgments

Just as Sherlock Holmes had Dr. Watson to assist him in his adventures, we had the following people who assisted us in the production of this book:

Greg Beston, who clarified a matter concerning a paper that he had submitted to the Society for American Baseball Research.

Eileen Canepari, membership services associate, Society for American Baseball Research, who sent us reels of microfilm in a timely fashion.

Louis Cicotello, who listened to his brother's progress reports on the book and designed the collage that appears in the introduction.

Pat Ervin, Fountain Creek Dezign Works, who created the key illustration for Louis Cicotello's collage.

Anna Louisa, who proofread most of the chapters of the manuscript and offered invaluable editing advice and who believes that Samuel Kingston played a bigger role in Ed Delahanty's death than he admitted.

Pamela Louisa, who graciously aided us with proofreading, editing, and indexing and who put up with Angelo Louisa while doing so.

Andy McCue, president of the Society for American Baseball Research and chairperson of its Bibliography Committee, who sent us statistics on the annual number of books on baseball that have been published from 1838 to 2008.

Marian McDonald, who compiled the first draft of the index.

John Schneiderman, formerly of Criss Library, University of Nebraska at Omaha, who facilitated multiple requests for interlibrary loan materials.

Troy Soos, the master mystery writer, who took time from his busy schedule to contribute a thoughtful foreword for our book.

Floyd Sullivan, who not only co-authored a chapter for the book but spent a considerable amount of time doing research at the Chicago History Museum to help us check and edit Gene Carney's chapter.

Acknowledgments

Lucy Sullivan, who assisted Floyd Sullivan with the research that he did at the Chicago History Museum.

Stephanie Viola, Criss Library, University of Nebraska at Omaha, who picked up from where John Schneiderman left off in facilitating our requests for interlibrary loan materials.

All the people who joined us in authoring or co-authoring chapters for the book: Dennis H. Auger, the late Gene Carney, Jerrold Casway, Timothy M. Gay, the late Daniel E. Ginsburg, David C. Ogden, Floyd Sullivan, and Robert Trumpbour.

All the people who assisted us and/or offered us advice in determining how many books have been published on particular sports: Judy Anghelescu, collection development librarian, Omaha Public Library; Joanne Ferguson Cavanaugh, manager, Charles B. Washington Branch of the Omaha Public Library; David Kelly, reference librarian, Library of Congress; Myron J. "Jack" Smith, Jr., professor of library science and history and director of Garland Library, Tusculum College; and John Thorn.

All the people who found or attempted to find newspaper articles and/or other materials to help us proofread the manuscript: Olivia L. Bravo, special collections librarian, Kanawha County Public Library; Robert Cochran; Ryan Kunhart; Daniel Levitt; Gabriel Schechter; Ronald M. Selter; Steve Steinberg; Patricia Sullivan; William Wagner; Catherine Smythe Zajc; and John Zajc, executive director, Society for American Baseball Research.

All the people who aided us in acquiring photographs or other visual material: Dennis H. and Elaine Auger obtained a photograph of the late Dick Thompson and helped us with the search for an image of the West Baden Springs Hotel; Jerrold Casway contributed a contemporary photograph of the International Bridge for his chapter; Douglas W. DeCroix, editor of the Western New York Heritage Press, handled our request for a vintage picture of the International Bridge from that organization; Paul Hogroian, photo duplication services, Library of Congress, facilitated the acquisition of images from the nation's oldest federal cultural institution; Pat Kelly, photo archivist at the National Baseball Hall of Fame Library, always responded quickly to our numerous inquiries regarding subjects in the library's photograph collection and supplied us with the largest quantity of images (29!) for the book; Larry Lester, historian and author, provided us with a photograph of Jewbaby Floyd; Susan Sutton, coordinator of

Acknowledgments

visual reference services, Indiana Historical Society, conscientiously searched the society's photograph collection and selected the best image of the West Baden Springs Hotel for our book; Barbara Thompson graciously shared a photograph of her late husband, baseball historian Dick Thompson, and granted us permission to use it; and Erin Tikovitsch, rights and reproductions, Chicago History Museum, expedited our order for a photograph of Ed Delahanty.

And all the people who provided encouragement while we worked on the manuscript: Olivia L. Bravo, Sarah Case, Arthur D. Hittner, Ryan Kunhart, Anna Louisa, Pamela Louisa, Elizabeth Price, Brent J. Ruswick, and Mike Sowell.

Angelo J. Louisa *and* David Cicotello

Foreword
by Troy Soos

Baseball has provided the inspiration for novels, poetry, plays, songs, movies, and television. Some of these works have been entirely fictional, but others have incorporated actual events and people from the game's rich history into their plots. Bernard Malamud's 1952 novel *The Natural*, for example, was partly based on the shooting of Philadelphia Phillies first baseman Eddie Waitkus by an obsessed fan. The movie *Field of Dreams* (adapted from W. P. Kinsella's *Shoeless Joe*) memorably includes Joe Jackson and other members of the 1919 White Sox.

Every form of drama requires characters in situations of conflict. Starting nearly with the beginning of the game itself, baseball has had a wealth of both shady characters and intense conflicts. As early as 1865, while baseball was still ostensibly an amateur game, three New York Mutual players were expelled for crooked play which was euphemistically termed "willful and designed inattention" (this was not the club's only scandal, perhaps not surprising since it was financed in part by Tammany Hall's spectacularly corrupt Boss Tweed). In 1877, the National League's second season, four players from the Louisville team received lifetime bans for conspiring with gamblers to throw games. Five years later, Richard Higham became the first and only major league umpire to be banned, also for fixing games.

Corruption was not the only misconduct to afflict early baseball. As the 19th century progressed, the last vestiges of a gentleman's game disappeared and violence often marred the sport. During the 1890s, as exemplified by pugnacious teams such as Ned Hanlon's Baltimore Orioles and Patsy Tebeau's Cleveland Spiders, hard play sometimes turned into outright assault. Tragically, the increase in brutality resulted in more than one death:

in separate incidents, two minor league umpires were killed on the field of play by enraged bat-wielding players. Off the field, baseball players were involved in murder and mayhem as well. Perhaps the most tragic case was that of Marty Bergen: after the 1899 season, the mentally disturbed Boston catcher killed his entire family before taking his own life.

Throughout baseball history, there have been killers and thieves, robber barons and gangsters, drug dealers and gamblers. Battles have raged between penurious owners and indentured players, between established leagues and encroaching upstarts, and between zealous fans of rival teams (in one notorious incident, an argument between a Brooklyn Dodger supporter and a New York Giant partisan ended in murder). White racists fought to maintain baseball's color line, aging veterans clashed with young rookies vying for their roster spots, head-hunting pitchers targeted batters, and Ty Cobb battled just about everyone. Baseball, in fact, has had all the villains and heroes, crimes and tragedies, motives and madness necessary for a novelist to weave together a murder mystery.

However, baseball history is so filled with intrigue and suspense that there is really no need to introduce a fictional element at all. As this book convincingly demonstrates, there are real-life mysteries that stand on their own without the help of literary license or Hollywood embellishments.

Scholars and editors Angelo J. Louisa and David Cicotello present nine of the most fascinating baseball mysteries in this work. Any one of these puzzles could provide enough fodder for a novel, but the editors and contributors forgo fiction in favor of meticulous research. The results of their studies prove that historians are every bit as capable at detective work as the private eyes of crime fiction.

Jerrold Casway leads off with a century-old mystery that would frustrate the most intrepid cold case detective: the 1903 death of Ed Delahanty, who had won the American League batting title the previous year and would later be inducted into the Baseball Hall of Fame. Delahanty's body was found at the bottom of Niagara Falls, but how it got there has been a question that has never been resolved.

Psychological and emotional pressures can lead to tragic actions, both in crime fiction and in life. The deaths of Red Sox star Chick Stahl and National League president Harry Pulliam during the first decade of the 20th century are treated here with insight and understanding by Dennis H. Auger, Angelo J. Louisa, and Floyd Sullivan.

Foreword by Troy Soos

Niagara Falls, as illustrated in *The Falls from Prospect Park* (1896) by A. Castaigne. Ed Delahanty's body was found at the bottom of it (Library of Congress, Prints & Photographs Division, Cabinet of American Illustration [LC-USZC4-1448]).

Foreword by Troy Soos

Of course, not all mysteries involve death. Some of the most interesting have involved disappearances of people or objects. But how does a baseball game vanish from history — especially when one of the pitchers is future Hall-of-Famer Pete Alexander? David Cicotello investigates that question as he searches for the truth behind the legend.

In their chapters, Gene Carney, Daniel E. Ginsburg, and Timothy M. Gay focus on various gambling scandals that have tainted the game and, in one case, even stained the reputations of the great Ty Cobb and Tris Speaker. A study by David C. Ogden sheds some much-needed light on one of the most famous pitcher-batter confrontations in Negro League history, and a chapter by Robert Trumpbour examines whether a team owner has been falsely blamed for betraying an entire city.

By exploring the darker side of the game, the writers who contributed to *Mysteries from Baseball's Past* have also contributed to a better understanding of the game's history. They have discovered previously unknown material and provided plausible explanations consistent with the available information.

However, despite the outstanding work of the authors, these are not cases that can simply be stamped "Solved" and shelved away. History rarely provides the neat denouements of fiction. Much mystery remains, and many questions are yet to be definitively answered. That's because these stories are true. And that's what makes them truly compelling.

TROY SOOS is a writer, historian, and teacher who has published 11 books, including the Mickey Rawlings historical baseball mysteries (*Murder at Fenway Park, The Cincinnati Red Stalkings, Hanging Curve,* and three others) and *Before the Curse: The Glory Days of New England Baseball, 1858–1918* (rev. ed., McFarland, 2006).

Introduction: When the National Pastime Meets a Good Mystery

ANGELO J. LOUISA
and DAVID CICOTELLO

Ever since the middle of the 19th century, baseball has been referred to as the national pastime,[1] and despite the fact that association football — or as Americans refer to it, soccer — ranks first as the most popular sport in the overwhelming majority of countries in the world, baseball continues to be the leading subject for the production of sports books. Even professional American football, which has been the top spectator sport in the United States from 1965 to the present,[2] does not have as many books published about it as baseball has.[3] And sociologist and baseball historian David Quentin Voigt has proclaimed, "Indeed, it may fairly be said that among all of mankind's games and sports, only chess [a game, but not a sport], with its advantage of over a thousand years of existence and its international exposure, surpasses the literary outpourings devoted to baseball!"[4]

So what is it that attracts both writers and readers to baseball books, to either create them or to buy and enjoy the fruits of the creative process? Perhaps it is the nature of the game itself. As Thomas R. Heitz, then librarian of the National Baseball Hall of Fame Library, stated in his foreword to Myron J. Smith, Jr.'s *Baseball: A Comprehensive Bibliography*:

> Baseball is our nation's trademark. It reflects in countless ways the lessons of life. Baseball is metaphor for the strivings of common men for excellence and immortality. Baseball brings out our best and sometimes our worst.

Introduction (Louisa and Cicotello)

Baseball Mysteries, Louis Cicotello, paper collage, 2010.

Introduction (Louisa and Cicotello)

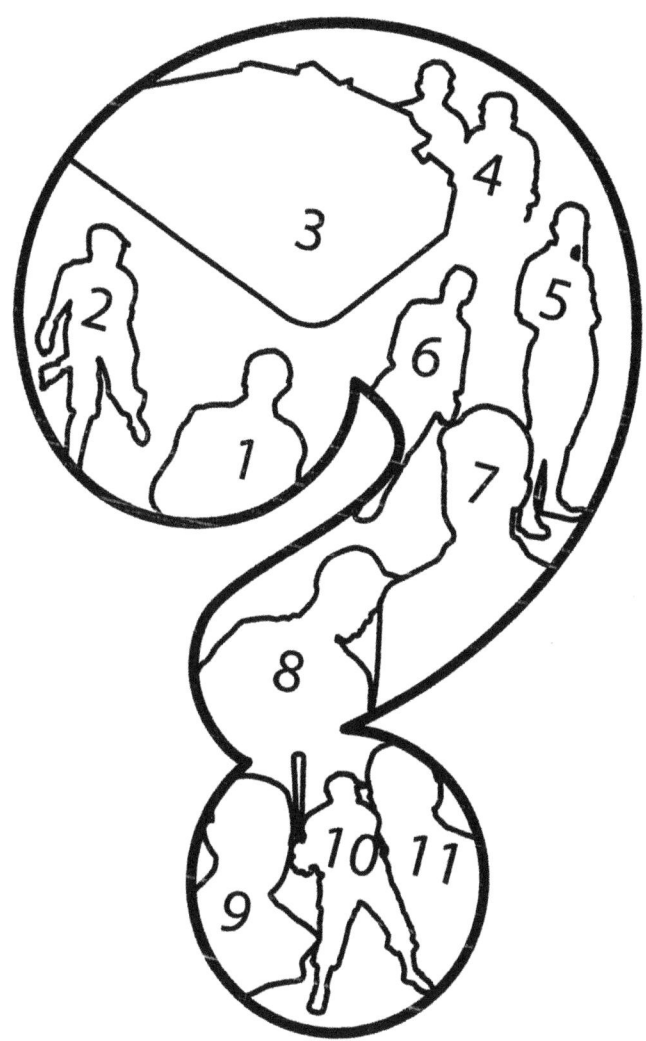

Baseball Mysteries, Louis Cicotello, paper collage, 2010. All of the illustrations except number 1 are from the National Hall of Fame Library, Cooperstown, New York. 1. Harry Pulliam (Library of Congress, Prints & Photographs Division, Bain Collection). 2. Wilbur Cooper. 3. Ebbets Field. 4. Ty Cobb and Tris Speaker. 5. Jimmy O'Connell. 6. Eddie Cicotte. 7. Chick Stahl. 8. Satchel Paige. 9. Ed Delahanty. 10. Josh Gibson. 11. Walter O'Malley.

Introduction (Louisa and Cicotello)

> Some win, some lose; some are rained out, while others remain on the bench. Some hit in the clutch to come from behind; others strike out with the bases loaded.[5]

Or consider the observations of an anonymous SABR member quoted by Theresa M. Danna in her chapter in *Baseball and American Culture: Across the Diamond*, edited by Edward J. Reilly:

> I love the rhythms of the game—the day-in-day-out of the long season, the leisurely pace, the ordered taking of turns at bat.... I love the lore of baseball and its characters.[6]

"[T]he lore of baseball and its characters"—could that be the answer? Baseball has certainly had its share of descriptive lore and colorful characters, both of which have easily lent themselves to be written and read about.

Or perhaps it is the size of the ball. In 1992, the famous journalist George Plimpton wrote:

> Some years ago I evolved what I called the Small Ball Theory to assess the quality of literature about sports. This stated that there seems to be a correlation between the standard of writing about a particular sport and the ball it utilizes—that the smaller the ball, the more formidable the literature.[7]

Leaving aside golf, which Plimpton admitted had an advantage over baseball because the latter "[did] not have much international appeal,"[8] it is not difficult to show that baseball surpasses all other sports in the number of quality works written about it.

But whatever the reason, in the minds of many readers, baseball has retained the title of the national pastime.

And it has been said that everyone loves a good mystery. Whether it be viewing such movies as *The Maltese Falcon*, *Murder on the Orient Express*, or *Lone Star*, watching episodes of *NCIS*, *Mystery!* (now a segment of *Masterpiece*, the former *Masterpiece Theatre*), or even the dramedy *Psych*, or reading novels by Tony Hillerman, P. D. James, or Ellis Peters, a myriad of people are fascinated by mysteries. The enduring allure of certain mystery films like *Rear Window* and *Chinatown* and the high ratings of various mystery-related television shows speak for themselves.[9] And as a fictional literary genre, the mystery is the second most published type, being outdone by only romance novels.[10]

Introduction (Louisa and Cicotello)

Nor have fictional mysteries monopolized the market. The Princes in the Tower, the lost Roanoke colony, Jack the Ripper, Amelia Earhart's disappearance, the Bermuda Triangle, the assassination of John F. Kennedy, and other nonfiction mysteries have had their share of books, chapters, and articles written about them and some of the topics have even been made into movies or *History Channel* productions.

So, why do people love mysteries? Is it because human beings are inherently curious and, thus, want to know the unknown? Is it a desire to solve problems? Is it the unpredictability factor: that because many people have predictable, mundane lives, they long to watch television shows and movies and read stories that have unpredictable elements? Or when it comes to viewing or reading mysteries involving crimes, is it the desire to catch the culprit, or at least to discover who the culprit was? No doubt, the answer depends on the mystery lover.

But what happens when the national pastime meets a good mystery — or specifically, nine good mysteries? *Mysteries from Baseball's Past* attempts to answer that question by providing a detailed look at nine intriguing puzzles that have mystified the baseball world.

Included in this collection are the untimely death of a superstar, two controversial suicides, a game that may never have been played, three scandals, a legendary pitcher-batter confrontation that may not have taken place, and the hidden reasons behind a beloved Brooklyn team moving to Los Angeles. Certain mysteries may be familiar to some readers, but all the contributors engaged in original research, with considerable attention given to the investigation of primary materials, resulting in provocative interpretations being presented or new questions being raised. Also, every chapter is sufficiently documented, though each author was responsible for the details and accuracy of the notes for his particular chapter.

The mysteries are arranged in chronological order, but the book need not be read that way. Each mystery can stand alone, so the reader can choose the chapter that he or she would like to peruse first and proceed from there.

Of course, this is not to say that there are not common issues and personages found in the book. For example, attempts to fix games figure prominently in four chapters, obsessive concern about protecting the image of the sport to the extent of not seeking out the truth or the embellishment of accomplishments to inflate a star's stature can be found in six chapters, and the larger-than-life figures of John McGraw, Ban Johnson, and Judge

Introduction (Louisa and Cicotello)

Kenesaw Mountain Landis, the czar of baseball (National Baseball Hall of Fame Library, Cooperstown, New York).

Landis appear and reappear in several parts of the book.

The primary purpose of this work is to both entertain and inform those who read it. And with a variety of topics, writing styles, chapter lengths, and conclusions, there should be something that interests everyone.

However, the book also serves as a testament to the resilience of professional baseball. Although much has been written about the trials and tribulations of the sport today, *Mysteries from Baseball's Past* shows that professional baseball has been plagued with bizarre player behavior, corruption, cover-ups, injustices, and mythmaking for a long time, and yet, it not only has survived but also continues to thrive.

NOTES

1. According to baseball historian Jules Tygiel, *Porter's Spirit of the Times* and the *New York Clipper* started calling baseball the "national game" in 1855, but "[o]n December 5, 1856, the *New York Mercury* coined the phrase 'the national pastime.'" Jules Tygiel, *Past Time: Baseball as History* (New York: Oxford University Press, 2000), 3.

2. Bryan Curtis, "The National Pastime(s)," *The New York Times*, February 1, 2009, http://www.nytimes.com/2009/02/01/weekinreview/01curtis.html, and http://www.nfl.com/history/chronology/1961-1970. Also see "Football Reaches Historic Popularity Levels in Gallup Poll," January 19, 2007, http://www.gallup.com/poll/26188/football-reaches-historic-popularity-levels-gallup-poll.aspx?version=print.

3. Although it is impossible to find exact statistics on how many books have been published on particular sports, searches done by Judy Anghelescu and Joanne Ferguson Cavanaugh of the Omaha Public Library and by the editors of this book using BooksIn Print.com, the Library of Congress, and other bibliographical materials all indicate that baseball heads the list. However, in doing such searches, it is important to distinguish between the different types of football that are played throughout the world — in particular, to separate soccer from American football — so as not to skew the results. It is not advisable to use Amazon for such searches because even if an advanced subject search is done on American football, books on Australian football, Canadian football, Gaelic football, rugby, and soccer will appear on the list; books containing excerpts on a particular sport, but not

Introduction (Louisa and Cicotello)

dealing directly with that sport, will show up in an advanced subject search done on the sport; and drill-down searches are misleading due to the number of times that a book is cross-referenced in multiple categories and, hence, is counted more than once. Nor is it advisable to use WorldCat, which not only includes books on Australian football, Canadian football, Gaelic football, rugby, and soccer under the general subject heading of football, but also counts game programs as books and at times has duplicate records for the same book. As for how many books on baseball have been published, no one knows for sure, but Andy McCue, the president of the Society for American Baseball Research and the chairperson of its Bibliography Committee when this book was written, has statistics to show that the approximate number equals 18,437, with 7,425 alone being published between 1990 and 2008, an average of 391 a year. Microsoft Office Excel attachment from Andy McCue to Angelo J. Louisa, October 15, 2009. According to McCue, "[The data] includes hardbound and paperbound books, as well as pamphlets. It does not include a fair number of items from the 19th century where we don't know how they were bound. It does not include team yearbooks. It does include fiction about baseball. As it is a volunteer project, I'm sure things have been missed." E-mail message from Andy McCue to Angelo J. Louisa, October 15, 2009.

    4. Myron J. Smith, Jr., comp., *Baseball: A Comprehensive Bibliography* (Jefferson, NC: McFarland, 1986), vi.

    5. Ibid., xi.

    6. Theresa M. Danna, "Home Base: A Survey of Backyard Baseball Diamonds," in *Baseball and American Culture: Across the Diamond*, ed. Edward J. Reilly (New York: The Haworth Press, 2003), 14.

    7. George Plimpton, "The Smaller the Ball, the Better the Book: A Game Theory of Literature," *New York Times*, May 31, 1992, http://www.nytimes.com/books/97/06/08/nnp/26049.html.

    8. Ibid.

    9. A few of the more popular mystery-related shows from television's past are *Columbo*—first, one of the parts of *The NBC Mystery Movie* (later retitled *The NBC Sunday Mystery Movie*), and then, one of the parts of The *ABC Monday Mystery Movie* (later retitled *The ABC Saturday Mystery Movie* when the show was moved to the last day of the week)—*Murder, She Wrote*, and *Unsolved Mysteries*.

    10. Ben Williams, "Martin Hegwood," Mississippi Writers & Musicians, http://www.mswritersandmusicians.com/writers/martin-hegwood.html.

1

Delahanty's Disappearance: Where Is the King of Swatsville?*

JERROLD CASWAY

One of the most puzzling happenings in baseball history was the bizarre death of Ed Delahanty. Considered one of the greatest batsmen of baseball's formative years, Delahanty, a year after winning the American League batting title, disappeared without a trace on the evening of July 2, 1903. A week later, a bloated and disfigured body was discovered at the foot of Niagara's Horseshoe Falls. The carcass was blackened and the legs broken, with the left leg nearly severed at the thigh. The stomach was torn open, exposing the entrails. The undertaker blamed the body's extreme decomposition to intoxication. Once the body was identified as the missing Delahanty, the shocked baseball public wanted to know what happened to the sport's reigning batting star.

Delahanty's death is best understood by the circumstances of the contractual bidding war between the two major leagues. Under contract with three different teams, Delahanty was tortured by troubling gambling debts, disturbing marital problems, and declining on-field skills. The talented outfielder's tribulations began in 1901 when he was lured by a large guaranteed contract to jump leagues and join the Washington Nationals of the fledgling American League. In spite of his 1902 successes in Washington, the city and his contract failed to live up to his exaggerated expectations. This was particularly evident when the New York Giants, under John McGraw, were offering Delahanty more than double the salary he earned during his prime

---

*Editors' Note: This chapter is a modified version of "The Fall," which was published in Ed Delahanty in the Emerald Age of Baseball by Jerrold Casway. It appears here by permission of University of Notre Dame Press. ©2004 by University of Notre Dame.

years with the Philadelphia Phillies. Believing he was entitled to the best possible contract, Delahanty was willing to forego his last year in Washington. Offered a guaranteed three-year pact with New York at $6,000 per annum, "Del," as the ballplayer was called, saw a grand opportunity to end his illustrious career. Unfortunately, McGraw and the Giants' new owner, John Brush, manipulated Delahanty by encouraging the hitter's gambling addictions. Heavily in debt, Del was susceptible to McGraw's enticing offers, which eventually led to him receiving an advance of $4,000 from the New York club without even playing a game for the Giants. He also received $1,600 in advance money from the final year of his 1903 Washington contract. These conflicting arrangements were compounded by the fact that Del was legally bound to his original team, the National League Phillies. Thus, the King of Swatsville, as he was also called, was contractually tied to three teams in two different leagues.

Edward James "Del" Delahanty (1867–1903), the King of Swatsville, pictured here with a troubled expression in June 1903. Was this a portent of his death later that year? (Chicago History Museum).

These contract disputes were to be settled in a court of law and by the peace commission of major league executives and owners that ended the war between the American and National leagues. Meeting in Cincinnati, the commission tried to resolve the matter by refusing to acknowledge Delahanty's pact with New York and thereby supporting Washington's claim to Del's services. The Giants' front office, however, was not deterred.

Ed Delahanty was disquieted by these decisions. He was carrying large racetrack losses and was determined he was best served by finishing his career in New York. When the 35-year-old slugger reported to Wash-

1. Delahanty's Disappearance (Casway)

ington's 1903 training camp, he was discontented and out of shape. He performed listlessly and rumors circulated that he was drinking heavily. Whatever chance Del had of playing in New York revolved around the Giants' recruiting efforts of another star, George Davis.[1]

For the next few months, Delahanty brooded and his level of play fell off. He was slow afield and often misplayed balls. On one occasion he was threatened with a suspension for insubordination. For their part, the Washington front office and management did all that they could to appease their former captain. Meanwhile, the team was mired in last place, winning only six out of 34 games between May 14 and June 25. During those weeks, Delahanty raised his batting average to .340, going 28 for 72 in June. But the more he hit, the less Washington was willing to let him leave.[2]

While the team continued to slide, Delahanty's dysfunctional life began spiraling downward. His finances were in desperate straits, his wife was ailing and distraught, and his state of mind and the Giants' appeals were at an impasse. Del's only antidote for his stress and anxiety was drinking. But alcohol never sat well with Delahanty, an infrequent binge drinker, whose overindulgence brought out a dark and sullen side to the good-natured, weak-willed ballplayer. For obsessive gamblers like Delahanty, liquor was self-destructive, as events on Washington's Midwestern road trip confirmed.

Washington would lose 10 out of the 12 road games, seven by shutouts, with Delahanty's last game being played on Thursday, June 25, before family and hometown friends in Cleveland. The Nationals were blanked, 4–0, but Del stroked a single, the 2,597th hit of his 16-year career. The hit also kept a 16-game batting streak alive. That evening, the Delahantys

George Davis, whose playing status with the Giants pushed Delahanty over the edge (National Baseball Hall of Fame Library, Cooperstown, New York).

hosted a dinner for the ballplayers and all seemed well, but the next day Del was an entirely different person.

The newspapers reported that the National League president, Harry Pulliam, without the consent of the owners, yielded to John Brush's lobbying and gave the Giants a favorable decision about George Davis' status[3]—a decision that pushed Delahanty over the edge. He ranted about his situation, began drinking heavily, and did not make it to the ballpark.

After a 1–0 loss, the Nationals returned to the hotel and did not find Delahanty, who was out drinking with his Cleveland cronies. When he did appear, Del was mean-spirited and difficult to handle. Only the timely intervention of his mother pacified him.

The next morning, the cycle began anew when the local papers reported that Davis played his first game with the Giants.[4] In a quandary, Delahanty wired McGraw for advice and lapsed into a hysteria fueled by alcohol. He stormed about the hotel threatening players and even vowed to take his own life.[5] However, after much cajoling, he settled down and was babysat by the injured Jimmy Ryan as Washington finished out their games in Cleveland. Ryan was confident that the upcoming Lake Erie boat trip to Detroit would revive the slugger's spirits.[6]

Del responded well to the cruise, and according to John R. Robinson in an article in the August 1, 1903, issue of *Sporting Life*, he "appeared in a rational frame of mind" the morning of June 28.[7] But no sooner had his teammates left for the ballpark than Delahanty started drinking. There is no evidence as to what caused this relapse. Perhaps there were continued reports about his erupting crisis or he received a telegram from McGraw. This time when his teammates returned to the hotel, they found Del on the verge of a hallucinating breakdown. The frightened players called a doctor and telegraphed Delahanty's mother that she was needed. One commentator related that Del was nothing but a big overgrown boy by nature.[8] An immature and spoiled adolescent man, Delahanty, depended on strong women in his life—a dominating mother and a manipulative and aspiring wife. He probably resented this dependence, but in his time of need, he required his mother's attention and his wife's comfort. After Bridget Delahanty calmed down her son, she took him to a nearby church where she counseled him about the evils of drink. In the presence of a priest, Del swore off whiskey.[9]

Back at the hotel, Delahanty quietly recuperated until he read stories

1. Delahanty's Disappearance (Casway)

about his anguish in the local papers. Humiliated, the King of Swatsville was made to look like a misguided adolescent, scolded by his mother and a priest. These stories festered in him throughout the day. On the morning of July 2, he awakened to new problems and pressures when he learned that an injunction was issued against Davis playing in New York. Not knowing how this would affect him, Delahanty likely wired John McGraw. In the meantime, he was told that McGraw's Giants were about to leave New York on a Midwestern road trip. Dispirited that he might be without alternatives, Del reneged on his one-day-old sobriety pledge. In his confused state of mind, he sent off a letter to his wife, in which he enclosed a lapsed accident insurance policy and confessed that he hoped he would die in a train accident. Soon after, bolstered by his drinking, Del took matters into his own hands. He packed his suitcase and satchel, left his Washington uniform and cap in his room, and purchased a ticket on the overnight Michigan Central train #6 from Detroit to Buffalo, where he was scheduled to arrive at 11:00 P.M. From there, he would travel on to New York City.[10]

Delahanty had a Pullman sleeping berth which entitled him to the buffet car that served tobacco and drinks. At first, the troubled ballplayer attracted little attention. He silently fretted about his fate, smoked a cigarette, and ordered a whiskey to sooth his nerves. But then, for the next few hours, an intoxicated Delahanty continued to run afoul of the head conductor, John Cole. Tempers flared and threats were made by both men. Eventually, the sulking slugger settled down and dozed in the smoking parlor. When the train stopped at the border-crossing station at Bridgeburg, the disoriented Delahanty stirred, believing the train had crossed the Niagara River and was in Buffalo, his first destination.[11]

Startled by this realization, Delahanty hurried back to his sleeping berth to fetch his bags. But in the dimly lit aisle, he went to the wrong berth. Confusion erupted and harsh words were exchanged. Within moments, conductor Cole was alerted to the disruption. When he arrived, he found Delahanty in the grasp of the porter and two conductors. They escorted Del up the aisle and evicted him from the train.

Upset by his ejection, Delahanty found himself in front of the Bridgeburg Station in Fort Erie, Ontario, but his valise and satchel remained on the Pullman. Moments later, after the recoupling of the engine, the train departed across the bridge for the United States. Left unattended with the

Mysteries from Baseball's Past

The International Bridge, also known as the International Railway Bridge, ca. 1900 (©Western New York Heritage Press, Inc., use by permission).

lights of his destination faintly visible in the night, Ed Delahanty pondered his options.[12]

It was a moonless and lightly clouded evening, with the temperature in the mid–60s. The harbor of Black Rock, on the American side, was five minutes away by train. Fifteen minutes beyond that was the city of Buffalo. No one appeared to assist Delahanty from the one-story platformed building. In the guardhouse at the bridge's entrance was an elderly bridge tender, Samuel Kingston. The old man had no idea that train #6 had left a passenger at the station platform. Alone and distraught, the King of Swatsville bore his despair in silence. Remembering that he had to get to New York before McGraw went west, Delahanty decided to follow the Michigan Central over the darkened single-track railroad bridge. Prohibited to pedestrian traffic, the bridge had no side railings, the footing was treacherous, and the only lumination came from summer marine lights. The structure was not the place for an unfamiliar traveler, especially one who had been drinking.

Delahanty ignored, or did not see, the wooden sign warning pedes-

1. Delahanty's Disappearance (Casway)

trians to keep off the bridge. As he passed under the foreboding iron archway, he resisted the frightening reality of his venture. Shrouded in darkness, he began to tread warily along the left train rail on the north side of the 20-foot-wide span. Less than six inches away, at the edge of the bridge, was a double iron chord or girder. In a matter of about 10 minutes, Del made his way to the third span, when the track ahead of him became illuminated by the headlights of an oncoming freight train. The train had waited at the Black Rock Station for Delahanty's Michigan Central to pass before resuming its journey.

A recent interior interior view of the International Bridge (courtesy Jerrold Casway).

With the freight train bearing down on him, there was little the befuddled ballplayer could do. He tried clearing his head, and in the oncoming light, he saw the iron chord at the side of the bridge. Suppressing his mounting panic, Delahanty stepped from the wood frame onto the two-foot-wide chord and braced himself against the vertical truss that linked the bridge to its external frame. After a few frightening moments, Del tried to steady his nerves and balance in a new veil of enveloping darkness. Alone on the iron girder, Delahanty was alerted to the sound of the rushing Niagara River and his deteriorating predicament. He realized that he would need all his athletic dexterity and strength to get him through the evening.

Just as the freight train exited the bridge, a small light appeared to make its way toward the unmoving Delahanty. Samuel Kingston had seen someone go onto the bridge. He knew nothing about the abandoned passenger but was attentive to smugglers along the river. With his bull's-eye lantern in hand, he set out to investigate the situation. He later testified that he saw a large man standing on the chord against the first upright column and put his light on him. The recovering Delahanty, stunned and upset by his discovery, cried out, "Take that light away or I will knock your damned brains out." The old watchman later testified that his intent was to find out why this man was on the bridge and escort him off to safety. Reluctant to take any unnecessary chances, Kingston stepped back and asked Delahanty if he had a pass or permit to travel on the bridge. Del responded by repeating his former threat. Kingston said he thought the man was drunk or crazy and was afraid he would jump into the river. Acting quickly, the watchman tried to grab Delahanty. He reported he threw his arm over the angry ballplayer and caught him by the collar of his coat, pulling him down. Both men tumbled onto the track and Kingston got his foot stuck between the ties. Lying astride the tracks with his lantern light out, the old man struggled to his feet and heard a splash. He ran to the side of the bridge and said he saw Delahanty's head above the surging water hollering for help. The ballplayer called out several times until he vanished from sight. Shaken by this calamity, Kingston ran back to the station to alert the bridge foreman, who ordered a tugboat search below the International Bridge. The rescuers found no body. Only a derby hat was recovered by the watchman from the top of the iron chord.[13]

What happened to Delahanty perplexed investigators because every party had a stake in contrary conclusions. The Michigan Central Railroad and the Grand Trunk Railway Company were occupied with liability issues, the Delahanty family had religious and personal concerns, and Sam Kingston and conductor Cole were wary about their responsibilities. To unravel this mystery, the agenda of each party has to be weighed and taken into account. The legal responsibility for Delahanty's death would eventually be determined by a Canadian appellate court, but the actual cause of this misfortune had three possibilities: foul play, suicide, or an accident.

1. Delahanty's Disappearance (Casway)

Foul play was the most convenient and tolerable explanation. If proven, the actions of the railway or Delahanty's behavior would not be open to judgment. Everything would be explained and questions resolved if someone had waylaid the finely attired ballplayer, took his money and jewelry, and pushed him off the bridge. Kingston and the Grand Trunk Railway Company would not be liable, and the Delahanty family would be relieved of the religious stigma of suicide or Del's shameful dissipation.

Initially, conductor Cole proposed a solution because he could not recall any jewelry on his troublesome passenger. He suggested that the man could have been robbed in Detroit.[14] However, most opinions about a robbery took their cue from Del's angry and disbelieving 20-year-old brother, Frank. The younger Delahanty, who played for Syracuse in the New York State League, was one of the first people on the scene. He told reporters in Buffalo that stories of suicide or intemperance had no foundation. He spoke of foul play and suggested his brother was held up and murdered.[15] This opinion was supported by the talk of smugglers and crimes along the Niagara border. One story in particular created confusion. It described the plight of a wealthy farmer from nearby Tonawanda who was robbed and thrown into the river sometime after Delahanty's disappearance.[16] However, in the investigation of Ed Delahanty's death, no evidence of a crime was ever uncovered. So whatever happened on the bridge that night was known only to the frightened old watchman and the deceased Delahanty. As for the ballplayer's valuables, if his clothes were washed off his body, then anything he was carrying would have been scattered along the course of the Niagara River or was at the bottom of the Horseshoe Falls.[17]

The issue of suicide was the most controversial and sensitive scenario for the Irish Catholic Delahantys. They and many of Del's friends refused to acknowledge that Delahanty's psychological anguish might have pushed him to such a desperate act. No one was more steadfast or apologetic than his mother, who told Cleveland reporters, "I am confident that he has not taken his own life, unless he did it while rendered insane by heat [whiskey], for he was in the best of spirits when with me. No, he was not despondent. He had no reason at all to be so."[18] Mrs. Delahanty's remarks were part of her denial, which was consistent with her misapprehension about her son's troubled lifestyle.

The possibility of suicide owed much to the prejudiced assessment

Mysteries from Baseball's Past

of Sam Kingston, who spoke of the distressed man looking out over the river from the bridge's girder.[19] His description fit Delahanty's panicked behavior in Cleveland and Detroit. But the question that remained was whether Del's vocal and frequent threats of self-harm were whiskey-induced pleas, a way of reaching out for help and relief, or statements of intent. For example, his remarks to his wife about not surviving a train wreck could have been an appeal for her love and support.[20] What Delahanty might have been saying was that he regretted what he had done to upset his wife, and though he could not take his own life, maybe a train crash would do it for him. This threat was not his first. He frequently alluded to hurting himself during his tirades. Supporting this belief was an unverified story that Del's teammates once stopped him from turning on the gas in his Washington hotel room when he became despondent about his marriage.[21]

All these accounts confirm Delahanty's pained state of mind. They do not, however, prove he committed suicide on the International Bridge. The fact that he made these intoxicated threats around people who could look after him reveals that he may have been crying out for help. So, perhaps the only way to appreciate whether Delahanty wanted to die is to put this presumption into the context of his flight from Detroit.

Delahanty's disappearance and death followed the much publicized suicide of the popular Detroit pitcher, George "Winnie" Mercer. Troubled by family problems, Mercer compounded his situation with the loss of thousands of dollars in gambling and racetrack debts. Unfortunately, part of the money he lost came from game receipts of his traveling off-season all-star troupe. On January 12, 1903, Mercer wrote letters of farewell and apology and put a rubber tube from a gas jet into his mouth. The last words of the 28-year-old pitcher were "Beware of women and a game of chance."[22] Mercer's suicide stunned the sporting world, and it inevitably became a gauge for explaining Delahanty's original disappearance.

Also fueling this theory was the association of suicide with the International Bridge or Niagara Falls. On the afternoon of the Delahanty incident, an electrical engineer attending a local conference committed suicide by going over the falls. Part of the confusion surrounding Del's vanishing was identifying the dead engineer.[23]

But the critical point dispelling suicide talk was Delahanty's intentions. Being distraught over professional and personal problems did not

1. Delahanty's Disappearance (Casway)

deter Del from going to New York. His one-way ticket was for Manhattan, where he intended to meet with his manipulative benefactors, John McGraw and John Brush. Although it was widely believed that they were in contact with Delahanty throughout the Davis affair, neither man ever acknowledged their scheduled rendezvous. The *Washington Post* reported that most people believed that Del was in touch with the New York ballclub and expected to play there.[24] Fred Postal, Washington's president, publicly stated that Brush was responsible for Delahanty's death. He asserted that the Giants' president was always tampering with the big outfielder and never let him get satisfied with his situation. "Brush and McGraw," he said, "do not know ... the baseball war is over."[25] President August "Garry" Herrmann of Cincinnati endorsed these sentiments. Herrmann confessed that Delahanty would be alive and appearing in his outfield if New York had not obstructed his trade efforts.[26] Another overlooked piece of evidence was the fact that Delahanty left his Washington uniform in Detroit and packed his spiked baseball shoes and glove in his leather satchel.[27] In other words, Delahanty intended to leave the Nationals and believed McGraw and Brush would find a way for him to stay in New York. This corroboration was probably what Del was waiting for when he took the Michigan Central to Buffalo. Aside from his New York destination, Delahanty also wanted his wife to meet him in Washington. Although he did not tell her about his change of plans and the purpose of his stopover in New York, all evidence indicates that Delahanty had a plan and purpose for this trip. These intentions and incentives were not the actions of a man bent on self-destruction. As a *Sporting News* editorial related, "Delahanty's death was due to dissipation and not to design."[28] Nor does a lapsed insurance policy mean anything. The troubled ballplayer just overlooked its deadline. It was customary to forward these indemnities ahead.[29] When sober and rational, the Catholic Delahanty did have an opinion on suicide. Speaking with his teammates, he declared that "no one but a coward would ever drown himself."[30] So if Delahanty did not take his own life, what happened the evening of July 2 on the International Bridge?

According to news reports of interviews with Sam Kingston and railroad officials, Delahanty either jumped into the river or ran east towards the United States and an open drawbridge. In his original statement, the shaken watchman said the draw was raised to allow a steamship to pass. This story put the blame on Delahanty for running up the unlit bridge to the waiting chasm. The problem with this version was that the drawbridge was at least two spans away and Kingston would have had to have gone some distance to see the struggling Delahanty in the swirling water. Nor could anyone explain the automatic gate that guarded the opening.[31]

The befuddled Kingston, upset with the notion that he had a role in Delahanty's death, stuck to the drawbridge story.[32] But this description of the fall did not endure the police investigation or the family's lawsuit against the railroad. In sworn testimony, Kingston eventually asserted that after he fell on the tracks, with his foot wedged between the ties, Delahanty "got away ... and went some little distance further on."[33] He also confessed he did not know whether Delahanty was running or how he got into the river. Kingston did relate that the man on the bridge went to the other [south] side of the span and then recrossed the track and fell in on the north side, where he had originally been standing.[34] With the drawbridge defense eliminated, the question is narrowed to how Delahanty fell off the bridge.

There are two possibilities worth considering. One had Delahanty losing his footing when Kingston lunged at him; the other was that he tripped on the raised tie and/or the chord in his effort to elude the elderly watchman. Both explanations were plausible given Delahanty's physical condition and the darkened state of the bridge. Of the two, the latter met the criteria of the incident. The footing was unstable under the best of circumstances and no side rail or rope existed along the bridge's edge. A person stumbling over the tie or the chord would be less than a body length from the precipice. Had both men fallen on the tracks in a scuffle, the younger and stronger Delahanty would have recovered sooner. Without an avenue of escape, the confused athlete could have easily slipped or staggered over the unprotected side. Evidence for this was the fact that both men's hats remained on the bridge. If Delahanty had fallen when Kingston grabbed him on the chord, his derby would have likely followed him into the Niagara. Instead, each man lost his hat on the bridge. The crushed watchman's hat was found between the ties, and Delahanty's derby was mistakenly picked up and worn by Kingston.[35] The only reasonable conclusion was that the unstable Delahanty lost his balance and tumbled over the unsecured side.

Ed Delahanty fell about 25 feet into the blackened void and the chilled, fast-moving river. The treacherous midstream current flowed as

1. Delahanty's Disappearance (Casway)

rapidly as eight miles per hour. It was a capturing torrent that ensnared anything in its midst, even a strong and accomplished swimmer like Delahanty would be in trouble. What doomed Delahanty was the surprise and jolt of the fall, the cold water, the darkness, and the strength of the current, though the greatest handicap was his intoxication. Drunk people who fall into water often get disoriented when the water enters their inner ears. They become confused and swim downward, instead of up toward the surface.[36] But Delahanty did not stumble out of a boat, he toppled 25 feet into a surging river in the darkness of night. He never had time to right or compose himself before being overwhelmed by the elements and his panic. Shouting for aid, he was unaware that Squaw Island was a few hundred feet to his right. The current quickly carried him forward to the river's widest expanse, below Grand Island, before taking him west into the Chippawa Channel. He probably drowned before the confluence, north of Navy Island. Ahead lay dangerous rocks and rapids that began Delahanty's 26-mile journey to the Falls of Niagara. On the morning of July 9, Delahanty's body was discovered. His corpse was taken to the Morse Funeral Home in Drummonville, now Niagara Falls, Ontario. Del's unclaimed baggage from the train, which included his wife's season ticket book, suggested the victim's identity. But physical verification of the body which included his gold front teeth, his disfigured "baseball fingers," and his surviving necktie, confirmed what everyone had already suspected. The following morning Delahanty's remains were embalmed and placed in a metal-lined container and carrying crate and taken by the Michigan Central Railroad to Buffalo on its way to Cleveland. On Saturday morning, after a High Mass at Immaculate Conception Church, the King of Swatsville was interred at the family plot at Calvary Cemetery.[37]

Delahanty's widow, Norine, the mother of their five-year-old daughter, was not yet 25 years of age. She had never worked and was accustomed to the comforts of better living. Nor did she have any meaningful prospects. Her husband's estate amounted to his last paycheck. All the cash and jewelry he carried were lost in the river. His road trip insurance policies had lapsed and the benefits from his lodge memberships were not forthcoming because of dues in arrears. Her only recourse was to bring suit against the railroad for selling her husband liquor and then leaving him unattended in sight of his ticketed destination.

On May 4, 1904, a jury decided in Mrs. Delahanty's favor. She was awarded $3,000 and her daughter was to receive $2,000. However, their vindication was short-lived. The railroad appealed the judgment to an appellate court in Toronto, which overturned the lower court's decision. Unable to afford a new appeal, Norine and her daughter went on with their lives. In 1906, the widow remarried and moved to Mobile, Alabama.[38]

Although the appellate court denied Delahanty's family exoneration and restitution, it did lay out the events of that tragic evening. Thanks to sworn testimony and police reports, the facts of Delahanty's death were clarified. The railroad company believed it was acting in the best interest of its passengers, and Delahanty was judged to be capable of taking care of himself. It contested that the slugging outfielder went on a nonpedestrian bridge under his own power and suffered the consequences. The company, for obvious reasons, never dismissed the notion of suicide, but the record is quite clear about Delahanty's intent and missteps on the night of his senseless death.[39]

NOTES

1. For the details behind the contract war and Delahanty's troubles, consult Jerrold Casway, *Ed Delahanty in the Emerald Age of Baseball* (Notre Dame: University of Notre Dame Press, 2004), 242–247.
2. For Delahanty's problems with the Washington ballclub, see Ibid., 250–258.
3. *Sporting Life*, July 4, 1903; *Washington Post*, June 26, 1903.
4. *Cleveland Press*, June 27, 1903.
5. *Sporting Life*, July 11, 1903.
6. *Washington Post*, July 5, 1903; July 8, 1903; *Buffalo Morning Express*, July 8, 1903; July 9, 1903; *Boston Globe*, July 8, 1903; *Sporting Life*, July 18, 1903.
7. *Sporting Life*, August 1, 1903.
8. *Washington Evening Star*, July 6, 1903.
9. *Detroit Times*, July 1, 1903.
10. *Washington Post*, July 5, 1903; July 6, 1903; July 8, 1903; *Washington Star*, July 4, 1903; *Boston Globe*, July 8, 1903; *Cleveland Plain Dealer*, July 8, 1903; *Buffalo Morning Express*, July 8, 1903; July 9, 1903; *Buffalo Evening News*, July 8, 1903; *Niagara Falls Gazette*, July 9, 1903; *Detroit Evening News*, July 8, 1903; *Detroit Times*, July 8, 1903; *Philadelphia Press*, July 8, 1903. The court transcripts discussed the actual ticket destinations. Court Transcript, 1904, 46, 85, Randall Papers, Packet 5 (Letters, Papers, and Documents of Norine Delahanty-Lerio), Mobile, Alabama.
11. Court Transcript, 1904, 19–20, 48, 59.
12. For details of his ill-fated train trip, consult Ibid., 16–23, 26–30, 47–48, and 57–82. Also see *Buffalo Evening News*, July 9, 1903; July 10, 1903; *Buffalo Morning Express*, July 9, 1903; July 11, 1903; *Cleveland Press*, July 9, 1903; *Niagara Falls Gazette*, July 6, 1903; *Philadelphia Inquirer*, July 10, 1903. For contemporary summaries that do not include court

1. Delahanty's Disappearance (Casway)

testimony, see Norm Nevard, "The Strange Fate of Hall-of-Famer Ed Delahanty," *Baseball Digest*, July 1954, 13–16; Robert Summers, "His Ticket Said New York City, But Fate Said Niagara Falls," *Buffalo Courier Express Magazine*, September 8, 1974; Frank Fitzpatrick, "A Baseball Mystery is 85 years Old," *Philadelphia Inquirer*, July 3, 1988; Joel Stashenko, "Delahanty's Death Obscured his Baseball Achievements," *Richmond Times*, September 26, 1992; and Mike Sowell, *July 2, 1903: The Mysterious Death of Hall-of-Famer Big Ed Delahanty* (New York: Macmillan, 1992), 262–263.

13. The description of the bridge and the details of Delahanty's last moments come from court testimony. See Court Transcript, 1904, 2–11. Also consult *Boston Globe*, July 8, 1903; *Buffalo Evening News*, July 3, 1903; July 8, 1903; *Buffalo Morning Express*, July 8, 1903; July 9, 1903; July 11, 1903; *Cleveland Plain Dealer*, July 9, 1903; July 10, 1903; *Cleveland Press*, July 8, 1903; *Daily Cataract Journal*, July 9, 1903; July 11, 1903; *Niagara Falls Gazette*, July 9, 1903; *North American*, July 9, 1903; *Philadelphia Press*, July 9, 1903; *Sporting Life*, July 18, 1903; *The Sporting News*, July 11, 1903; *Washington Evening Star*, July 8, 1903; *Washington Post*, July 8, 1903; July 12, 1903. For modern accounts, see citations in note 12.
14. *Daily Cataract Journal*, July 11, 1903.
15. *Cleveland Press*, July 9, 1903.
16. *Buffalo Evening News*, July 14, 1903.
17. For the foul play scenario, consult *Buffalo Morning Gazette*, July 11, 1903; *Cleveland Press*, July 9, 1903; *Daily Cataract Journal*, July 11, 1903; *Philadelphia Inquirer*, July 10, 1903; *Washington Evening Star*, July 8, 1903; *Washington Post*, July 9, 1903.
18. *Cleveland Plain Dealer*, July 8, 1903.
19. *Buffalo Evening News*, July 3, 1903.
20. *Boston Globe*, July 8, 1903; *Buffalo Evening News*, July 8, 1903; *Niagara Falls Gazette*, July 9, 1903; *Washington Post*, July 5, 1903.
21. *Buffalo Evening News*, July 9, 1903; *Washington Post*, July 10, 1903.
22. *Sporting Life*, January 24, 1903; *The Sporting News*, January 24, 1903; *Washington Post*, January 14, 1903. Initially, there was speculation among Mercer's friends that he was murdered. *Sporting Life*, January 24, 1903.
23. At first, it was said that the man jumped off the International Bridge. His death was probably confused with reports about Delahanty's fall later that evening. The engineer's body was recovered in the Whirlpool, below the falls, on Friday, July 3. His body could not have gotten to that location in one day. *Niagara Falls Gazette*, July 3, 1903.
24. *Washington Post*, July 5, 1903.
25. Ibid., July 12, 1903. *The Sporting News* said that Delahanty was convinced that Brush had smashed the peace settlement and he could play in New York. *The Sporting News*, July 18, 1903.
26. *Washington Evening Star*, July 11, 1903.
27. Court Transcript, 1904, 16; *Buffalo Evening News*, July 8, 1903; *Cleveland Plain Dealer*, July 9, 1903; *Niagara Falls Gazette*, July 9, 1903; *Sporting Life*, July 18, 1903; *The Sporting News*, July 11, 1903; *Washington Post*, July 9, 1903.
28. *The Sporting News*, July 18, 1903.
29. *Washington Evening Star*, July 8, 1903.
30. *Philadelphia Press*, July 12, 1903.
31. *Boston Globe*, July 8, 1903; *Boston Herald*, July 10, 1903; *Buffalo Evening News*, July 3, 1903; July 8, 1903; *Buffalo Morning Express*, July 8, 1903; July 9, 1903; July 11, 1903; *Cleveland Plain Dealer*, July 9, 1903; *North American*, July 10, 1903; *Philadelphia Inquirer*, July 10, 1903; *Philadelphia Ledger*, July 10, 1903; *The Sporting News*, July 11, 1903; July 18, 1903; *Washington Evening Star*, July 8, 1903; *Washington Post*, July 8, 1903.
32. *Buffalo Morning Express*, July 9, 1903.

33. Court Transcript, 1904, 54.
34. Ibid., 11.
35. *Buffalo Evening News*, July 8, 1903; *Buffalo Morning Express*, July 9, 1903; *Daily Cataract Journal*, July 9, 1903; Court Transcript, 1904, 7.
36. Sally Squires, "The Hazard of Drunk Boating, High Seas," *Washington Post*, Health Section, July 2, 1996, 10.
37. For the identification and care of the body, see Casway, 276–282.
38. For the lawsuits and Norine Delahanty's tribulations, see Ibid., 284–286. Also consult the court transcripts in the Randall Papers, Packet 5.
39. For a full description of Delahanty's life and fate, see Casway, chapters 15–17.

2

The Suicide of Chick Stahl

Dennis H. Auger

In a 1907 newspaper account, Charles Sylvester Stahl of the Boston Americans was described as "one of the best outfielders and batsmen in the game's history."[1] The Indiana native was establishing Hall of Fame credentials, but his tragic end overshadowed a successful 10-year major league career which included contributing to four championship teams between 1897 and 1906. Statistically, Bill James and Derek Gentile provide a perspective on Stahl's accomplishments. The former ranks him 51st all-time among center fielders, while the latter names the left-handed hitter number 416 among baseball's best ever.[2] These rankings are based on a .305 lifetime batting average, five .300 seasons, and Stahl's ability to produce extra-base hits, highlighted by a career total of 118 triples. But perhaps the most impressive testimonial to Stahl's prowess is derived from the pen of Francis Richter, the influential founder and editor of *Sporting Life*. In his 1914 book entitled *History and Records of Base Ball*, Richter lists the six greatest outfielders covering the 1900–1912 period.[3] Stahl's name appears with Ty Cobb, Tris Speaker, Willie Keeler, Sam Crawford, and Fred Clarke, all Hall of Famers. Thus, "Chick," as he was known, was one of the premier players of his era.

After successive championships in 1903 and 1904,[4] the Boston Americans fell precipitously. In the parlance of the day, the 1906 club achieved the moniker "champion tailenders" following a last-place finish with a 49–105 record. Besides losing 20 consecutive games early in the season, the team scored the fewest runs and had the highest earned run average in the junior circuit. It was an aging ballclub riddled by injuries and dissension. Manager Jimmy Collins was suspended when he left the team without permission, and the manager's close friend, Stahl, was appointed the new skipper of the club. This decision was in sharp contrast to Chick's mid-summer declaration that he would never manage. "Not for me, [Stahl had said,] life is too short; let somebody else do the worrying."[5] The team chemistry soon reached its nadir when Hobe Ferris assaulted teammate Jack Hayden during a game for lackadaisical play. This altercation was described as "the most disgraceful affair ever predicated of any players on the ball field."[6] The interim manager was unable to change the team's fortunes and compiled a 5–13 slate.

The offseason was marked by personal and professional changes in Stahl's life. *Sporting Life* designated the 33-year-old as "a benedict,"[7] a reference used in the early 1900s to indicate a long-term bachelor entering the married state. At St. Francis De Sales Church in Roxbury, Massachusetts, "Charles Sylvester Stahl's love romance culminated on November 14 in his marriage to Miss Julia Harmon, a pretty little brunette."[8] The couple, who had met at a church function, honeymooned at Hot Springs, Arkansas, and Buffalo, New York, where they were Jimmy Collins' guests. On December 11, a second significant event occurred. At the insistence of John Taylor, the Boston owner, and with the blessing of Collins, Stahl accepted the club's managerial position. His official statement included this excerpt: "I will get the club on a sound basis[;] if I didn't[,] I wouldn't have agreed to manage the club, for yours truly doesn't intend to manage any lemon-champions."[9]

With the arrival of spring training in 1907, a sense of optimism permeated the team. Catcher Lou Criger had recovered from a debilitating illness, while Jimmy Collins returned physically and mentally invigorated. In addition, the new manager discarded the lax training methods from the

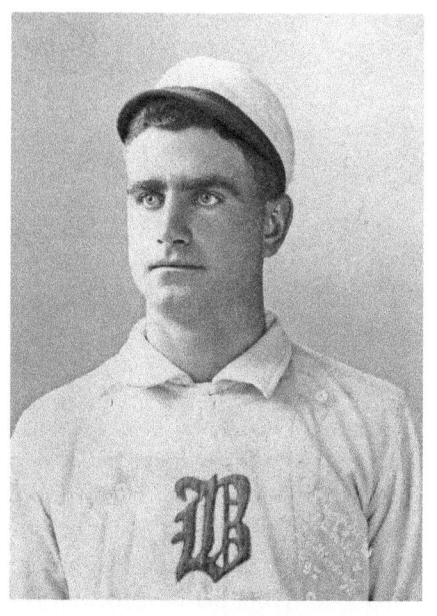

Charles Sylvester "Chick" Stahl (1873–1907), one of the premier players of his era (National Baseball Hall of Fame Library, Cooperstown, New York).

2. The Suicide of Chick Stahl (Auger)

previous year. So, as the team departed from Little Rock, Arkansas, for engagements in other locales, Stahl stated, "All the boys are in fine condition and we could not have picked out a better training place."[10] This picture of stability was fractured when Chick resigned the managerial post on March 25 while the team was in Louisville, leaving him as acting manager until a replacement was named. The veteran player would then be given the duties and responsibilities associated with being team captain. A sense of serenity appeared to have returned to Stahl, implied by the telegram wired to his wife on the evening of March 27 from West Baden, Indiana, which read, "Cheer up, little girl, and be happy. I am all right now and able to play the game of my life."[11]

Jimmy Collins, Chick Stahl's friend and roommate (National Baseball Hall of Fame Library, Cooperstown, New York).

It was evident that the "Fort Wayne boy" had never been comfortable with managing. In 1906, he had resisted the position and said in a self-deprecating manner, "I would make a nice manager, why I couldn't release a man even if he was no good at all."[12] Stahl's inner turmoil was further verbalized when he came forth with this candid observation after his resignation: "This handling of a baseball team both on and off the field is not what it is cracked up to be, and I am glad to be relieved of the responsibility. Releasing players grated on my nerves and they come so frequently at this time of the year that it made me sick at heart."[13]

On the morning of March 28, Stahl ate his customary breakfast and visited the players in their rooms just prior to practice. He then returned to his suite, swallowed four ounces of carbolic acid, and suffered excruciating pain. Despite sending out an alarm for medical assistance, there was nothing that his roommate Jimmy Collins or the other players could do. The dying man's last words were, "Boys, I couldn't help it, it drove me to it."[14] Because the coroner ruled the death a suicide, the funeral could not take place in Stahl's parish, even though Chick was a practicing Roman

The West Baden Springs Hotel, the state-of-the-art resort where Chick Stahl committed suicide (Indiana Historical Society, Bass Photo Company Collection).

Catholic. The Church's canonical laws did not permit a Catholic burial since taking one's life was believed to be a total rejection of God's love and authority. On March 31, the funeral rites were performed by the Benevolent Order of Elks and the Fraternal Order of Eagles at Stahl's residence. Accounts of "[t]he scenes at the Stahl home before the funeral possession [sic] left were pathetic in the extreme. The young bride of a few months was almost prostrated and the grief of the aged mother of the deceased was pitiful to behold."[15] The funeral cortege, attended by thousands, accompanied the player's remains, which were buried in Lindenwood Cemetery in Fort Wayne.

However, the tragic story still had another chapter. On November 15, 1908, Julia Stahl's body was discovered "in the dark hallway of a tenement"[16] in South Boston. Earlier that day she had been in "a drinking place."[17]

What have baseball historians published about the deaths of Charles

2. The Suicide of Chick Stahl (Auger)

and Julia Stahl? In *Baseball's Most Wanted*, Floyd Conner writes that Julia "was a drug addict and committed suicide a year after [Chick's] death. In addition, another woman claimed she was pregnant with Stahl's child and threatened to make the news public if he didn't marry her,"[18] so he took his own life. Derek Gentile, author of *The Complete Boston Red Sox*, narrates that Stahl did not kill himself due to managerial stress, "[b]ut decades later, the real story emerged. Stahl, who was married, had had an affair with what would now be called a baseball 'groupie.'... The woman was pregnant, and came to Stahl for child support. Stahl, mortified, could not face his wife and teammates."[19] John Snyder, in *Red Sox Journal*, amplifies Gentile's comments by stating that Chick's marriage "was not a happy union due to Stahl's infidelity. He had been carrying on a liaison with Lulu Ortman in his home town of Fort Wayne, Indiana, for at least five years.... In addition, Stahl had impregnated a third woman from Chicago during a casual affair. The mistress blackmailed Stahl, threatening to make the news public...."[20] Unable to deal with this, he killed himself. The author also asserts that Julia was "a drug addict" and probably a prostitute.[21]

The above statements are representative of what has been published about the deaths of the Stahls. Several themes arise here. All the authors in question are well known and respected in baseball circles. They speak with a certain authority, as do others who will be cited later. Their information is presented as factual. But the underlying concern is that they do not provide documentation to substantiate their accounts. Without identified sources, what has become accepted in mainstream baseball literature is open to question. The task is to examine the origin of their views.

Extensive research shows that baseball historian Glenn Stout is the primary impetus behind the blackmail theory. Stout points out that the press of the day initially attributed Stahl's demise to managerial stress, but that Frederick O'Connell of the *Boston Post* reported that "domestic troubles are hinted at," "a great trouble was generally admitted," and "many know the true cause."[22] The trouble was never identified because the young reporter contracted pneumonia shortly after Stahl's suicide and died a month later. However, Stout is unequivocal in identifying the cause when he states that "Chick Stahl was driven to his death by the specter of scandal initiated by a women [sic], a women [sic] who was not Mrs. Stahl. She was a 'Baseball Sadie' [i.e., a groupie]."[23] Stout expands on his contention by writing that "[w]hile the Americans played in Chicago late in the 1906 season, Stahl ... had a brief affair with an anonymous woman who is said to have made a habit of sharing her bed with ballplayers."[24] During spring training in 1907, this woman came to Little Rock informing Stahl that she was pregnant and demanded financial support and marriage; if he failed to comply with her demands, she would blackmail him by publicizing the pregnancy. The recent groom saw no way out and ended his life. Stout concludes that "the basic ingredients of the story are generally accepted. Two of baseball's most noted historians, Harold Seymour and David Q. Voigt, refer to the sad tale in their multivolume histories of the game."[25]

However, even though Stout presents specific details about the affair and the blackmail, "the trouble," to quote Frederick O'Connell, is that his story is factually problematic.[26] The documentation to confirm what he wrote is limited to one footnote which cites Harold and Dorothy Seymour's *Baseball.* That text reads, "There is reason to believe that a woman who asserted she was his pregnant wife hounded Chick Stahl, playing manager of the Boston Red Sox, into committing suicide."[27] But Seymour does not offer any proof and no source is provided. Furthermore, "[a] search through his [the Seymour] papers and notes at Cornell University revealed no trace of information concerning Chick Stahl."[28] As for Voigt, he writes that Stahl, "distraught over fear of exposure, swallowed carbolic acid and died in agony at the age of thirty-four."[29] Voigt's footnote refers to Al Stump, who wrote an article entitled "Dames Are the Biggest Headache," which appeared in the September 1959 issue of *Baseball Digest.* The story line and methodological issues are no different. To summarize, the blackmail proponents fail to provide documentation and identifiable sources confirming the veracity of the theory in question. They have never been able to specify a named or unnamed source, e.g., an ex-ballplayer, supporting the threat or scandal. The blackmail contention is based on conjecture and unfortunately is often being presented as historical fact.

Two observations come to mind. One is that Stump was the first to write about the anonymous Chicago woman, which was 52 years after Stahl's death. For this story not to have come out earlier and with more specific detail would have required an incredible conspiracy of silence. It would have necessitated that everyone — including friends, family, baseball personnel, the woman, and jealous individuals — all refrained from making it known. This belies human nature and the seemingly innate tendency to gossip. Was it not O'Connell in March 1907 who stated "many" knew? The other comment concerns the phrase, "It drove me to it." If the "it" referred to the anonymous woman, would it not make more sense that Stahl, in his moment of intense emotional and physical pain, would have blurted out, "She drove me to it," instead of making an inanimate reference?

In *Diamonds in the Rough,* Joel Zoss and John Bowman dismiss the blackmail theory because "little evidence has been offered to support this claim."[30] They propose another explanation, primarily based on an article published in the November 21, 1908, issue of *Sporting Life*. The paper reported that Mrs. Stahl was "fully and richly dressed" and "wore jewelry valued at $2,000, all of which, with the exception of a gold-mounted comb and wedding ring, was missing from the body when found."[31] Also, "[a]fter completing an autopsy, Medical Examiner McGrath announced that death was due to natural causes, 'probably exhaustion brought on by the use of drugs and alcohol.'"[32] For Zoss and Bowman, this means Mrs. Stahl died from a drug overdose. They argue that Julia lived in an era of extensive drug abuse. The fact that she went "to her rendezvous wearing her wealth of jewelry when it was her habit to wear only the wedding ring that was found on her body suggests that she may have been on her way to make a major buy or to pay a major debt."[33] From this article, the authors surmise that "the 'it' that drove Chick Stahl to take his life may well have been his or his wife's addiction."[34] However, if the authors had read the next issue of *Sporting Life*, they would have realized that the police determined Julia was not wearing the jewelry in question because it had been found in her house drawer.[35] Thus, the drug deal or payment theory collapses. Concerning the coroner's statement, the wording was likely addressing the initial police suspicion that Julia's drink had been drugged. Furthermore, there is no evidence offered by the two writers that she had a drug problem when Chick was alive or that he ever had one. In fact, he was the best hitter on that 1906 club, led the American League in games played[36] and outfield putouts,[37] and was in fine physical condition in 1907.[38]

So, what did happen to Julia? She was at "a drinking place ... where men and women mingle about the tables."[39] Four men, ranging in age from 18 to 31, admitted being in the company of Mrs. Stahl and, according to a subhead in the Pawtucket *Evening Times*, had been "Giving Her Whiskey to Drink."[40] They left her in the doorway of a building nearby, believing she had simply passed out. At 10:15 P.M. that evening, Julia was found dead.

In examining Julia's death, Stout connects it to Chick's alleged unfaithfulness. "Now I don't know if his wife got wind of it [the affair with the Chicago woman] over the winter or, and this is hearsay — I couldn't find any evidence of it — but I think he might have gotten a dose [syphilis], and given it to his wife. That split them up."[41] The result was that "Chick lived the rest of the winter in Fort Wayne, and she lived the rest of the winter in Boston."[42] This separation would have occurred shortly after their honeymoon in November 1906. The other indicator that Stahl had been infected with syphilis was his use of carbolic acid. This deduction is questionable because at the turn of the 20th century, carbolic acid was used as a disinfectant for a myriad of ailments. In addition, it was often ingested to commit suicide. But what about the alleged separation and marital discord between the Stahls? This is contradicted by a story in the Fort Wayne *Journal Gazette* which describes the occasion when Charles and Julia were guests at a party given by a Mr. and Mrs. Schneider in February 1907 in Fort Wayne. Mrs. Schneider was quoted as saying, "It would be impossible to conceive of two people happier than they were at that time ... I never saw a man and wife more devoted to each other than were Mr. and Mrs. Stahl."[43] This clearly undermines Stout's statements.

What is Glenn Stout's theory about Julia's death? "I think by that time [1908] she was a prostitute. And I think that she had syphilis too, 'cause she died of edema of the brain, which is also a symptom of syphilis."[44] However, the prostitution allegation is suggested by "[h]er manner of dress"[45] and because she had been drinking with men at an establishment. Following this logic, one is left with the conclusion that any well-attired woman who is at a bar which catered to both genders must be engaging in promiscuous sex for money.

The more troubling contention that Julia had syphilis is based on the death certificate which, according to Stout, stated she died from "natural causes — specifically an edema, or swelling, of the brain."[46] Edema is a symptom of syphilis, but it occurs years after initial infection and in the tertiary phase of the disease, i.e., the final phase. It must be remembered that late 1906 is the time frame advanced as the date of her infection. Furthermore, the presence of brain swelling would have been preceded by *tabes dorsalis* which is defined as "a slow degeneration of the nerve cells and nerve fibers that carry sensory information to the brain."[47] Its onset is usually in mid-life and symptoms might not occur for "decades after the initial infection."[48] Common symptoms include weakness, nutritional problems, unsteady gait, diminished reflexes, loss of coordination, intense pain, dementia, and hearing and visual impairment.[49] All things considered, "[Julia would have been] quite young for that to happen."[50] If she had *tabes dorsalis* and edema due to syphilis, her daily living skills would have been severely compromised. On the day of her death, the widow was seen as an attractive and well-dressed individual, who visited friends at different places and took a streetcar to the drinking establishment. That would not have been possible with tertiary syphilis.

Thus, how does one account for edema of the brain? Mrs. Stahl was a woman of petite stature, and being female, would have had a lower tolerance and metabolism rate for alcohol than men. The men who left her in the doorway thought she had passed out. In all probability, the alcohol had reached the deepest recesses of her brain center anesthetizing her vital signs, resulting in edema and death. Or she could have been poisoned if the liquor that she drank had been drugged or made from homemade alcohol with methanol. Another possibility is that she had intracranial bleeding, i.e., an aneurysm which would exclude alcohol as a factor. In the end, however, the most likely and logical choice is that she died from an alcohol overdose,[51] overhydration being consistent with the cited medical examiner's statement and the death certificate's conclusion. Julia did not commit suicide nor did she die from syphilis. Moreover, the Catholic Church guarded against scandal. If Julia had taken her own life or been involved in "loose living," she would have been denied a funeral mass, but she was not. And at that mass, Father E.J. Farrell eulogized her, emphasizing "that she had always been regarded as an exemplary and devout young woman."[52]

Historical research is not an infallible endeavor. The printed word about Chick Stahl, however, is marked by a preponderance of misinformation, confused facts, innuendos, and unsubstantiated theories and rumors. In addition to the ones previously cited, there are others. John Snyder's statement that Stahl was unfaithful to his wife because he had a five-year relationship with Lulu Ortman is not corroborated by anyone. Snyder probably misread the 1907 newspaper story which reported that Ortman had fallen in love with Stahl five years prior, but it was not ongoing. It had ended in 1902. Another story makes reference to a woman, not

Ortman, who tried stabbing Stahl. But this has never been authenticated in any fashion. Based on such examples, it appears that baseball writers have not complied with the standards of historical research. A "herd mentality" permeates the Stahl literature, i.e., "once somebody says it, it's taken as gospel without checking the facts."[53]

Stahl's persona is commonly portrayed as that of a narcissistic womanizer whose unethical behavior led to his act of self-destruction. This impression fails to take into account the complexity of the man. At the time of Chick's suicide, some Washington players observed that they knew "for a year or more he had some secret trouble which did not seem to be connected with base ball and that his loud laughter and jollity were often a mask."[54] This inner turmoil clearly predated the alleged affair and blackmail.

What was this trouble? Dick Thompson uncovered a long forgotten story and concluded that the truth was not to be found in the Boston press reports but in Fort Wayne.[55] The March 30, 1907, issue of the Fort Wayne *Journal Gazette* contained an extensive article about Stahl's chronic history of depression. The headline and subheads appeared as follows: "Meditated Self-Slaying," "Chick Stahl Had Often Talked About Suicide," and "Base Ball Player Had Entertained Dangerous Ideas About Self-Destruction."[56] "Close friends ... were not surprised at his suicide"[57] and another friend since boyhood related that Stahl had "talked about killing himself several times when he was discouraged about his affairs...."[58] This confidant, who was a city official, reported that about five years previously he heard Chick "tell the barber who was shaving him that it would be a good thing for him to put the razor through his neck."[59] The article also stated that "more than once before that time and more than once afterwards he [Stahl] was heard to say things that indicated a suicidal tendency."[60] This mental anguish and talk of taking his own life was present as far back as 1889 when Stahl was playing amateur ball, and even then "[s]ometimes the slightest disappointment would sink him into almost a stupor of depression, and on these occasions[,] his team mates and manager used to fear that he had designs on his own life."[61] Clinically, such overreaction to life's problems is symptomatic of a mood disorder. These mood swings and suicidal gestures surfaced in March 1907 and were witnessed by the manager's "closer friends on the team."[62] Late in spring training, Stahl told a Memphis photographer, "Well, I guess that will be the last picture ever taken of

2. *The Suicide of Chick Stahl* (Auger)

me."[63] These documented facts confirm a pattern of Stahl's behavior which cannot be denied.

Some commentators have referred to Stahl's mental condition as "general melancholy" or "simple despondency." However, such descriptions fail to grasp the intricate nature of Chick's clinical depression. He suffered from a psychiatric illness during his entire adulthood. The evidence is unmistakable. Depression was indeed the Indiana ballplayer's main trouble which "many" witnessed and knew about.

But there is more to the character study of Charles Stahl. It is crucial to address his religious beliefs and practices. During the late 19th century, Roman Catholics were in love with baseball. Parish priests often played and organized games, as exemplified by Father Michael McGivney (1852–1890), whose process of being declared a saint has been initiated.[64] Catholics were plentiful on major league rosters and close bonds between players and priests were common. When Harry Dolan of the Boston Doves died from typhoid fever in March 1907, the funeral mass was celebrated by Father F.J. Ryan, "a life long friend of the deceased."[65] This period was also marked by anti–Catholicism and the Church offered a safe haven for worship and recreation. Stahl, a practicing Catholic, lived in this social milieu and he met his wife at church. In a story dated March 31, 1907, Frederick O'Connell wrote: "Born of German Catholic parents[,] Stahl never forgot his religious duties during the base ball season. Only a week ago last Sunday[,] Stahl did his Easter duty [*sic*] in Little Rock. He never missed mass if it was possible for him to attend."[66] Easter Duty refers to the Catholic practice of going to confession and receiving communion during the Easter season, which continues until Pentecost Sunday, 50 days after Easter Sunday. And Stahl adhered to this Church precept, demonstrating that he was a man of faith.

It is also important to remember that during Stahl's lifetime, Catholic morality was heavily influenced by Jansenism. This view stressed that human nature was corrupt and that a believer needed to observe an ultra-rigid moral code. Only in so doing could one avoid mortal sin and its accompanying consequences, which included eternal damnation in the fires of hell. Special vigilance had to be taken to avoid sins of the flesh, i.e., sexual sins. The German theologian, Father Bernard Haring, notes that "[d]uring the last centuries, the faithful were particularly troubled by the specific emphasis given by many moralists and by the Roman Universal

Inquisition who taught that all sins in thought, desire and deeds against the sixth commandment are *ex toto genere suo* mortal sins,"[67] which means "deadly in all degrees and dimensions."[68] In other words, masturbation or taking pleasure in a sexual thought was as seriously sinful as fornication, adultery, and sodomy. During Stahl's lifetime, American priests used moral manuals to guide them in confessional matters. The theme was straightforward: "There is no *parvitas materiae*— no small or slight matter — in the sixth and ninth commandments; all sexual sins contain grave matter."[69]

As a Catholic, Stahl would have found comfort and support in his heritage. On the other hand, as he struggled with depression, his coping skills would have been compromised as he tried to deal with an unhealthy and unrealistic demand for perfectionism, which the Church of his day expected. Furthermore, if Stahl was sexually promiscuous, one likely reason for this behavior would have been to self-medicate his depression. But ironically, this would have increased his guilt due to the inability to live up to the moral dictates of his conscience. And this vicious cycle would have intensified the depression.

However, there is another dimension to this issue. On March 30, 1907, a syndicated story reported that David Murphy of Fort Wayne committed suicide by swallowing carbolic acid: "It is believed that the suicide of 'Chick' Stahl, who was an intimate friend of Murphy, had much to do with influencing Murphy. He left a note saying: 'Bury me beside Chick.'"[70] From a psychologist's perspective, Murphy's language and behavior indicates that this relationship might have been more than platonic, at least in his mind. Was it sexual? Was Murphy delusional? Was it an unreciprocated sexual obsession? If it was mutual, this would only heighten Stahl's moral conflict and depression.

The Chick Stahl story is truly tragic. A man of religious faith, he fulfilled his Easter Duty and, a few days later on Holy Thursday, committed suicide, thus prohibiting a Catholic burial. His premature death was a loss to family and friends. They described the beloved Chick as a virtuous man who demonstrated care, compassion, wisdom, generosity, courage, and loyalty throughout his life. Explanations for Stahl's self-destruction have been examined in detail, but perhaps the best theory was presented by Dick Thompson when he wrote, "I think O'Connell did know the truth, but the truth was not that Stahl was responding to a blackmail threat. It was that he was responding to his own haunted emotions."[71] Depression,

2. The Suicide of Chick Stahl (Auger)

which includes a chemical imbalance, was the underlying issue. The role of psychosocial stressors such as managing and the alleged (but unproven) womanizing would be secondary and exacerbating factors. In the end, Stahl experienced what Catholic mystics describe as the dark night of the soul, i.e., an overwhelming depression combined with a feeling of total abandonment by God. If Chick Stahl were alive today, therapy, medication, and spiritual direction would be available to him. This "might have allowed him to lead a long and productive life."[72]

Offering masses for the repose of souls has been a centuries-old Catholic tradition. The purpose is to honor and remember the deceased, asking God to forgive and grant them eternal rest. These memorial masses are usually celebrated on the anniversary of the death of the person in question. This writer has such a mass celebrated for Charles Sylvester Stahl on a yearly basis.

Richard J. "Dick" Thompson, the baseball researcher who believed Stahl's inner demons were to blame for the star's demise (courtesy Barbara Thompson).

Notes

1. This quotation is taken from an April 6, 1907, article found in Stahl's file in the National Baseball Hall of Fame Library in Cooperstown, New York. However, the newspaper from which the article comes is not identified.

2. Bill James, *The New Bill James Historical Baseball Abstract* (New York: Free Press, 2001), 755; Derek Gentile, *Baseball's Best 1,000: Rankings of the Skills, the Achievements, and the Performance of the Greatest Players of All Time* (New York: Black Dog & Leventhal, 2004), 329.

3. Francis C. Richter, *Richter's History and Records of Base Ball: The American Nation's Chief Sport*, The McFarland Historical Baseball Library, eds. Gary Mitchem, Marty McGee, and Mark Durr, no. 4 (Jefferson, NC: McFarland, 2005), 417.

4. Alfred H. Spink, *The National Game*, 2d ed. (Carbondale: Southern Illinois University Press, 2000), 315. In 1904, the National League pennant was won by the New York

Giants, but since they refused to play the Americans in the World Series, "the title of World's Champions went to Boston by default."

5. *Sporting Life*, August 4, 1906, 7.
6. This quotation is taken from an article found in Ferris' file in the National Baseball Hall of Fame Library in Cooperstown, New York. However, the newspaper from which the article comes and the date of the article are not identified.
7. *Sporting Life*, November 24, 1906, 3.
8. Ibid.
9. *Sporting Life*, December 15, 1906, 3.
10. [Pawtucket] *Evening Times*, March 23, 1907.
11. [Fort Wayne] *Journal Gazette*, March 30, 1907.
12. Ibid., March 29, 1907.
13. Ibid.
14. Ibid.
15. Ibid., April 1, 1907.
16. [Pawtucket] *Evening Times*, November 19, 1908.
17. Ibid., November 17, 1908.
18. Floyd Conner, *Baseball's Most Wanted: The Top 10 of the National Pastime's Outrageous Offenders, Lucky Bounces, and Other Oddities* (Dulles, VA: Brassey's, 2000), 352–353.
19. Derek Gentile, *The Complete Boston Red Sox: The Total Encyclopedia of the Team* (New York: Black Dog & Leventhal, 2004), 321.
20. John Snyder, *Red Sox Journal: Year by Year & Day by Day with the Boston Red Sox Since 1901* (Cincinnati: Emmis Books, 2006), 47.
21. Ibid., 48.
22. Glenn Stout, "The Manager's End Game," in *Sports in Massachusetts: Historical Essays*, eds. Ronald Story and Martin Kaufman (Westfield: Institute for Massachusetts Studies, 1991), 132.
23. Ibid., 133.
24. Ibid.
25. Ibid., 134.
26. I discussed Stahl's suicide in less detail in *Deadball Stars of the American League*, ed. David Jones (Dulles, VA: Potomac Books, 2006), 418–421.
27. Harold Seymour and Dorothy Seymour Mills, *Baseball: The Golden Age* (New York: Oxford University Press, 1989), 102.
28. Chris Christensen, "Chick Stahl: A Baseball Suicide," *Elysian Fields* 20, no. 2 (2003): 29.
29. David Quentin Voigt, *American Baseball*, vol. 2, *From the Commissioners to Continental Expansion* (University Park: The Pennsylvania State University Press, 1983), 71–72.
30. Joel Zoss and John Bowman, *Diamonds in the Rough: The Untold History of Baseball* (Chicago: Contemporary Books, 1996), 344.
31. *Sporting Life*, November 21, 1908, 8.
32. Ibid.
33. Zoss and Bowman, 344.
34. Ibid.
35. *Sporting Life*, November 28, 1908, 8.
36. Pete Palmer and Gary Gillette, eds., *The 2005 ESPN Baseball Encyclopedia* (New York: Sterling, 2005), 155.
37. Pete Cava, "Requiem for a Ballplayer: Indiana's Chick Stahl," *Traces* 16, no. 3 (2004): 43.

2. The Suicide of Chick Stahl (Auger)

38. *Sporting Life*, April 6, 1907, 5.
39. [Pawtucket] *Evening Times*, November 17, 1908.
40. Ibid., November 19, 1908.
41. Peter Golenbock, *Red Sox Nation: An Unexpurgated History of the Boston Red Sox* (Chicago: Triumph Books, 2005), 27–28.
42. Ibid., 27.
43. [Fort Wayne] *Journal Gazette*, March 29, 1907.
44. Golenbock, 28.
45. Stout, 135.
46. Ibid.
47. "Neurological Disorders: Tabes Dorsalis," May 16, 2008, 1, http://www.mamas health.com (accessed May 16, 2008). Besides this article, medical information has been provided by Vincent Marcaccio, MD, from Mineral Spring Primary Care Associates in North Providence, Rhode Island.
48. Ibid.
49. Ibid., 1–2.
50. E-mail message from Vincent Marcaccio, MD, to Dennis Auger, May 15, 2008.
51. Ibid. Dr. Marcaccio, an expert in treating substance abuse disorders, is in agreement with this view. Also, he is the physician who raised the poisoning and aneurysm possibilities.
52. [Pawtucket] *Evening Times*, November 19, 1908.
53. The "herd mentality" was discussed in *Blue and Gold Illustrated* 24, no. 16 (April 2005): 23.
54. *Sporting Life*, April 13, 1907, 6.
55. Dick Thompson, "In Name Only," *The National Pastime* 20 (2000): 56; Dick Thompson, "Stahl's Suicide," *The Baseball Research Journal* 28 (1999): 7.
56. [Fort Wayne] *Journal Gazette*, March 30, 1907.
57. Ibid.
58. Ibid.
59. Ibid.
60. Ibid.
61. Ibid.
62. [Pawtucket] *Evening Times*, March 29, 1907.
63. [Fort Wayne] *Journal Gazette*, March 30, 1907.
64. For information on Father McGivney, see Douglas Brinkley and Julie M. Fenster, *Parish Priest: Father Michael McGivney and American Catholicism* (New York: HarperCollins, 2006).
65. *Sporting Life*, April 13, 1907, 7.
66. Frederick O'Connell, "Worried to Death." This article is found in Stahl's file in the National Baseball Hall of Fame Library in Cooperstown, New York, and was syndicated and appeared in a St. Louis paper dated April 6, 1907. However, the original date of the article is March 31, 1907.
67. Bernard Haring, *Free and Faithful in Christ: Moral Theology for Clergy and Laity*, vol. 1, *General Moral Theology* (New York: Seabury Press, 1978), 407.
68. Ibid., 406.
69. Leslie Griffin, "American Catholic Sexual Ethics," in *The Encyclopedia of American Catholic History*, ed. Michael Glazier and Thomas Shelley (Collegeville, MN: The Liturgical Press, 1997), 45.
70. [Pawtucket] *Evening Times*, March 30, 1907.
71. Thompson, "In Name Only," 56.
72. Ibid.

3
The Strange Death of Harry C. Pulliam

Angelo J. Louisa and Floyd Sullivan

At 9:30 A.M. on Wednesday, July 28, 1909, Harry Pulliam, the president of the National League, arrived at his office at 26th and Broadway in New York City and started reading the correspondence that he had received. After getting about halfway through, he stopped and began staring out his window. Then, at 1:00 P.M., he told his stenographer that he felt ill and was leaving for the day. He did not say where he was going or when he would return, but since Pulliam was a bachelor who lived alone at the New York Athletic Club, he may have gone there to rest, though no one at the club knew that he was in his room until approximately 9:30 that evening. It was at that time that a telephone operator on the ground floor of the club noticed a flashing light on his switchboard, indicating that the telephone receiver in Pulliam's room had been lifted. After attempting to contact Pulliam several times without receiving an answer, the operator notified one of the hotel clerks who sent a bellboy named Thomas Brady to Pulliam's room to check on him. Brady either found the door unlocked or opened it with a passkey after knocking and getting no response — newspaper accounts disagree — and entered the room. What he saw next may have horrified him. There, lying on the floor or, as one newspaper reported, the divan, dressed only in his underclothes, was the mortally wounded Pulliam. He had been shot once through the head, the bullet entering his right temple, fracturing the frontal bone, blowing out his right eye, passing through the upper portion of his left eye, and exiting the left side of his skull. Also, apparently lying on the floor — though some newspaper accounts do not mention it — was a .38 caliber revolver.[1]

3. The Strange Death of Harry C. Pulliam (Louisa and Sullivan)

Hotel authorities immediately called the club physician, Dr. J.J. Higgins of West 56th Street, and the Manhattan coroner, Dr. George Shrady. When the men arrived, they discovered Pulliam semiconscious and in pain, but still able to talk a little. Shrady tried to find out what had happened by asking the only witness present: Pulliam himself. What followed depends on which newspaper version is to be believed. According to the *New York Times*, Shrady asked, "How were you shot?" To which Pulliam supposedly responded, "I am not shot."[2] The *Chicago Daily Tribune* also reported Shrady's question, but said that Pulliam replied, "What do you mean? I don't understand what you mean."[3] The *Atlanta Constitution*, *Cincinnati Enquirer*, and *Los Angeles Times* all stated that Shrady, assuming that Pulliam's wound was self-inflicted, was more direct in his approach

A photograph taken in January 1909 of Harry Clay Pulliam (1869–1909), left, the president of the National League, seated with the other members of the National Commission, Organized Baseball's governing body from 1903 to 1920. Others, left to right: August "Garry" Herrmann, the owner of the Cincinnati Reds; Byron Bancroft "Ban" Johnson, the president of the American League; and John E. Bruce, the commission's secretary (Library of Congress, Prints & Photographs Division, Bain Collection, [LC-USZ62-91940]).

and inquired, "Why did you shoot yourself?" Pulliam at first did not reply, but once the question was repeated, he allegedly answered, "Why! Whose shot?" or "Who's shot?" or "Why, who is shot?" And when asked the question again, he said either "What shot?" or "Who's shot?"[4] Shrady and Higgins agreed that any further questioning would get them nowhere and would only worsen Pulliam's already critical condition. So, they did what they could to make him comfortable and put him in bed, where he lapsed into a coma and died at 7:40 the next morning.[5]

For many people associated with the National League, Pulliam's death was not only tragic but also a major setback to the growth of Organized Baseball. A man of integrity and diplomacy, Pulliam had been a highly successful administrator. After being elected as president of the senior circuit as a compromise choice on December 12, 1902, he immediately went to work to achieve peace between the two warring major leagues, something that was accomplished by the middle of the next month.[6] And though Pulliam should not receive all the credit for ending the interleague conflict — he was only one of eight representatives, four from each league, selected to address the issues[7]— his desire to negotiate and his willingness to put the interests of Organized Baseball as a whole over any bias that he may have had for his own league can be seen in the terms of the treaty, as summarized by Arthur Hittner:

> Each league agreed to respect the reserve rights of the other league's clubs, which bound players indefinitely to their respective teams. A uniform player contract was adopted for use in both circuits. Claims over disputed players were resolved. Finally, the American League was permitted to field a team in New York for the 1903 season in exchange for abandoning its plans to move into Pittsburgh.[8]

Once peace was attained, Pulliam then turned his attention to bringing order and respectability to the National League. In doing so, he almost always supported the decisions of his umpires, fined and suspended players and managers for what was then termed "rowdyism" on the field, and struggled to curb the divisiveness of the club owners. Concerned about the safety of the players, as well as that of his men officiating the games, he "recommended that the sale of liquids in bottles be prohibited at all baseball grounds and that no intoxicants be sold in the grandstands."[9] Equally concerned about the accuracy of baseball statistics, he "ruled that if, when a ball is batted to a fielder, and that fielder attempts to force another player,

3. The Strange Death of Harry C. Pulliam (Louisa and Sullivan)

but fails, the bats[man] should be given a fielder's choice instead of a hit, unless it was clear that the fielder could not have thrown him out at first."[10] He even spoke out against the spitball, saying in 1908:

> It's unclean; it prevents good fielding; it handicaps scientific batting; it's a freak, and so has no place in straight sport.... I am strongly opposed to the use of that style of delivery for the reasons I have stated, and for others, too. It is possible that between now and the time for holding the next annual meeting of the National League, there will be framed some legislation to which both leagues will agree, and which will do away with this offensive style of pitching.... The "spit ball" is no more an essential part of base ball than is the dog-faced boy of the three-ringed circus. Both are freaks, without which the big show would be much better off.[11]

However, Pulliam's attempts to improve his league went beyond the field of play. He criticized the New York Giants for not having better locker rooms for the visiting teams and the umpires[12]; he started a Hall of Fame in the National League offices in New York, where photographs of select baseball stars and championship teams could be placed[13]; and he moved the National League meetings from a Broadway hotel to the Waldorf-Astoria.[14] Furthermore, he tried to better the sport in general by supporting the establishment of the Baseball Writers Association of America, in part because the organization intended to institute uniform scoring practices.[15] And he wanted to help former ballplayers who were struggling to survive. As *The Sporting News* reported three weeks after Pulliam died, "The late Harry C. Pulliam was a firm advocate of a beneficiary for permanently incapacitated players. For several years prior to his death[,] he had worked for the establishment of a home for decrepit stars of the diamond."[16]

But despite Pulliam's accomplishments and noble intentions, or perhaps because of them, those close to him were not surprised to learn about his death. A dandy who wore wide-brimmed hats and gala-colored waistcoats, "Haberdashery Harry," as one sportswriter referred to him, could be a charming fellow.[17] He was an educated gentleman, a raconteur, a lover of nature, and a former newspaper writer with a penchant for quoting Shakespeare.[18]

Unfortunately, though, Pulliam also had his own set of demons with which to contend. An overly sensitive perfectionist with high ideals, he let the pressures of his office get the best of him and became defensive when confronted with any form of criticism.[19] This defensiveness either led to or exacerbated the bouts of depression or, as it was termed in the early 20th century, melancholia from which Pulliam suffered, a condition that was probably further worsened by the opposition that Pulliam's policies received from John Brush, the owner of the New York Giants, John McGraw, the manager of the Giants, and to a lesser extent, some of the other National League magnates. Pulliam's friends in Pittsburgh, a city where Pulliam had lived and served as the secretary of the Pirates before becoming the head of the National League, claimed that since 1907, Pulliam "had talked unreservedly of suicide."[20] And Barney Dreyfuss, the owner of the Pirates and Pulliam's onetime partner and longtime supporter, said upon learning about Pulliam's death, "It's awful, but I expected it."[21]

Thus, when Pulliam passed away on that July morning in 1909, his death was assumed to be a suicide brought about by a fragile emotional state and the stress that came with the position that he held. In particular, it was thought that the verbal beating that he took from the New York media and fans concerning the infamous Merkle incident pushed him over the brink. Much has been written about this incident, but for those readers unfamiliar with it, the known facts are these:

- On September 23, 1908, the New York Giants, the Chicago Cubs, and the Pittsburgh Pirates were battling it out in the last few weeks of a three-team pennant race, with the Giants in a virtual tie with the Cubs (New York was slightly ahead on percentage points, .635 to .629) and the Pirates only a game and a half behind the leaders going into the day.
- The Giants faced the Cubs in a single game in the Polo Grounds that afternoon.
- In the bottom of the ninth of that game, with the scored tied, 1–1, and with two outs, the Giants had Moose McCormick on third and Fred Merkle, a rookie, on first, when the batter, Al Bridwell, singled to center. McCormick scored what appeared to be the winning run, but Merkle, viewing McCormick crossing the plate, did what he had seen veteran players do in similar situations: he ran about halfway to second and then headed for the clubhouse, thinking that the game was over and his team had won. At the same time, the Giant faithful surged onto the field to celebrate the victory, producing a chaotic scene.

3. *The Strange Death of Harry C. Pulliam* (Louisa and Sullivan)

- However, in the midst of the chaos, Cub second baseman Johnny Evers, knowing that technically a force out at second would nullify McCormick's run, shouted to the Cub center fielder, Art Hofman, to throw him the ball. This Hofman did, but his throw was off target. Several Cub players, as well as Giant coach Joe McGinnity, realized what was going on and all of them went for the ball, with McGinnity apparently wrestling it away from his opponents and supposedly throwing it into the stands. But somehow Evers retrieved the thrown ball or received another ball from his teammates, tagged second base, and appealed to the base umpire, Bob Emslie, that Merkle was out and the run should not count.
- Emslie responded that he had not seen the play and asked the plate umpire, Hank O'Day, for assistance. O'Day, in turn, told Emslie that Evers was right, ruled that Merkle was out, and took the run away from the Giants, leaving the game a 1–1 tie because play could not be resumed.
- When the Giants protested the ruling to the National League office, Pulliam, as was his habit, supported his umpires, keeping the game a draw and saying that it would have to be replayed at the end of the season if it was needed to determine the pennant winner. The Giants then appealed to the National League board of directors, but the board upheld Pulliam's decision and scheduled the game to be replayed on October 8 if necessary.
- And as events turned out, the makeup game certainly was necessary. New York and Chicago ended the regular season tied for first, so the game was played in the Polo Grounds, with the Cubs winning, 4–2, and capturing the pennant and with the Giants and their followers blaming O'Day and Pulliam for robbing them of what was rightfully theirs.[22]

The resulting barrage of criticism was, and still is, believed by some sportswriters and historians to be the catalyst that aggravated Pulliam's already weakened psyche, leading to his eventual "nervous breakdown" in February of 1909, his leave of absence between February and June of that year, and his subsequent suicide in July. According to this theory, Pulliam returned too soon to his job, not giving himself enough time to recover from the wear and tear of the previous six years.

Mysteries from Baseball's Past

However, the reasons for Pulliam's suicide — if it was indeed a suicide and not murder — may be far more complex and murky than just a talented but troubled idealist who cracked under the strain of a position for which he was not emotionally suited. And the clues to understanding these reasons come from several key factors:

1. Pulliam's genes.
2. Another unsolved baseball mystery: Who was behind the attempt to bribe the officials who umpired the makeup game on October 8?
3. Pulliam's own words and actions, in particular between October 1908 and July 28, 1909.
4. Pulliam's alleged homosexuality.
5. The piece of correspondence that Pulliam was supposedly reading on July 28, 1909, when he told his stenographer that he was not feeling well and was going to take the rest of the day off.

Turning to the first factor, Charles Ebbets, the owner of the Brooklyn Superbas, stated in February of 1909 that he "understood that there was a tinge of insanity somewhere in [Pulliam's] family,"[23] and the descendents of one of Pulliam's siblings have admitted that mental illness did indeed affect at least a few of their ancestors.[24] One of Pulliam's sisters, Grace, committed suicide eight years after Pulliam died and may have been the woman A.R. Cratty was referring to when he wrote, "A dear relative [of Pulliam] lost her reason early in life."[25] And one of Grace's twin sons spent his adult life in a mental institution.[26]

These findings may explain Pulliam's bouts of depression and talk of suicide as early as 1907, but they also raise the question of why Pulliam did not end his life sooner than late July of 1909. Was there something that occurred in 1908 or 1909 that served as a catalyst for pushing Pulliam over the brink? If Pulliam was indeed suffering from a type of psychoneurotic or psychotic disorder, could a serious external event or one or more individuals involved in a serious external event have led to his death? And that is where the second and most detailed factor enters the picture.

In October of 1908, Bill Klem, one of the two umpires scheduled to officiate the New York–Chicago makeup game, claimed that he had been approached the day before the game by Dr. Joseph Creamer, the Giants'

3. The Strange Death of Harry C. Pulliam (Louisa and Sullivan)

team physician, and offered a bribe of $2,500 if the Giants emerged victorious.[27] According to Klem, Creamer went further to say that he represented the Sullivans — "Big Tim," the powerful Tammany Hall ward boss, habitual gambler, and in the words of Mike Dash, "Tammany's most important conduit to New York vice,"[28] and "Little Tim," Big Tim's cousin and one of his lieutenants[29] — who had bet $20,000 or $25,000 on New York to win.[30] And when Klem declined the bribe by replying, "I don't know who is even going to umpire the game, and I could not do anything like that, [name removed, probably "Doc,"] why I have just made good at the business, and you would not want me to be marked like that," Creamer is said to have retorted, "I have been the go-between for these fellows many times in [deleted word or words] and it ain't going to hurt you, because McGraw or the players don't know anything about it."[31] However, perhaps just as interesting, in the ensuing conversation in which Creamer was unsuccessful in convincing Klem to accept his bribe even if he could get the amount raised to $3,000, the doctor allegedly let slip that he was waiting for John Brush.[32]

Klem reported the incident to the National League office the next morning and asked to be removed from officiating the game. At the same time, the umpire scheduled to work with Klem, Jimmy Johnstone, arrived at the office, told his own story about being approached on the evenings of October 6 and 7 by two different men whom he did not know but who offered him bribes if he would make sure that New York would win, and also asked to not umpire that day.[33] Pulliam was out of town, but John Heydler, the National League secretary, listened to Klem's and Johnstone's accounts and then told them that it was impossible to get another pair of officials to replace them on such short notice. So, the two men just had to make the most of the situation and umpire to the best of their abilities.

Later that day, as Klem and Johnstone were walking underneath the grandstand from their dressing room to the field of play to start the game, Creamer is said to have reappeared, tried to bribe Klem again, and added after Klem refused to budge, "Why, the big fellow [implying Big Tim Sullivan] said he never knew you lived here, and I can get you a job here for all the winters of your life"[34] and "Well, if we win the game[,] I am going to see that you get some of this money."[35]

Klem met with Pulliam on October 11 and 12 and told him about both incidents, and then, at Pulliam's request, he put into writing his version of what happened and submitted it to Pulliam in the form of a letter dated October 14, 1908. Similarly, after Johnstone talked with Pulliam in early December — a conversation in which the umpire said that he believed that Creamer represented the Sullivans[36] — he sent the National League president his written version of the bribery attempts as a letter dated December 5, 1908. In it, Johnstone reiterated in detail what he told John Heydler the morning of October 8, but there is one confusing line in which Johnstone stated that he saw Creamer attempting to give Klem money on October 7 as well as October 8, though Klem's letter makes no mention of Johnstone being present when Creamer approached him on the 7th.[37]

Whatever occurred, Pulliam said nothing about the letters until he read them to the National League owners at the December 1908 meeting of the senior circuit's board of directors, which led to a lengthy discussion about how to handle the problem. The always money- and image-conscious magnates were at loggerheads attempting to decide how to investigate the matter and what to tell the press, but they did agree to send a two-man committee of Charles Ebbets and August "Garry" Herrmann to visit John Brush, who was not present at the meeting, and apprise him of what had happened. This Ebbets and Herrmann did, with the latter suggesting that Brush join the rest of the owners and look at the letters himself. However, Brush, who hated Pulliam because he felt that the president showed partiality in his decisions, and who thought that the other magnates were against the New York club — something that Chi-

John Brush, the owner of the New York Giants and one of Harry Pulliam's enemies (National Baseball Hall of Fame Library, Cooperstown, New York).

3. The Strange Death of Harry C. Pulliam (Louisa and Sullivan)

cago Cubs owner Charles Murphy believed was "a newspaper fable"[38]— did not want to attend the meeting and probably would not have done so if Pulliam and some of the owners had not refused to let the letters out of the meeting room. But considering the fact that the accused Creamer had been the Giants' team physician, Brush probably thought it would be in his best interests to make an appearance, tell what he knew about his employee to the owners as a group, and help them determine how to resolve the matter.

Brush arrived the next day, and after listening to the other magnates' ideas about conducting an investigation and giving a statement to the press, he explained that he had not hired Creamer nor had he known that Creamer was working for his club until the season was over and Creamer had presented him with a bill for the services that he had rendered.[39] Brush said that he became furious, and when he looked into Creamer's claim, he found that the doctor's employment stemmed from a misunderstanding between Creamer and Fred Knowles, the secretary-treasurer of the New York club. According to Brush:

> [Creamer] claimed that in his talk with Knowles on 72nd [S]treet that he considered that an engagement by Knowles had been made with him to make [a road] trip with the club. He insisted upon that. Knowles insisted that that was not the case, and that so far as he was concerned he had extended the invitation to him as he would to anybody else, who said[,] "I wish I could take the trip"; and Knowles said[,] "Come on, it is a nice trip"; and he joined the club.
> During the conversation, and as a final conclusion, I realized that in a suit [Creamer's] statement in the hands of a jury probably would be believed....
> ... [A]nd feeling that [Creamer] would bring a suit that I did not like to become involved in[,] I paid his bill.[40]

Brush went further to say that in the presence of John McGraw, he severely criticized Knowles for his part in the affair and told him "that from that time on[,] he had no authority whatever as [s]ecretary and [t]reasurer of the New York [c]lub to contract for anything with anybody to the extent of one penny."[41] And then he added:

> I hardly know [Creamer]. I have hardly known any of the physicians that we have ever had in the club. We have had a new one nearly every year, and their bills have usually been presented for the special things they did.... He certainly never waited for me, as Klem states in his letter....

> The only conversation that I ever had with him in my life since his connection with the club was on the occasion of an accident or injury to some player, if I met him; but that is a rare case; that is usually attended to by Mr. McGraw. I was associated more with him in Pittsburg during the last Series there when he sat in a box than during all the summer put together. I do not know that I ever saw him after that except out on the field.[42]

As for advice to the owners regarding how they should proceed, Brush felt that they needed more information before going to the press with what they knew at that time, and in expressing his views, he brought up the idea of forming a committee to investigate the situation.[43] After Brush had finished talking, Pulliam voiced his support for Brush's idea and then boldly stated:

> I want to say what I think, and what everybody thinks, that Mr. Brush is an honest man. We think you are just as much interested in this as we are, and we think you won't stand for a wrong condition. As proof of that[,] I am willing to make you chairman of that committee with full power to act.... I am willing to be the good soldier and to play my part, and to show you my confidence in you, if a committee is appointed[,] I will appoint you chairman of it.[44]

Pulliam's remarks were followed by another lengthy discussion, during which Garry Herrmann proposed and the magnates unanimously approved:

> that a [s]pecial [c]ommittee of three be appointed, of which John T. Brush ... shall be the [c]hairman, to make a thorough and full investigation of this entire matter, and to report the results of that investigation back to this [l]eague at as early a period as possible, and that that committee be employed with authority to employ counsel, if necessary, and to present all the facts with reference of submission of the same to the [d]istrict [a]ttorney of this county, if they deem the same advisable.[45]

The committee of three was later raised to four, with Herrmann, Ebbets, and Pulliam being chosen to join Brush.[46]

Also during the discussion, Herrmann presented the draft of a statement that he had composed for the owners to give to the newspapers, a revised version of which was eventually released to the press as the official National League statement on the bribery case. In it, the magnates summarized the attempts to corrupt Klem and Johnstone, commended the umpires for refusing to give in to those who approached them, mentioned

3. *The Strange Death of Harry C. Pulliam* (Louisa and Sullivan)

who was on the committee that would be investigating the matter, described the committee's powers, and said that they desired "to punish all persons connected with this disreputable proceeding."[47] However, the magnates did not identify Creamer or the Sullivans by name, explaining that they had "grave doubts as to the truths of certain statements alleged by the person who approached one of the umpires; and it is for that reason, as well as having in mind the proper punishment of all guilty parties, that all names be withheld for the present."[48] But they added that "none of the persons whose names are withheld at this time are in any way connected with [O]rganized [B]aseball."[49]

Before adjourning, the letters written by Klem and Johnstone were turned over to John Brush, and the owners formed a gentleman's agreement that all questions concerning the Creamer affair and the National League's investigation of it should be directed to Brush as chairman of the investigating committee and no other magnate should say a word about it.[50]

In addition to everything else that transpired during the meeting, it is interesting to note that prior to Brush's explanation of his virtually nonexistent relationship with Creamer, Charles Ebbets informed the other owners that Harry Stevens, the Polo Grounds concessionaire, had told him the previous evening that Creamer was not connected with the Sullivans,[51] reinforcing the need to discover who was really behind the bribery attempts.

Unfortunately, however, the results of the investigation did nothing to solve the case, and instead, raised more questions than they answered. At the National League's annual meeting in February of 1909, Ebbets announced to the other magnates that on December 22, 1908, he and John Brush had made an appointment with DeLancey Nicoll, the former district attorney of New York City, who also happened to be a Tammany man. Ebbets went on to say that the two owners discussed the Creamer affair with Nicoll, showed him the letters of the two umpires, and asked him if "a crime had been committed that would be punishable under the law if the guilt of the person or persons could be proven."[52] Nicoll studied the matter and responded with a short letter dated January 14, 1909, in which he not surprisingly stated, "[T]he acts detailed by you to me and set forth in the letters exhibited by you to me do not constitute a crime in the [s]tate of New York, and that no prosecution for them would be entertained by the [d]istrict [a]ttorney of this [c]ounty."[53] Of course, the fact that Ebbets and Brush could have gone to a number of New York attorneys for advice but chose a lawyer who was connected with Tammany Hall and, by inference, the Sullivans is puzzling to say the least.

Ebbets next read the innocuous report that he, Brush, and Herrmann wrote about the affair, in which they reviewed the 1908 National League pennant race in general, naively described how difficult it would be to fix a baseball game, praised the integrity of the national pastime, extolled the honesty of Klem and Johnstone, and in essence, said much about nothing.[54] Pulliam, who was not present at the time and who apparently had no hand in the composition of the report, had appended a note indicating that he agreed with what had been written,[55] but he did not comment in writing on the lack of a search for additional information.

Then, in spite of the fact that the report did not mention Creamer by name or say anything about attempting to discover who was behind the accused doctor, the owners who were present — Brush again was absent — unanimously voted to approve it and thus brought an end to the investigation, making Garry Herrmann's December promise that the inquiry would be "thorough and full" look like a joke.

But the problems began even before the investigation started. First, the owners were too quick to believe John Brush's explanation at face value and to elect Brush the chairman of the committee looking into disreputable behavior of one of Brush's employees — a clear-cut conflict of interest — something which they compounded by turning over the only two pieces of evidence that they had on the bribery affair to Brush. Rightly or wrongly, Pulliam has received much of the blame for this mistake, and his motives certainly have to be questioned. In his defense, Pulliam may have just been bending over backward to show that although he and Brush were enemies, he was willing to trust Brush's integrity enough to suggest that the Giant owner be put in charge of the investigation committee. Also, this would help to mitigate Brush's and anyone else's feelings that Pulliam was partial in his rulings. Or perhaps this was not the case at all. Perhaps Pulliam was receiving some covert form of outside pressure to endorse Brush so that the Giant owner was not accused of being the sinister force behind Creamer. But even if Pulliam was being manipulated, what about the National League magnates who voted unanimously for Brush's appointment, without even one of them suggesting that this was a conflict of interest?

3. The Strange Death of Harry C. Pulliam (Louisa and Sullivan)

Nor should the magnates have put Charles Ebbets on the investigation committee. Ebbets "had long been active in Brooklyn's Democratic politics and had strong support in Tammany Hall,"[56] something that should have made him ineligible to serve.

Furthermore, the magnates were too quick to dismiss the Sullivans as being the real villains, despite Creamer referring to them by name during his first conversation with Bill Klem and implying Big Tim during his second conversation with the umpire, and despite Jimmy Johnstone telling Pulliam that he thought that Creamer placed the bribe for the Sullivans. Not surprisingly, Charles Ebbets presented the best defense for Big and Little Tim, citing as evidence what Harry Stevens told him, but some of the other owners, as well as Pulliam, also said that they believed that the Sullivans were innocent.[57] However, as Harvey Woodruff, the sporting editor of the *Chicago Daily Tribune*, would later discover "[Creamer was] a staunch Tammany man, and always ha[d] been regarded as one of 'Big Tim' Sullivan's henchmen."[58] And when Little Tim was dying in late 1909, the *New York Times* reported that "Dr. J.H. Creamer ... a neighbor, called in other prominent physicians, ... [and once Sullivan had died,] Dr. Creamer said the cause of death was Bright's disease and endocarditis."[59] Could this Dr. Creamer have been Joseph Creamer?

Once they had gone through the farce of approving the vague and ineffectual investigation report, the magnates proceeded to debate the pros and cons of whether the report should be given to the public, and if so, in what form.[60] It was during this debate that several disturbing pieces of information came forth.

- First, Ebbets admitted that he had talked privately to Little Tim Sullivan,[61] who, as might be expected, denied that the Sullivans had anything to do with the matter, and who confided to Ebbets that "[h]e sent for the man [meaning Creamer] and told him what he thought of it."[62] Ebbets went further to say that Sullivan mentioned that DeLancey Nicoll had also spoken to him about what had happened.[63] Ebbets' indiscretion, of course, was in direct violation of the gentlemen's agreement that the owners had made the previous December, but no one seemed to mind.
- Second, Garry Herrmann said that he had heard that Creamer did not represent the Sullivans, but instead represented three members

of the Giants: John McGraw, Christy Mathewson, McGraw's ace pitcher, and Roger Bresnahan, the New York catcher.[64] Although unsubstantiated, this rumor was plausible considering that the Giants felt they deserved the pennant even without winning the makeup game and that they had been accused of trying to bribe certain Philadelphia players to throw some late-season games against New York.[65] As Fred Snodgrass, the Giant outfielder, would tell Lawrence Ritter, "[W]e thought the pennant was ours by right, anyway. We thought the call on Merkle was a raw deal, and any means of redressing the grievance was legitimate."[66]

- And third, Ebbets, who was voicing John Brush's request, made a motion that the names of Creamer, the Sullivans, McGraw, Mathewson, and Bresnahan be stricken from both the December and the February minutes, something that the magnates unanimously approved.[67] Brush was particularly concerned that Creamer's name be removed, for he feared that if it were to remain in the minutes, someone in the future might not realize that Creamer "had been discharged [from his position with the Giants] before this matter was divulged."[68] This statement was true as far as it went, but Creamer had not been discharged from his position when the matter had occurred, making Brush's request cast more suspicion on the Giant owner.

Finally, failing to arrive at a consensus over what to do next, the owners called in Ban Johnson, the president of the American League, apprised him of the situation, and asked him for advice. Johnson, in turn, recommended that the matter be referred to the National Commission,[69] Organized Baseball's three-person governing body, consisting at that time of Johnson himself, Garry Herrmann, and John Heydler, who was subbing for Pulliam. This was done, with the commissioners eventually giving Creamer's name "to every major league club owner ... , with instructions to such club owners to bar him from their respective grounds for all time to come," though Creamer was never mentioned in the official statement released to the press about this matter.[70] That piece of the puzzle was announced to the world by Harvey Woodruff in an article in the April 24, 1909, issue of the *Chicago Daily Tribune*, in which Woodruff not only brought forth Creamer's name, but also revealed the doctor's connections

3. The Strange Death of Harry C. Pulliam (Louisa and Sullivan)

with the Giants and Tammany Hall.⁷¹ A follow-up article without a byline published the next day in the *Chicago Sunday Tribune* added Creamer's side of the story, which did nothing more than muddy the waters:

> It is a job to ruin me. I never saw Klem or Johnstone to speak to that day or any other day. I did not go outside the grandstand to meet them before the game in question, and I never tried to bribe anybody in my life. I have not decided what I shall do yet, but I have been advised to seek legal redress.
>
> ... I have been interested in sports for nearly twenty years and nobody has ever accused me of wrongdoing before. I cannot understand why the umpires have mixed me in this[,] unless it is a conspiracy of some kind.⁷²

However, Creamer never attempted to clear his name, and even though the *New York Evening Journal* began publicly asking who were the people behind the physician (obviously, the newspaper assumed that there was more than one person), no one was willing to provide an answer.⁷³ So, barring the possibility that Klem made up the story that he had described in his letter to Pulliam, and, thus, Creamer was really innocent, the primary suspects continue to remain to this very day the Sullivans, John Brush, John McGraw and/or one or more of his players, or some gambler or gambling syndicate not associated with the Sullivans.

But what does any of this unsolved mystery have to do with Pulliam's death? Well, for starters, Pulliam's reaction to the alleged bribery incident was extremely inconsistent and indicates that perhaps the president knew more than he was admitting. After receiving Klem's letter accusing Creamer, Pulliam locked it away and waited nearly two months before reading it to the owners at their December meeting, taking them by surprise when he did so. This surprise was followed by another when Pulliam said he was willing to appoint John Brush — arguably his number one enemy in all of Organized Baseball — as the chairman of the committee investigating Brush's team doctor. Then, once the magnates had issued their December statement to the press, Pulliam, according to Francis C. Richter, the editor of *Sporting Life*, told the newspapermen present "that in order not to defeat the ends of justice, the names of the persons involved are withheld for the present, but the [p]resident of the [l]eague is authority for the statement that the alleged bribers will not be shielded."⁷⁴ This comment led *Sporting Life* to later state, "President Pulliam intimated at the time the scandal originated that he would get to the bottom of it."⁷⁵ But even though Pulliam was one of the members of the investigation committee, it appears that, either by choice or by the maneuvering of Brush, Ebbets, and Herrmann, he had no hand in writing the useless report that the committee had presented to the owners in February of 1909, though as mentioned earlier, he did add a note indicating that he approved of its contents. Nor was he forthcoming with any information for public consumption, despite pleas by both *The Sporting News* and *Sporting Life* to do so.[76] A writer for the *Los Angeles Times* first noticed the problem when Pulliam visited his city between the December 1908 and February 1909 National League meetings and wrote about it after Pulliam's death:

> When Pulliam was in Los Angeles last winter[,] he showed every disposition to avoid answering directly questions put to him about baseball matters, although it seemed as though his mind was absorbed by the subject. Evidently his troubles centered in the baseball situation. If that was the case at that time[,] he must have had some extraordinary load on his mind.... Were [the] magnates, in their greed for gold, doing things which the sensitive honor of the gentleman from Kentucky did not approve of?[77]

Thus, did Pulliam know more than he was willing to tell, and if so, why was he hesitant to tell it?

In addition to these inconsistencies, Pulliam's mental health declined precipitously from the time that he became aware of the scandal until he went on his leave of absence on February 20, 1909. Garry Herrmann, in attempting to convince the other owners that Pulliam was not in his right mind, reported to them that their president was "doing things now that I never knew him to do before."[78] Among the things that Herrmann and a Mr. Logan, presumably Herrmann's friend and fellow Cincinnati Red stockholder, Thomas Logan, brought to the owners' attention were the use of profanity and vulgarity, the "spending [of] money now at the rate of a thousand dollars a week or more"— apparently Pulliam was known to be a spendthrift, but not at that rate — excessive drinking, telling offensive stories, and insulting people.[79]

However, in describing Pulliam's bizarre behavior, Logan also mentioned that Pulliam had said to him in early February that the National League magnates were crooked,[80] and in response to Logan telling him that the magnates' paid his salary and he should not be badmouthing his employers, he replied, "God damn them, I hate to look at them."[81] But was this only Pulliam's melancholia going to extremes, or was he aware of

3. The Strange Death of Harry C. Pulliam (Louisa and Sullivan)

some illegal or unethical dealings that he was unable to disclose? And based on the owners' handling of the bribery incident — the lack of a thorough investigation, Brush and Ebbets' seeking advice from a lawyer tied to Tammany Hall, the innocuous report, Ebbets' discussing the incident with Little Tim Sullivan, the striking of names from the December and February minutes, and the possible scapegoating of Joseph Creamer — were they trying to cover something up?

The combination of Pulliam's frayed emotional state and his conflict with the magnates came to a head in two incidents in mid–February of 1909. The first occurred on February 17 during a dinner given by Charles Comiskey, the owner of the Chicago White Sox, at the Chicago Automobile Club. Pulliam was one of the scheduled speakers, and when his turn came, he proceeded to castigate the National League magnates by stating:

> My days as a base ball man are numbered. The National League doesn't want me for president any more. It longs to go back to the days of dealing from the bottom of the pack, hiding the cards under the table, and to the days when the trademark was the gum shoe. Because I am for dealing above board and playing in the open[,] my days are numbered. I can't afford to quit, or I would resign now from my position, which pays $9,000 a year. But I will have to quit at the end of this year, for the club owners of the National League want to revert to the old methods.[82]

So, what did Pulliam mean when he said that the owners desired "to go back to the days of dealing from the bottom of the pack, hiding the cards under the table" and "because I am for dealing above board and playing in the open[,] my days are numbered"? Was he implying that the owners, or at least certain owners, were keeping information from him — perhaps information related to the bribery scandal? And/or was he suggesting that one or more people were covertly attempting to manipulate him or force him to quit?

The second incident happened the very next day after the majority of the magnates, troubled by what Herrmann and Logan had told them and convinced that their president needed professional help, had contacted Pulliam's brother who lived in Wisconsin and one of Pulliam's male "intimates" from Louisville and asked them to take charge of what they perceived to be a sick man.[83] Pulliam objected and made his escape via train to St. Louis, but not before George Dovey, the owner of the Boston Doves, disguised himself as a cabbie and tried to take Pulliam in the opposite direction of the train station so that he would miss his departure time.[84] However, the nimble Pulliam thwarted Dovey's plan by leaping from the taxi before it could gain much speed and sprinting to the station through the wintry Chicago weather, while his topcoat and luggage remained in the cab.[85] That same evening, the magnates gave Pulliam an indefinite leave of absence and appointed John Heydler as acting president.

But if someone was blackmailing or putting some other form of pressure on Pulliam to either keep him quiet or drive him out of the presidency, who was the perpetrator and how was he operating? In answer to the first part of that question, the obvious suspects would be the same people suspected of being the sinister force behind Joseph Creamer: the Sullivans, John Brush, John McGraw and/or one or more of his players, or some gambler or gambling syndicate not associated with the Sullivans. Each had a motive and most of them had the power to carry out any threats that were made.

For Big Tim Sullivan, who controlled the gambling interests in New York City, a man of integrity like Pulliam, who wanted to clean up Organized Baseball, would have been viewed as a threat that needed to be manipulated or eliminated. And Sul-

Timothy "Big Tim" Sullivan: New York politician, crime lord, and Tammany man (Library of Congress, Prints & Photographs Division, Bain Collection, [LC-DIG-ggbain-13653]).

3. The Strange Death of Harry C. Pulliam (Louisa and Sullivan)

livan's power was immense. Mike Dash, in explaining the influence that Sullivan wielded in the early 1900s, wrote in his *Satan's Circus: Murder, Vice, Police Corruption, and New York's Trial of the Century*:

> According to the [*New York*] *Times*, Sullivan devoted a good deal of his energies to heading a secret "gambling commission," consisting of four members, which not only collected and shared out the millions raised in protection money, but in effect licensed all the betting premises that operated in the city. Tim's committee, the paper charged, met weekly in an apartment just off Broadway and consisted of "a commissioner, who is at the head of one of the city departments, two state senators, and the dictator of the pool room syndicate of this city." It required little knowledge of local politics to identify three of these men as Sullivan, Frank Farrell [the gambling tycoon and later co-owner of the New York Highlanders], and State Senator [Hugh] McLaughlan [*sic*], the last representing the interests of the Democrats of Brooklyn. As for the mysterious "head of one of the city departments," only the most naïve of the *Times*' readers could have failed to recognize a reference to Bill Devery, then still chief of police [and later co-owner of the New York Highlanders]. The brilliance of Tim's system would have been immediately apparent to any reader who guessed the men's identities. Between them[,] the four members of Sullivan's committee controlled the police, Manhattan [and Brooklyn] politics, and the State Gambling Commission. The scheme was airtight.[86]

So, if Creamer, "a staunch Tammany man," "one of 'Big Tim' Sullivan's henchmen," and possibly the neighbor and physician of Little Tim Sullivan, was indeed the man who approached Klem, and if he said what Klem claimed that he said, it is not implausible to believe that the Sullivans, or at least Big Tim, would have wanted the matter buried and forgotten and may have stooped to any means to do so.

For John Brush, Pulliam was an enemy who needed to be removed from the presidency. The two men had clashed over Pulliam's decisions that went against the New York club, and as mentioned earlier in this chapter, the president had been critical of the Giants' locker rooms for visiting teams and umpires. Brush, in turn, opposed Pulliam's reelection as president for several years (1905–1907) or was not present when the voting for the presidency took place (1908).[87] And no doubt Pulliam's handling of the Merkle incident would have only intensified Brush's desire to rid himself of the meddlesome Southerner. Thus, the question remains that since Brush was unable to muster enough support among the other owners to prevent Pulliam's contract from being renewed year after year, would he have been willing to use some other method to silence his opponent — especially if Brush had had a hand in the bribery scandal? Keep in mind that Creamer was Brush's employee, that according to Klem, Creamer said that he was waiting to meet Brush when he had his first conversation with the umpire, and that Brush's explanation of his lack of knowledge regarding Creamer left something to be desired. Furthermore, Brush's modus operandi casts more suspicion on the Giant owner. As Charles C. Alexander wrote in his biography of John McGraw, Brush "preferred to avoid publicity and work in quiet (some said sinister) ways to achieve his ends."[88]

Like his employer, John McGraw also viewed Pulliam as an enemy. Pulliam's campaign to eliminate rowdyism certainly went against how the fiery New York manager played the game, and McGraw received more than his share of fines and suspensions from the league office. Nor was McGraw intimidated by Pulliam's position, even having once called the president to accuse him of being Barney Dreyfuss' lackey.[89] As for McGraw's involvement in the bribery scandal, the evidence is mixed. On one hand, if Klem is to be believed, Creamer said that McGraw and his players were not aware of what he was doing. On the other hand, McGraw was a known gambler who, as Charles Alexander has stated, "had close associations with various big-time gamblers, track and casino owners, and real

John McGraw, the manager of the New York Giants and another one of Harry Pulliam's enemies (National Baseball Hall of Fame Library, Cooperstown, New York).

3. The Strange Death of Harry C. Pulliam (Louisa and Sullivan)

estate hustlers ... [and] never was willing to put as much distance as he should have between himself and elements inside and outside baseball that could and sometimes did damage the integrity of the sport."[90] For example, in 1906, McGraw opened a pool hall in New York City, for which he had to pay protection money to Tammany Hall, and by October of 1908 — the time of the bribery scandal — it was rumored that one of his silent partners was the young Arnold Rothstein, the criminal mastermind and high-stakes gambler who is best known for his alleged role in fixing the 1919 World Series.[91] Or a dozen years later, when McGraw ran afoul of the Volstead Act, he was represented in court by William Fallon, one of the best and most notorious defense attorneys for lawbreakers during the 1920s.[92]

And then there is the matter of whether Klem was telling the truth about what Creamer had said. The owners may have implicitly trusted Klem and taken his word at face value, but in the second of a four-part article for *Collier's* in 1951, the umpire admitted that he and McGraw "developed a strange off-the-field relationship" and that "[they] frequently dined together during spring training and, in the few years when [McGraw's] team was not in the pennant race, [they] would dine after a game."[93] Obviously, the 1908 Giants were in the pennant race, but this does not take away from the fact that Klem and McGraw were friendly when they were not arguing with each other on the field and raises the question that Klem may have lied in his letter to Pulliam to protect McGraw.

The last two among the group of usual suspects — one or more of McGraw's players and a gambler or gambling syndicate not associated with the Sullivans — are less likely to be responsible for Pulliam's demise, but for somewhat different reasons. The New York players were certainly disgruntled over the outcome of the Merkle game and felt that the pennant had been stolen from them, and one or more of them may have been behind the alleged bribe — remember that McGraw's men had been accused of attempting to control the outcome of some late-season games against the Phillies. Also, there may have been particular Giant players who harbored grudges against Pulliam because of previous penalties that he had imposed on them for disruptive behavior on the field. But presumably most, if not all, of these men would not have had the connections to retaliate in a covert fashion, though such retaliation cannot be completely ruled out.

Mysteries from Baseball's Past

As for the gamblers not associated with the Sullivans, they may have offered the money for the bribe, and they may have had the power to make life miserable for Pulliam, but if Klem was both truthful and accurate, the first possibility could not have occurred, unless Creamer had falsely stated that he represented the Sullivans to cover for someone else — something a loyal Tammany man, like the accused doctor, would not have done. However, it is interesting to note that Klem said in 1951, "I will go to my grave wondering where the money [Creamer] offered me came from. Certainly not from Tammany Hall, because they didn't care ten dollars' worth. And certainly [Creamer] himself had neither the bank account nor the property to raise any large sum."[94]

Of course, even if the first possibility is eliminated, the second remains. Some gambler or gamblers totally unrelated to the bribery scandal may have wanted Pulliam removed from office for whatever reason and may have had enough "dirt" on him to have wreaked havoc with his emotional state in attempting to make their wishes a reality.

But what about the second part of the question: If there was indeed someone trying to control Pulliam or force him out of office, how was he operating? Because Pulliam had a reputation as an honest and honorable man, it would have been difficult to find any skeletons in his closet that could have been wielded as weapons against him. Or would it?

Dennis and Jeanne Burke DeValeria, the authors of *Honus Wagner: A Biography*, believe that Pulliam was gay, though they admit that they have not found any concrete evidence verifying their theory. In the words of Dennis DeValeria:

> There is no doubt in our minds that Pulliam was gay....
> ... [M]ost of what we know of the man was from the day-to-day newspaper digging we did. So our opinion was not garnered from a single source or piece of info. Over the years we covered that overlapped Pulliam's career in Louisville, Pittsburgh, and New York[,] there were numerous mentions of his natty attire or of him being a "dandy." (Purple waistcoats and hats with feathers tended to get a sportswriter's attention when worn by a woman, but especially when worn by a man.) All in all, there were just far too many wink-wink, nudge-nudge types of references to ignore.
> Did this place undo strain on him? I would say most definitely: He was in a man's world in baseball circles and no doubt that even then there were narrow-minded people who would have made his life uncomfortable to say the least. Did it have a bearing on his suicide? No way of knowing.[95]

3. *The Strange Death of Harry C. Pulliam* (Louisa and Sullivan)

Nor does it appear that the DeValerias were exaggerating when it comes to references that in an early 20th-century way may imply but not prove that the genial gentleman from Kentucky was a homosexual. For example, W.A. Phelon wrote in the March 6, 1909, issue of *Sporting Life*, "Harry Pulliam is not as strong, physically, as most of [the National League magnates]...."[96] And Francis Richter referred to Pulliam as "gentle" and said that "his disposition was sweet, kindly and charitable...."[97] Or Pulliam himself announced when he was addressing the National League owners in December of 1908, "I want to ask you not to interrupt me because I am not built like other people."[98]

Also, the fact that Pulliam was a 40-year-old bachelor with at least two, if not more, male "intimates"—as they were termed in 1909—only adds to the speculation that he was not heterosexual. One of these men was Henry Feuchtwanger, a Pittsburgher, about whom George Dovey once said, "[He] is perhaps closer to Mr. Pulliam in a social sense than any of us, and that he exercises some influence on him."[99] A.R. Cratty would later describe Feuchtwanger as a "loyal, companionable friend of the league chief," who had formed "a bond of union" with Pulliam.[100] Another of these close male associates was a Mr. Russell from Louisville who, along with Pulliam's brother-in-law, George W. Cain, met Pulliam at the Cincinnati train station on February 20, 1909.[101] Russell then proceeded to assist Cain in escorting the National League leader out of the city to "some thoroughly quiet place for a two months' rest," after a doctor provided by Garry Herrmann had advised Pulliam to take a long vacation.[102] Russell may also have been the fellow referred to only as "one of [Pulliam's] Louisville intimates" who the National League magnates had contacted during their Chicago meeting to try to persuade Pulliam to accept a leave of absence.[103]

As for his attitude towards women, Pulliam was praised for being "gallant to the ladies,"[104] but it does not appear that he ever had a serious romantic relationship with the fairer sex. True, when he was getting ready to bolt to St. Louis on February 18, Pulliam had let it be known that he was planning to marry "a prominent South Side St. Louis woman" and "going to Honolulu for a wedding trip."[105] But once in St. Louis, he denied the story and "said he did not care to discuss this matter, as he considered it a purely personal one."[106] Did this blatant contradiction reflect the confused state of Pulliam's mind, or did Pulliam make up the wedding story to neutralize any accusation that he was a homosexual?

Then, there was Pulliam's flashy apparel. As a writer for the *Cincinnati Enquirer* summed it up: "All colors of the rainbow were utilized by him in the 'color scheme' of his fancy waistcoats, and his entire eccentricity in dress ran in this direction."[107] In Pulliam's days, such flamboyant attire worn by a male was oftentimes viewed as a sign of homosexuality.

And finally, on March 2, 1909, not long after Pulliam began his leave of absence, umpire Clarence "Brick" Owens, disgruntled over the fact that his contract to officiate in the National League was not being renewed, let it be known that he had "'the goods' on Pulliam for something."[108] Owens went further to say:

> I have something on Pulliam that will stir him up more than he is now.
> I intended to make everything public before this, but don't want to attack Pulliam while he is in his present condition. I will wait until he is better, and then give out my side of the case....[109]

"'The goods' on Pulliam for something"? What did Owens mean? Did it have anything to do with the possibility that Pulliam was gay, or was there some other skeleton that Owens wanted to pull out of Pulliam's closet? Could Owens have been referring to Pulliam's extravagant lifestyle — the one which Garry Herrmann and Thomas Logan had revealed to the National League owners? Could Pulliam have been in debt to one or more powerful figures? Or do Owens' comments relate to Pulliam's excessive drinking? Unfortunately for future historians, Owens never carried out his threat, so "the goods" and the secret behind them may have died with the umpire.

Pulliam returned from his period of recuperation in June of 1909 and was reinstated by the National League magnates after a lengthy and heated discussion in which Charles Murphy, John Brush, and, initially, Charles Ebbets attempted to have him permanently removed from office. As *Sporting Life* reported:

> After a stirring five-hour session[,] it was decided that Harry Pulliam is to continue as president of their organization and that he is well enough to resume his duties. The Kentuckian will be back on the presidential job on or about June 19. A meeting of the National League magnates has been called for Chicago on June 16, when the authority conferred on Secretary John A. Heydler to assume the duties of president and to represent the old organization on the National Commission will be rescinded and Mr. Pulliam will be restored to his former standing.

3. The Strange Death of Harry C. Pulliam (Louisa and Sullivan)

> Mr. Pulliam had the support of five clubs at the start of the session and of six of them at the end. President Ebbetts [sic], of Brooklyn, deserted the Murphy-Brush faction when it was shown to him that Mr. Pulliam was in fit physical condition to resume his duties.[110]

At the time of the owners' decision, Pulliam said, "I feel strong again and entirely capable of again performing my official duties."[111] And others who saw him shortly after his reinstatement agreed with his assessment. For example, an article in the July 3, 1909, issue of *Sporting Life*, with a dateline of June 28 and the appropriate title of "Pulliam Redivivus," stated that "Pulliam looks splendid and never was in better physical trim."[112] Francis Richter would later add while writing about Pulliam's death that "he showed no signs of his long illness, and friends congratulated him upon his recovery...."[113] However, Richter was also quick to point out that Pulliam was "oppressively melancholy" at the opening of Forbes Field on June 30 and at the funeral for Israel Durham, the owner of the Philadelphia Phillies, the very next day, and that he had been afflicted with several bouts of melancholia while working in Cincinnati in July.[114] A.R. Cratty confirmed what Richter had observed at the Pirates' new ballpark, saying that Pulliam was "most taciturn" and that he talked "in a subdued tone."[115] But Cratty went further to say that Pulliam was "glancing furtively ever and anon, as if he was distrustful of every one."[116] And an article in the *Cincinnati Enquirer* at the time of Pulliam's death supported Richter's statement about what had happened in Cincinnati.[117]

So, why did the well-rested and revitalized Pulliam begin to once again suffer from depression after only a few weeks back on the job? Was this just his psychoneurotic or psychotic disorder raising its ugly head for no apparent reason, or did some external matter trigger it? Was he upset over the deaths of Durham and George Dovey, who had died on June 24? Both men were his allies and he would miss their support. Or was something else bothering him? And why did he appear to Cratty to be distrustful of everyone? If someone had been blackmailing him or putting pressure on him to resign, could the threats or other forms of intimidation have begun anew?

Francis Richter believed that Pulliam "nursed some deep personal trouble which was not caused directly, but was simply aggravated, by base ball."[118] "Some deep personal trouble"? But what was the source of that deep personal trouble?

Mysteries from Baseball's Past

Whatever the cause, the closest thing to a smoking gun may have been the item of mail that Pulliam was reading when he stopped and began looking out his window before telling his stenographer that he was not feeling well and was going to leave his office. But then again, the piece of correspondence may not have been a smoking gun at all. Some people suffering from depression have difficulty concentrating — even without external distractions.

In any case, it is not known what became of that piece of correspondence or any of the mail that Pulliam was looking at that day. Pulliam's stenographer was a Miss Caylor, believed to have been Lenore Caylor, the daughter of the deceased O.P. Caylor,[119] a lawyer, newspaper columnist, and one of the founding fathers of the American Association. But it is uncertain if she had seen the contents of what Pulliam had read that day and/or what she had done with Pulliam's mail.

In addition to the unknown whereabouts of what Pulliam was reading on the day before he died, there are several other mysterious matters regarding his death. There is no evidence as to where he was between the time that he left his office and the time when his mortally wounded body was first seen by Thomas Brady. Newspaper accounts disagree on whether Brady found Pulliam's hotel door unlocked or opened it with a passkey. No suicide note was ever discovered. And when the authors of this chapter contacted the New York Police Department and requested a copy of the police report for the incident, they received instead a copy of the coroner's report and nothing more. None of these matters proves or disproves anything. But when taken together, they certainly raise the possibility that Pulliam may have been murdered, or if he did indeed commit suicide, the reason or reasons for it may be more complex than just his being unable to handle the stress of his job.

Pulliam's own understandably confused state after he had been shot only adds to the mystery. The shock of being struck by a bullet at close range and the part of his brain damaged by that bullet no doubt greatly affected Pulliam's short-term memory, rendering the best witness to the incident incapable of explaining what had happened.

Thus, the issues surrounding Pulliam's death raise more questions than they answer. Did Pulliam have a hereditary illness that ultimately put him in such a severe state of depression that he felt ending his life was the only way to gain relief? Was someone exerting pressure on him to control

3. The Strange Death of Harry C. Pulliam (Louisa and Sullivan)

him or drive him out of the presidency of the National League? What effect did the events surrounding the attempted bribery scandal have in causing Pulliam's death? Did the Sullivans or John Brush or John McGraw or someone else directly or indirectly bring about Pulliam's demise? Was Pulliam gay, and if so, did the fear of being outed by a blackmailer or some other unscrupulous person play a hand in his pulling the trigger? Or did someone else pull the trigger? And what about the unknown piece of correspondence that Pulliam was reading at 1:00 P.M. on July 28, 1909, and the other unresolved matters regarding that fateful summer day?

Unless some new facts are unearthed, these questions will remain unanswered and this mystery will remain unsolved, allowing each researcher — or for that matter, each reader of this chapter — to weigh the evidence and decide for him/herself whether Pulliam pulled the trigger, and if so, why.

NOTES

1. Cf. "Harry Pulliam Tries Suicide," *Atlanta Constitution*, July 29, 1909; "Harry Pulliam Shoots Self," *Chicago Daily Tribune*, July 29, 1909; "Bullet," *Cincinnati Enquirer*, July 29, 1909; "Harry Pulliam Shoots Self," *Los Angeles Times*, July 29, 1909; and "Harry C. Pulliam Attempts Suicide," *New York Times*, July 29, 1909.
2. "Harry C. Pulliam Attempts Suicide."
3. "Harry Pulliam Shoots Self," *Chicago Daily Tribune*, July 29, 1909.
4. Cf. "Harry Pulliam Tries Suicide," "Bullet," and "Harry Pulliam Shoots Self."
5. "Pulliam, Self-Shot, Dies of his Wound," *New York Times*, July 30, 1909.
6. Arthur D. Hittner, *Honus Wagner: The Life of Baseball's "Flying Dutchman"* (Jefferson, NC: McFarland, 1996), 109.
7. Ban Johnson, Charles Somers, Charles Comiskey, and Henry Killilea for the American League; James Hart, August "Garry" Herrmann, Frank Robison, and Pulliam for the National League. Harold Seymour and Dorothy Seymour Mills, *Baseball: The Early Years* (New York: Oxford University Press, 1960), 322–323.
8. Hittner, 109.
9. "Rumors of Trades but No Transfers," *New York Herald*, December 11, 1907.
10. "Superbas Start To-Morrow on Last Half of Home Schedule," *Brooklyn Eagle*, June 29, 1908.
11. Charles H. Zuber, "The 'Spitball' Is Not in Favor with President Pulliam," *Sporting Life*, September 19, 1908, 26.
12. Cait Murphy, *Crazy '08: How a Cast of Cranks, Rogues, Boneheads, and Magnates Created the Greatest Year in Baseball History* (New York: Smithsonian Books, 2007), 178.
13. "Hall of Fame for Baseball Players!" *New York World*, March 10, 1903.
14. Sam Crane, *New York Evening Journal*, December 9, 1907; found in G.H. Fleming, *The Unforgettable Season* (New York: Holt, Rinehart and Winston, 1981), 5.

15. "Writers' Association," *Sporting Life*, August 15, 1908, 2.
16. "Caught on the Fly," *The Sporting News*, August 19, 1909, 6.
17. "His Old Home," *Cincinnati Enquirer*, July 30, 1909; William E. Akin, "Harry Clay Pulliam," in *Biographical Dictionary of American Sports: Baseball*, ed. David L. Porter (New York: Greenwood Press, 1987), 456–457; Dennis DeValeria and Jeanne Burke DeValeria, *Honus Wagner: A Biography* (New York: Henry Holt, 1995), 109; and William F. Kirk, "Chance Pays Some Attention to Giants," *New York American*, June 20, 1908.
18. "Pulliam's Rash Act," *Cincinnati Enquirer*, July 29, 1909; "His Old Home"; Francis C. Richter, "A Base Ball Tragedy," *Sporting Life*, August 7, 1909, 4; Akin, 457; and Bill Lamberty, "Harry Clay Pulliam," in *Deadball Stars of the National League*, ed. Tom Simon (Dulles, VA: Brassey's, 2004), 22.
19. "No Developments," *The Sporting News*, January 28, 1909, 1; Francis C. Richter, "Passing of Pulliam!" *Sporting Life*, August 7, 1909, 3; Richter, "A Base Ball Tragedy," 4; Lee Allen, *The National League Story: The Official History*, rev. ed. (New York: Hill and Wang, 1965), 122; and Harold Seymour and Dorothy Seymour Mills, *Baseball: The Golden Age* (New York: Oxford University Press, 1971), 10.
20. Richter, "Passing of Pulliam!" 3.
21. Ibid.
22. Most of the information for this section was taken from Harold Seymour and Dorothy Seymour Mills, *Baseball: The Golden Age*, 149–151, and David W. Anderson, *More Than Merkle: A History of the Best and Most Exciting Baseball Season in Human History* (Lincoln: University of Nebraska Press, 2000), 172–173.
23. Minutes of the National League Annual Meeting, February 1909, 133, National Baseball Hall of Fame Library, Cooperstown, New York. The authors are indebted to Bill Francis and Elizabeth Price of the National Baseball Hall of Fame Library for photocopying sections of these minutes, as well as sections of the Minutes of the National League Board of Directors, December 1908.
24. E-mail message from Floyd Sullivan to Angelo J. Louisa, August 4, 2008. The authors are grateful to Marlyce "Candy" Tingstad, the daughter of one of Harry Pulliam's nephews, for providing this information.
25. A.R. Cratty, "In Pittsburg," *Sporting Life*, August 14, 1909, 7.
26. E-mail message from Floyd Sullivan to Angelo J. Louisa, August 4, 2008. Marlyce "Candy" Tingstad also supplied this information, for which the authors thank her.
27. Minutes of the National League Board of Directors, December 1908, 273–274, National Baseball Hall of Fame Library, Cooperstown, New York. Although Creamer's name has been removed from the document, later findings show that the physician was indeed the person referred to by Klem.
28. Mike Dash, *Satan's Circus: Murder, Vice, Police Corruption, and New York's Trial of the Century* (New York: Crown, 2007), 81.
29. For more information on the Sullivans, in particular Big Tim, see Dash and David Pietrusza, *Rothstein: The Life, Times, and Murder of the Criminal Genius Who Fixed the 1919 World Series* (New York: Carroll & Graf, 2003).
30. Minutes of the National League Board of Directors, December 1908, 274. At the request of John Brush and the approval of the owners, all references to the Sullivans, Big Tim, and Little Tim — like those to Creamer (see note 27) — were excised from the minutes with a sharp instrument. But in the Minutes of the National League Annual Meeting, February 1909, the designated censor was not as careful and only scratched out the names with a pencil, leaving some of them readable if they are held up to a light. Thus, even though "the Sullivans" has been removed from the document, the information found in the February minutes confirms that Klem asserted that Creamer had told him that the Sullivans were

3. The Strange Death of Harry C. Pulliam (Louisa and Sullivan)

behind the bribe. The authors greatly appreciate Elizabeth Price's and Pamela Louisa's assistance in deciphering the scratched out names.

31. Ibid.
32. Ibid., 274–275.
33. For John Heydler's retelling of what Johnstone said, see ibid., 338–342, 344–345. However, Johnstone supplies the specific details of what happened to him in a letter that he would send to Pulliam in early December of 1908. The complete letter or parts of it may be found in several sections of the minutes, including pages 346–347.
34. Minutes of the National League Board of Directors, December 1908, 275–276.
35. Ibid., 276.
36. Ibid., 278.
37. Ibid., 273–279.
38. Ibid., 295.
39. For Brush's explanation of his relationship with Creamer, see ibid., 360–363.
40. Minutes of the National League Board of Directors, December 1908, 360–362.
41. Ibid., 361.
42. Ibid., 362–363.
43. Ibid., 365–366.
44. Ibid., 372–373.
45. Ibid., 408.
46. Ibid., 409–413.
47. Ibid., 415. For the complete statement, see ibid., 414–416.
48. Ibid., 415.
49. Ibid.
50. Ibid., 417–419.
51. Ibid., 358–359.
52. Minutes of the National League Annual Meeting, February 1909, 146–147.
53. Ibid., 147.
54. Ibid., 148–152.
55. Ibid., 153.
56. Burton A. Boxerman and Benita W. Boxerman, *Ebbets to Veeck to Busch: Eight Owners Who Shaped Baseball* (Jefferson, NC: McFarland, 2003), 21.
57. Minutes of the National League Board of Directors, December 1908, 278 and 287 (for Pulliam), 352 (for Murphy), 358–359 (for Ebbets), and 402 (for Dreyfuss); Minutes of the National League Annual Meeting, February 1909, 171 (for Murphy) and 172 (for Herrmann).
58. Harvey T. Woodruff, "'Dr. Creamer' Barred from All Major League Ball Parks," *Chicago Daily Tribune*, April 24, 1909.
59. "Little Tim Sullivan Is Dead at Forty," *New York Times*, December 23, 1909.
60. Minutes of the National League Annual Meeting, February 1909, 153–154.
61. Ibid., 163.
62. Ibid., 169.
63. Ibid., 163–165.
64. Ibid., 169. The names have been scratched out, but they can be read if the page is held up to a light.
65. Charles C. Alexander, *John McGraw* (New York: Viking, 1988), 135.
66. Lawrence S. Ritter, *The Glory of Their Times: The Story of the Early Days of Baseball Told by the Men Who Played It*, new enlarged edition (New York: Vintage Books, 1984), 108.
67. Minutes of the National League Annual Meeting, February 1909, 179–180.

68. Ibid., 180.
69. Ibid., 226.
70. "Court Decrees," *Sporting Life*, April 24, 1909, 7.
71. Woodruff.
72. "East Hears of 'Dr. Creamer,'" *Chicago Sunday Tribune*, April 25, 1909.
73. "Ovation to Chase," *The Sporting News*, May 13, 1909, 1.
74. Francis C. Richter, "Majors Meet," *Sporting Life*, December 19, 1908, 4.
75. "Latest News," *Sporting Life*, February 13, 1909, 2.
76. "Brush Censored," *The Sporting News*, February 11, 1909, 1, and "Latest News," 2.
77. "Pertinent Comment on Sports," *Los Angeles Times*, August 1, 1909.
78. Minutes of the National League Annual Meeting, February 1909, 108.
79. Ibid., 108–131.
80. Ibid., 130.
81. Ibid., 131.
82. "Comiskey's Dinner," *Sporting Life*, February 27, 1909, 3.
83. Minutes of the National League Annual Meeting, February 1909, 131–143, and "Pulliam to Take Indefinite Rest," *Chicago Daily Tribune*, February 19, 1909.
84. "Pulliam to Take Indefinite Rest."
85. Ibid., and "Long Rest Idea Suits Pulliam," *Chicago Daily Tribune*, February 20, 1909.
86. Dash, 82–83.
87. Richter, "Passing of Pulliam," 3.
88. Alexander, 99.
89. Ibid., 114.
90. Ibid., 7.
91. Pietrusza, 39.
92. Ibid., 175, and Alexander, 221–224, 227, 234.
93. William J. Klem with William J. Slocum, "Jousting with McGraw," *Collier's*, April 7, 1951, 51.
94. Ibid., 54.
95. E-mail message from Dennis DeValeria to Angelo J. Louisa, January 5, 2007.
96. W.A. Phelon, "Chicago," *Sporting Life*, March 6, 1909, 7.
97. Richter, "A Base Ball Tragedy," 4.
98. Minutes of the National League Board of Directors, December 1908, 273.
99. Minutes of the National League Annual Meeting, February 1909, 136.
100. Cratty, 7.
101. "Pulliam Is in a Bad Way," *Washington Post*, February 21, 1909.
102. Ibid.
103. "Pulliam to Take Indefinite Rest."
104. "Pulliam's Rash Act."
105. "Pulliam Says He Is to Be Married Soon," *Chicago American*, February 19, 1909.
106. "Long Rest Idea Suits Pulliam."
107. "His Old Home."
108. "Owen to Prefer Charges," *Washington Post*, March 3, 1909.
109. Ibid.
110. "Pulliam the Victor!" *Sporting Life*, June 12, 1909, 1.
111. Ibid.
112. "Pulliam Redivivus," *Sporting Life*, July 3, 1909, 2.
113. Richter, "Passing of Pulliam!" 3.

3. The Strange Death of Harry C. Pulliam (Louisa and Sullivan)

114. Ibid.
115. Cratty, 7.
116. Ibid.
117. "Pulliam's Rash Act."
118. "Richter, "Passing of Pulliam!" 3.
119. Tim Wiles, the director of research for the National Baseball Hall of Fame Library, discovered the possible identity of Pulliam's stenographer.

4

In Search of Wilbur Cooper and Pete Alexander's 1–0 Game

David Cicotello

In a 2004 biographical article on the Pittsburgh Pirates' left-handed ace Wilbur Cooper included in *Deadball Stars of the National League*, a description of a standout game in the pitcher's career is featured: Cooper triumphed over Grover Cleveland "Pete" Alexander in a contest that lasted 59 minutes at Forbes Field.[1] The author of that article had drawn upon several sources from which a composite account of that game emerged and selected details of it were published.[2] That author was me.

The ironic, unsettling, and mysterious fact which has surfaced since the publication of the article is that I likely, though unintentionally, contributed to the perpetuation of a fascinating story about a baseball game that may *never* have happened.

Constructions and Reconstructions of the Game

In preparing the Cooper essay, my research and reading included (but was not limited to) the usual suspects: previously published biographical articles, a collection of periodical literature and other documents from the National Baseball Hall of Fame Library, standard reference works on baseball history, selections from three books by Bill James, and online material.[3]

Details of Cooper's duel with Alexander appeared in several sources, though not all the "facts" (score, time of game, and venue) were found in a single source, and no date for the game was cited in any account.[4] In

4. In Search of Cooper and Alexander's 1–0 Game (Cicotello)

the earliest of these sources, a 1969 article honoring Cooper's election into the Fraternal Order of Eagles Hall of Fame, teammate Pie Traynor recalled that "[h]e [Cooper] and (Grover) Alexander were matched up one time and they finished in less than 58 minutes. Clyde Barnhart hit a home run and we won, 1–0."[5]

The next two sources were Cooper himself. Retired and living in Van Nuys, California, the left-hander gave two interviews near the end of his life. On the occasion of his 80th birthday in 1972, he was profiled in an article by Bernie Milligan, a columnist of the local paper. Here, the former pitcher recounted "incidents of games played in the days of Ty Cobb, Grover Cleveland Alexander, Edd Roush, Charlie Grimm, Rabbit Maranville, [and] Honus Wagner...."[6] Milligan also mentioned that Alexander and Cooper "once pitched against each other in Pittsburgh's Forbes Field and the game ended in 59 minutes."[7]

Harold "Pie" Traynor, who claimed to have witnessed the mysterious 1–0 game (National Baseball Hall of Fame Library, Cooperstown, New York).

Six months later, Mike Miller, another local writer, interviewed Cooper at his home. Reminiscing with the reporter, Cooper shared his scrapbook of memories, rated Honus Wagner as the greatest player he had ever seen, and "told [Miller] about the time when his team, the Pirates, was playing the Phillies and Grover Cleveland Alexander and he finished a nine[-]inning game in 59 minutes[.]"[8]

And finally, on August 8, 1973, the day after Cooper died, *Pittsburgh Post-Gazette* columnist Al Abrams wrote a lengthy obituary of the "greatest lefthanded [sic] hurler in Pittsburgh history."[9] While extolling Cooper's legacy, Abrams pointed out that baseball writers had overlooked the former Pirate pitcher in the Hall of Fame voting.[10] Included in the article was an acknowledgment that "'Coop' and Grover Alexander once pitched against each other at Forbes Field in a game that lasted only 59 minutes."[11]

It was the evidence from these sources that led me to conclude the game had occurred and to insert a summary description of it in the article. As it later turned out, that conclusion was flawed. But, at that juncture, the decision was made and further supported by other research concerning the pitching styles of the two protagonists.

Cooper and Alexander in Their Time

Arley Wilbur Cooper (1892–1973), the best left-handed pitcher in Pittsburgh Pirate history (National Baseball Hall of Fame Library, Cooperstown, New York).

For most of their major league careers, Wilbur Cooper and Pete Alexander pitched in the Deadball Era, a baseball epoch prior to 1920 that because of many factors, including the construction of the ball, produced low-scoring games and emphasized strategy over slugging.[12] Consequently, it was common for games to finish between 90 minutes and one hour and 45 minutes.[13] But in an era when the standard pace of action was quick, Cooper and Alexander earned reputations as fast workers on the mound.

Described as a "pitcher of rare abilities,"[14] Wilbur Cooper made his major league debut in 1912 and established a style based on control, a graceful delivery, and a quiver of pitches: "a sneaky fast ball [*sic*], a sharp curve, [and] a change of pace...."[15] Long before the contemporary prac-

4. In Search of Cooper and Alexander's 1–0 Game (Cicotello)

tice of a pitcher choosing a designated battery mate, the Pirate southpaw teamed with catcher Walter Schmidt for about eight years. As a result, the two "rarely had their signals crossed"[16] and Cooper formed the habit of working fast:

> I knew what he [Schmidt] was going to call, and he knew what I was going to pitch.... For the last five innings of one ball game, he didn't give me a sign. I just kept whipping 'em in there.[17]

Charles J. "Chilly" Doyle, baseball writer for the *Pittsburgh Sun-Telegraph*, covered most of Cooper's career with the Pirates. In a 1952 series of retrospective articles on his reportage, Doyle featured an installment on the Pirates' 1925 pennant-winning season. Cooper, "mound star of perfect habits, and a great teamworker,"[18] had been traded with Rabbit Maranville and Charlie Grimm to Chicago after the 1924 season. Revisiting owner Barney Dreyfuss' decision to send Cooper to the Cubs, Doyle posed the question:

> [W]hy punish the steadiest southpaw [Cooper] in the National League, a smoothie of graceful physique who could run off those thrilling 1–0 classics against Alex the Great [Grover Cleveland Alexander] in an hour and 30 minutes?[19]

Doyle's description of those memorable Cooper-Alexander matchups includes one element that comports with the score of the game in question, but the duration does not.

In an article about Cooper's election to the Pittsburgh Hall of Fame in 1959, Al Abrams asked the honoree to identify the best pitcher he ever faced:

> Grover Cleveland Alexander. He was the greatest. I remember hooking up with him in many a pitching duel, most of them taking a little more than an hour.[20]

Cooper's recollection about the length of the contests between the two pitchers foreshadows his remarks in the two interviews he gave in 1972 concerning the 1–0 game that was attributed to them. When questioned about the current state of the game, Cooper expressed his dislike for "lengthy, drawn-out [*sic*] and often dull contests."[21] In contrast, he recalled his rapid pace of delivery by stating, "I remember many a time, I'd be half through my windup by the time I got the signal from [Walter] Schmidt."[22]

As for whom Cooper praised as his most capable adversary, Grover

Cleveland Alexander was indeed the "National League's most dominant pitcher of the Deadball Era's second decade."[23] Based on his remarkable 1910 minor league season at Syracuse where he finished 29–11, the right-hander — now nicknamed "Alex the Great" — was promoted to the majors in 1911 and arrived in Philadelphia ready for stardom. Proving that his promotion was well deserved, the Nebraska farm boy soon showcased his pitching prowess.

With a mediocre team that finished 79–73 and in fourth place, Alexander nevertheless was outstanding: a 28–13 record over 367 innings; 31 complete games in 37 starts; a 227–129 strikeouts-to-walks ratio; and a 2.57 ERA. It was, as John Skipper points out in his biography of the famous right-hander, "the greatest rookie season of all time."[24]

Grover Cleveland "Pete" or "Alex" Alexander (1887–1950), one of the greatest pitchers to wear a major league uniform (National Baseball Hall of Fame Library, Cooperstown, New York).

On the mound, Alexander was "the picture of grace and efficiency."[25] He came to be known for his signature sidearm delivery, superb control, and "wicked" curve. With an "uncanny ability to hit the corners of the plate,"[26] Alexander, like Cooper, wasted little time pitching.

"Alex" — as he was called by his teammates — "knew what he wanted to do with each batter,"[27] and by quickening his pace of delivery, he kept the opponent from thinking too much between pitches. When asked for an explanation for his rapid style, Alexander answered that "he did not want the batters 'relaxing' on his time."[28] As a result, he completed most

4. In Search of Cooper and Alexander's 1–0 Game (Cicotello)

of his games in 90 minutes or less, except for those that went into extra innings.[29]

Clearly, Cooper and Alexander represented a pair of pitchers, one lefty and one righty, whose similar styles hastened the pace of a game in an era when contests were quickly completed. That the two could have finished a nine-inning game in less than an hour is conceivable. But did it happen?

Deconstructing the Game

Subsequent to the publication of the Cooper profile in *Deadball Stars of the National League*, Bruce Fleming, who had read the article, contacted me with the following question: What was the date of the 59-minute game?[30] That question begged an answer and the search for it was on. In the end, the search yielded some useful evidence to answer the question, which, in turn, not only established a case of reasonable doubt about the existence of the game, but also raised more questions to be answered.

Fleming, whose baseball research interest has focused on games completed in less than one hour, had identified eight such contests. However, the Cooper-Alexander matchup was not on the list.[31] And that discrepancy initiated a reexamination of the accounts of the game found in the original source material used in compiling the biographical article on Cooper.

In all four accounts, a *time for the game* is mentioned: three cited 59 minutes; one cited 58. In two, the same *venue* is identified: Forbes Field. In only one is the *score* listed: 1–0. The source of that information is Pie Traynor, who was Cooper's teammate for five years (1920–1924). It is Traynor who also provides another detail that does not appear anywhere else: that Clyde Barnhart of the Pirates hit a homer to produce the winning run. Barnhart was an outfielder–third baseman on the Pittsburgh roster during those same five seasons.

In revisiting the original sources, it became evident to me in hindsight that the variations in the accounts had created uncertainty now about whether the game had even occurred. *Moreover, the answer Fleming sought was nowhere to be found in the material consulted for my article.* As Fleming suggested, a search of Retrosheet would be in order to determine the relevant details—date and venue—of any games that ended in a 1–0 score in which Cooper and Alexander were the pitchers of record.[32] Once identified by its date, the time of the game could be checked in the Retrosheet archive, if provided there, or through ProQuest, if listed in the newspapers.

As pitchers in the National League, Cooper and Alexander had virtually overlapping careers. Cooper was with Pittsburgh from 1912 to 1924; Alexander was with Philadelphia from 1911 to 1917 and then with Chicago from 1918 to 1924. The two were teammates in 1925 with Chicago. Therefore, the arc of time for possible head-to-head games spanned 13 seasons: 1912–1924 (Scenario 1).

If the game occurred when Alexander was with the Phillies (as Cooper asserted in the Miller interview), then the time frame narrows to six seasons: 1912–1917 (Scenario 2). However, if Traynor is to be believed, the range shifts to 1920–1924, during which all four players (Cooper, Alexander, Traynor, and Barnhart) overlap. Furthermore, the possibility is limited to one game in that period in which Cooper and Alexander faced each other *and* in which Barnhart hit a solo home run to earn the 1–0 victory (Scenario 3). Given these multiple scenarios, a check of Retrosheet would be useful in order to possibly settle the disparate accounts of the game and the constituent details that were either missing or in question.[33]

The Retrosheet Results

According to the Retrosheet game logs, Cooper and Alexander appeared in games head-to-head *only four times* over 13 seasons. The first of those games occurred on September 13, 1915, at Forbes Field with Philadelphia prevailing, 4–2. The second contest was held on August 18, 1917, at Baker Bowl, the Phillies' home field, where the Pirates lost, 3–2. The following year, Alexander was traded to the Chicago Cubs. In the third game between the two on April 28, 1920, at Wrigley Field, the Cubs walloped the Pirates, 11–1. The fourth and final matchup occurred at Forbes Field on June 22, 1922, and Pittsburgh outlasted Chicago, 8–6.[34] None of the results of these four games are remotely similar to the game in question and *none lasted less than one hour.*[35]

Nor does Clyde Barnhart's role in the game and his winning home run agree with the anecdotal evidence. Barnhart, a lifetime .295 hitter,

4. In Search of Cooper and Alexander's 1–0 Game (Cicotello)

had eight solo blasts over the five seasons when he was Cooper's teammate (1920–1924).[36] And as it turns out, he *did* hit a solo home run against Alexander, but it was during the fourth head-to-head game on June 22, 1922, with no outs in the second inning, giving Pittsburgh an early 1–0 lead in the contest which ended 8–6.[37] Also, it is interesting to note that the batter following Barnhart in the Pittsburgh order that day was teammate and third baseman, Pie Traynor.

The result: There is *no* box score data to confirm the existence of a game matching Cooper against Alexander that finished under one hour at any of the venues and/or that ended 1–0 on a Barnhart home run. Yet, the game persisted in the memories of both Wilbur Cooper and his teammate, Pie Traynor. And what about Grover Cleveland Alexander?

Clyde Barnhart, who, according to Pie Traynor, hit a solo home run that won the mysterious 1–0 game for the Pirates (National Baseball Hall of Fame Library, Cooperstown, New York).

Pete Alexander: To Corroborate or Not to Corroborate

The case of the 1–0 game lay dormant until I contacted John Skipper in late 2006. The early conception and planning of this chapter were underway, and my intention was to obtain from Skipper any information that may be useful from his research on the other protagonist in this narrative. Nowhere had any evidence surfaced from Alexander's side; it was entirely from Cooper, supported by Traynor and the Pittsburgh sportswriters.

Skipper, like Fleming, found no confirmation of such a Cooper-Alexander matchup. In fact, he remarked that it was "strange that for two starting pitchers whose careers pretty well paralleled one another, they only faced each other four times...."[38] Skipper, like Fleming and me, checked the Retrosheet game logs; furthermore, he consulted other biographies of Alexander and searched his own records. He could find no reference to the game.[39]

Towards Resolving the Mystery

Is the 1–0 game a mere story unsubstantiated by the facts? Or are there other explanations?

In his essay "Legends as an Expression of Baseball Memory," Lowell D. Blaisdell cogently writes that "baseball is especially well suited to the intermingling of what once was with what yet is."[40] The lode of legends is deep in the history of baseball, and as he points out, the purpose "of a baseball legend is to lift an episode from the past, and imprint it memorably on the present."[41] Blaisdell's analysis of the characteristics, function, and staying power of legends in the collective memory of the national pastime may offer an alternate explanation: that while the narrators establish the plausibility of an event with certain facts, the narrative of it is enhanced or altered proportionally in the retelling process. "This ambiguity between fact and fiction"[42] is at the tantalizing center of legends. Perhaps this case, a 1–0 game in which the protagonists finish nine innings in less than one hour, suggests the stuff of legendary lore.

Contributing to the possibility that the 1–0 game is more legend than fact is the chief "witness" to this purported event: Pie Traynor. Besides Cooper, no other first-hand corroborators have been found yet to support Traynor's account that was published in the 1969 interview. James Forr, who co-authored a 2010 biography of the Pirate third baseman, recalled that he did not read "anything about that game"[43] in the course of his research. Moreover, as for Traynor's narrative, Forr surmised, "It seems like Pie (as he liked to do sometimes) was telling a little bit of a fish story."[44]

4. In Search of Cooper and Alexander's 1–0 Game (Cicotello)

Then, too, have all the possibilities been exhausted? In the search for Cooper-Alexander matchups, an interesting homestand of four games occurred between Philadelphia and Pittsburgh at Forbes Field, August 9–11, 1917 (a little more than a week prior to the second matchup on August 18). The Pirates beat Alexander in the first game, 5–1. The next day, Wilbur Cooper pitched a 1–0 shutout over Eppa Rixey. On August 11, Alexander defeated the Pirates in the initial game of the series-ending doubleheader, 4–3, with Philadelphia winning the second game, 3–2.[45]

Cooper's 1–0 victory occurred between the first and third games in the series in which Alexander was the starter for both. Pittsburgh manufactured the lone run off Rixey in the bottom of the seventh inning when Pirate right fielder Lee King reached base on an error, advanced on a sacrifice, and later came home on a single. The game finished in one hour and 26 minutes.[46] While neither Traynor nor Barnhart were on the team, and while the contest lasted 86 minutes, could this be the origin for the 1–0 score and also the occasion in which Alexander is substituted for Rixey? The blending or transforming of details would be consistent with the establishment of a potential legend.

A search of *all* other 1–0 games in which Wilbur Cooper was the victor yields only six: five happened between 1912 and 1919 and one during the 1920–1924 span when Traynor and Barnhart were his teammates. In addition, each game was completed in nine innings.

The first of these 1–0 contests matched Pittsburgh against Chicago at Forbes Field on May 31, 1915. Cooper outdueled Jimmy Lavender, who loaded the bases in the third inning on three walks and then hit Pirate right fielder Bill Hinchman, which forced catcher George Gibson home with the only run. The game lasted one hour and 36 minutes.[47]

Two years later at the Polo Grounds on July 23, 1917, Cooper both pitched and hit his way to the victory. After seven scoreless innings, the Pirates broke through with a run in the eighth against New York Giant pitcher Ferdie Schupp. Catcher Bill Wagner doubled and then scored one batter later when Cooper slammed a double down the left field line. The time of this game was one hour and 31 minutes.[48]

Later that summer in a battle of lefties, Cooper faced Rube Benton of the Giants on August 27 at the Polo Grounds. In the fourth inning, Pirate center fielder Max Carey reached first on a bunt and then went to second on a single by third baseman Tony Boeckel. As Carey stole third,

Mysteries from Baseball's Past

Giant catcher Bill Rariden bluffed a throw and then noticed Boeckel on his way to second. Rariden's peg caught Boeckel stealing. Meanwhile, Carey, who had rounded third during the action, scored the only run as he beat the throw to the plate. The game ended in one hour and 36 minutes.[49]

On August 29, 1918, in the front end of a doubleheader against St. Louis at Forbes Field, Pittsburgh left fielder Tommy Leach coaxed a walk in the bottom of the eighth off Cardinal starter Bill Doak, moved to second on a sacrifice, and raced home on a hit by right fielder Billy Southworth. It was enough for Cooper to close out the victory. The game lasted one hour and 38 minutes.[50]

In a masterful performance at the Polo Grounds on July 12, 1919, Cooper gave up only three hits and outpitched Giant hurler Fred Toney. Pittsburgh produced its run in the second inning, when Pirate second baseman George Cutshaw tripled and scored following a single by first baseman Fritz Mollwitz. Cooper faced only 30 batters and 20 of the 27 outs were on fly balls. Oddly, Toney had two of the Giants' three hits.[51] No time was cited in the box scores published in either the *New York Times* or the *Pittsburgh Post*.[52]

The final 1–0 contest occurred at Redland Field in Cincinnati on April 16, 1924. In his first start of the season, Cooper was matched up against Reds' pitcher Dolf Luque. Holding the Reds to only five hits, Cooper was provided the margin of victory in the ninth inning when Carey singled, moved to second on a sacrifice, stole third, and then scored on a single by Traynor. The time of the game was one hour and 25 minutes.[53]

This set of 1–0 scores confirms Wilbur Cooper *was* a consistently quick worker over the arc of his career and lends credence to one part of Charles Doyle's memory that the Pirate lefty completed games within 90 minutes or so. However, Doyle's recollection that Pete Alexander was regularly Cooper's opponent in these games is flatly refuted by the evidence. Is this discrepancy perhaps a case of a sportswriter's journalistic license with the facts? It seems likely.

Then again, John Skipper raises still more questions in the pursuit of this mysterious Cooper-Alexander 1–0 contest:

> I am not absolutely certain that the game ... did not take place.... I can't find any reference to [it]. But what about in the minor leagues? What about on a barnstorming trip? What about in an exhibition game? That's my hesitancy.

4. *In Search of Cooper and Alexander's 1–0 Game* (Cicotello)

I can't say for sure the game never took place. The only thing I can say for sure is that I can't find it.[54]

Elusive as it may be, the game may be out there waiting to be found.

NOTES

1. David Cicotello, "Arley Wilbur Cooper," in *Deadball Stars of the National League*, ed. Tom Simon (Dulles, VA: Brassey's, 2004), 181–182.

2. Bill Heufelder, "Cooper of the Pirates," *Eagle*, October 1969; Bernie Milligan, *Van Nuys News and Valley Green Sheet*, February 29, 1972; Mike Miller, "Wilbur Cooper: Pirate Great," *The View from Sierra Madre*, August 31, 1972; and Al Abrams, "Sidelights on Sports," *Pittsburgh Post-Gazette*, August 8, 1973. All of these articles were found in Wilbur Cooper's file in the National Baseball Hall of Fame Library, Cooperstown, New York. The author wishes to thank Miriam Velasquez of the *Los Angeles Daily News* who assisted him in locating the edition of the *Van Nuys News and Valley Green Sheet* in which Milligan's article was published.

3. Among the research materials consulted were the *Biographical Dictionary of American Sports: Baseball*, ed. David L. Porter (Westport, CT: Greenwood, 1987); David Finoli and Bill Ranier, *The Pittsburgh Pirates Encyclopedia* (Champaign, IL: Sports Publishing L.L.C., 2003); Wilbur Cooper's file in the National Baseball Hall of Fame Library, Cooperstown, New York; *The Baseball Encyclopedia: The Complete and Official Record of Major League Baseball*, 6th ed., ed. Joseph L. Reichler (New York: Macmillan, 1985); Bill James and Rob Neyer, *The Neyer/James Guide to Pitchers: An Historical Compendium of Pitching, Pitchers, and Pitches* (New York: Fireside, 2004); Bill James, *The Politics of Glory: How Baseball's Hall of Fame Really Works* (New York: Macmillan, 1994); Bill James, *The Bill James Historical Baseball Abstract* (New York: Villard Books, 1988); http://www.baseball-reference.com; http://www.cnnsi.com; and http://www.baseball-almanac.com.

4. In retrospect, the variations between and among the accounts were sufficient enough to have led me to propose that the game was more likely a legend of baseball lore.

5. Heufelder.

6. Milligan.

7. Ibid.

8. Miller.

9. Abrams, August 8, 1973.

10. The all-time franchise leader in victories (202) and complete games (263), Cooper is arguably the greatest pitcher in the history of the Pittsburgh Pirates, but as of 2010, he has not been elected to the Baseball Hall of Fame. In addition, he has yet to be the subject of a book-length biography.

11. Abrams, August 8, 1973.

12. For an excellent description of how baseball was played during the Deadball Era, see Benjamin G. Rader, *Baseball: A History of America's Game*, 2d ed. (Urbana: University of Illinois Press, 2002), 97–100.

13. David W. Anderson, *More Than Merkle: A History of the Best and Most Exciting Baseball Season in Human History* (Lincoln: University of Nebraska Press, 2000), 18. The author wishes to thank David Anderson, Ron Selter, and John Simpson of SABR's Deadball

Mysteries from Baseball's Past

Era Committee who responded to his request for research assistance concerning the length of games during this period.

14. John J. Ward, "Wilbur Cooper, Premier Pitcher of the National League," *Baseball Magazine* 27, no. 4 (September 1921): 455.

15. Al Abrams, "Sidelights on Sports," *Pittsburgh Post-Gazette*, January 27, 1959.

16. Heufelder.

17. Ibid.

18. Charles J. (Chilly) Doyle, "Wilbur Cooper Victim of a Cruel Release; Oil Smith Takes Over," *Pittsburgh Sun-Telegraph*, February 12, 1952.

19. Ibid.

20. Abrams, January 27, 1959.

21. Ibid.

22. Ibid.

23. Jan Finkel, "Grover Cleveland 'Pete' Alexander," in *Deadball Stars of the National League*, ed. Tom Simon (Dulles, VA: Brassey's, 2004), 209.

24. John C. Skipper, *Wicked Curve: The Life and Troubled Times of Grover Cleveland Alexander* (Jefferson, NC: McFarland, 2006), 29.

25. Finkel, 209.

26. Skipper, 29.

27. Ibid., 46.

28. Jerry E. Clark and Martha Ellen Webb, *Alexander the Great: The Story of Grover Cleveland Alexander* (Omaha: Making History, 1995), 3.

29. Skipper, 46.

30. E-mail message from Bruce Fleming to David Cicotello, August 19, 2004.

31. E-mail message from Bruce Fleming to David Cicotello, August 20, 2004.

32. Ibid.

33. I did *not* consult Retrosheet to fact-check the 1–0 game during the research and writing phases of the Cooper biographical article. The details of the game were included in the manuscript and altered slightly in the copyediting stage. The responsibility, however, is solely mine for what appears in *Deadball Stars of the National League*.

34. http://www.retrosheet.com game logs, retrieved November 16, 2009.

35. The times for each game were: 9/13/15, two hours and 29 minutes in 13 innings ("Thirteenth Lucky for Phillies," *New York Times*, September 14, 1915); 8/18/17, two hours and 28 minutes in 14 innings ("Clean Sweep for Phils," *New York Times*, August 19, 1917); 4/28/20, one hour and 41 minutes in nine innings ("Cubs Slaughter Pirates," *New York Times*, April 29, 1920); and 6/22/22, one hour and 47 minutes in nine innings ("Pittsburgh Beats Chicago by 8 to 6," *New York Times*, June 23, 1922).

36. *SABR Presents The Home Run Encyclopedia: The Who, What, and Where of Every Home Run Hit Since 1876*, eds. Bob McConnell and David Vincent (New York: Macmillan, 1996), 248.

37. http://www.retrosheet.com game logs, retrieved December 14, 2009.

38. E-mail message from John Skipper to David Cicotello, January 1, 2007.

39. E-mail message from John Skipper to David Cicotello, December 3, 2007.

40. Lowell D. Blaisdell, "Legends as an Expression of Baseball Memory," *Journal of Sport History* 19, no. 3 (Winter 1992): 228.

41. Ibid.

42. David C. Ogden, "Josh vs. Satchel: Legends, Their Leveling Effect and Their Cultural Longevity," in *Baseball/Literature/Culture: Essays, 2004–2005*, ed. Peter Carino (Jefferson, NC: McFarland, 2006), 120.

43. E-mail message from James Forr to David Cicotello, February 5, 2010.

4. In Search of Cooper and Alexander's 1–0 Game (Cicotello)

44. Ibid.
45. "Buccaneers Rout Alex," *New York Times*, August 10, 1917; "Phillies Humbled Again," *New York Times*, August 11, 1917; and "Phillies Take Two Games," *New York Times*, August 12, 1917.
46. *New York Times*, August 11, 1917.
47. "Only Run Scored by Pirates," *New York Times*, June 1, 1915.
48. "Cooper Restricts Giants to Ciphers," *New York Times*, July 24, 1917.
49. "Lone Run Made by Pittsburgh Pirates Proves Ample to Defeat Giants," *New York Times*, August 28, 1917.
50. Ed F. Balinger, "Pirates Divide Bargain with Tailenders," *Pittsburgh Post*, August 30, 1918.
51. "Giants, Baffled by Cooper's Curves, Relinquish Lead in Pennant Contest to Reds," *New York Times*, July 13, 1919.
52. Ibid., and Ed F. Balinger, "Cooper Hurls Giants from First Place," *Pittsburgh Post*, July 13, 1919.
53. "Carey's Work Wins for Pirates in 9th," *New York Times*, April 17, 1924.
54. E-mail message from John Skipper to David Cicotello, December 3, 2007.

5

The Mysterious Mr. Cicotte

Gene Carney

He pronounced it "SEE-cott," but in his 14 seasons at the top level of baseball, he must have heard at least a half dozen variations. Ring Lardner made the task of getting his name right the subject of a humorous poem.

> This pretty name of mine is not
> As some folks claim,
> just plain Si-cot;
> Nor is it, as some have it, Sic-ot,
> Although I'm sure
> I don't know why not.
> And furthermore, take this from me,
> I don't pronounce it Sick-o-tee;
> And you can also make a note
> That it is surely not Si-cote.
> You stand to win some easy cash
> By betting it's not succotash.

But there is no record that this ever bothered Eddie Cicotte. He just lived with it.

We have countless words from William Shakespeare, but we really have no definite idea what he looked like. We have numerous photographs of Eddie Cicotte and a fair number of words, but much of his life still remains a mystery.

Those who have written about the 1919 World Series, including Eliot Asinof, whose *Eight Men Out* has been the most influential secondary work on the scandal, never had access to the "hidden" words of Eddie Cicotte: those spoken in private to his team's lawyer, before he went to the grand

5. The Mysterious Mr. Cicotte (Carney)

Edward Victor "Eddie" or "Knuckles" Cicotte (1884–1969), a man of mystery (National Baseball Hall of Fame Library, Cooperstown, New York).

jury in 1920; the grand jury testimony itself; and his later depositions for an obscure trial in 1924. A few of those words made it into the newspapers then, but were generally overlooked, though today there is no excuse for pretending that Cicotte was the vindictive villain trying to get even with his skinflint owner, Charles Comiskey. The evidence suggests that "just ain't so."

Foreshadowings

It was not until his 11th season, at age 33, that Cicotte finally won 20 games. In fact, he went from 15–7 in 1916 to a splendid 28–12, with a microscopic 1.53 ERA in 1917. That burst helped take his Chicago White Sox to a pennant, and he added a win that October as the Sox beat McGraw's Giants in six games. Known as a heady hurler with a variety of pitches, Cicotte had acquired the nickname "Knuckles" for the pitch he threw so often, the knuckleball, but after 1917, the baseball world was calling him the master of another trick pitch, the shine ball.

The shiner acted like a knuckler, and there are several theories about how the ball was doctored to make it act so. Cicotte's catcher said that he rubbed dirt into the seams; others said that he rubbed one spot smooth with his uniform, or maybe he rubbed the ball on a waxy paraffin spot on his trousers. Cicotte himself said there was no shine ball and that was reported in *The Sporting News* in the spring of 1918:

> "It was a myth[,] pure and simple," said Eddie. "It was all a scheme of Hap's [Happy Felsch's] and mine to fool the batsman, who is always hanging around to be fooled."
> Happy Felsch assented to all that Eddie said about the origin of the shine ball as perfected by the alert White Sox pitcher. The whole blooming thing was cooked up on an off day at the Texas training camp, according to Hap.[1]

The Reach Guide confirmed that the pitch was fictitious, invented to confuse batters:

> He has been accused time and again of using the "shine ball," which is nothing more than a myth. Ball after ball has been taken out of the game and brought to the headquarters of the league for examination, and there never has been found any foreign substance on the sphere.[2]

5. The Mysterious Mr. Cicotte (Carney)

But it was too late—the shine ball had taken on a life of its own. Cicotte was asked about it again in 1956, when there was no reason to deny it, and he said that the pitch never existed.[3]

In his 1963 book, *Eight Men Out*, Eliot Asinof, who never talked with Cicotte, makes the controversial pitcher somewhat sympathetic by telling readers that the ace of the Sox staff decided to get into the fix of the 1919 World Series because he was denied a $10,000 bonus promised him by the team owner, Charles Comiskey.[4] (In the movie *Eight Men Out*, the subject of the bonus is moved up to 1919, providing a more immediate motivation.)

But Cicotte himself never spoke of a bonus, which he would receive for winning 30 games; nor is there any mention of it in his contract in either 1917 or 1919.[5] In both of those seasons, he did in fact have chances to win 30. So, he was not held back by his team to prevent him from earning a bonus. In 1917, Cicotte was the starting pitcher on September 2, 8 (there were no games on the 6th or 7th), 14 (there were no games between September 10–13), 19, 25, and 29. In 1919, he was rested between his starts on September 5 and 19, but he had complained about a lame arm. However, just before the 1919 Series, Kid Gleason contradicted Cicotte's complaints by saying, "Those stories about Cicotte having a sore arm were all wrong. He's ready [for the Series]."[6] Thus, the disagreement was, as Bob Hoie indicated in the early 1990s, "*exactly the opposite* of what one would expect if Cicotte had been artificially held back from winning thirty games in order to cheat him out of a bonus."[7]

It appears that Comiskey did reward Cicotte for winning 29 games in 1919 with a $3,000 bonus, and that was *after* the tainted series had been played. This was reported in the press during the Black Sox trial in the summer of 1921. It is probable that Cicotte's teammates knew about the $10,000 that he took before the World Series, which makes the $3,000 bonus from Comiskey look like hush money: keep the money, but *keep it quiet*.

One of the top pitchers in baseball in 1917, Cicotte was paid just $5,000 the following year (coming off a 28-win season, 29 counting his win in the World Series). However, salaries in baseball were depressed across the board, due to the war. In 1919, because the owners were still uncertain about whether the fans would return to baseball, Cicotte was paid around $5,000 again. So, his jump to $10,000 for 1920 reflected a raise that had been overdue. The other Black Sox players who signed new contracts for 1920 all received similarly generous raises; Happy Felsch was the only player to suggest that the boosts included hush money, but he may have said that just to help out Joe Jackson in Jackson's 1924 law suit against the White Sox for back pay.[8] When Felsch spoke to Eliot Asinof, during the author's research for *Eight Men Out*, he made no mention of hush money and said he got the raise for 1920 by writing a letter "demanding" it.[9]

Of course, the confusion about his name's pronunciation, the arguments over whether he had an extra weapon in his pitching arsenal, and the legend of the denied big bonus are but a prelude to the most important mystery of all that surrounds Eddie Cicotte: whether he pitched the 1919 World Series to win or to intentionally lose to the Cincinnati Reds.

The 1919 Series

Before going further, a recap of Cicotte's performance in the 1919 Series is necessary. Hurt by the absence of disabled veteran Red Faber, Chicago would logically pitch Eddie Cicotte, the ace of the staff, in Game One, and then yield the mound to the Sox southpaw, 23-game winner Lefty Williams. The only other starter available was a rookie, Dickie Kerr, and if he could not handle Cincinnati, the National League champions, Cicotte and Williams would have to carry the load in this experimental best-of-nine.

Cicotte started Game One shakily, hitting the hometown Reds' first batter square in the back with his second pitch. The runner scored, but the Sox rallied to tie the game at 1–1. In the fourth inning, the Reds had one man out and one on first, when Cicotte fielded a comebacker which looked like a sure double-play ball. Accounts differ about what happened next: shortstop Swede Risberg may have stumbled covering second or maybe Cicotte's throw was late or off-line. In any case, the runner was out at second, but the batter was safe at first. There were now two outs, and the next batter popped one over short that Risberg fielded, but could not hold. Given two extra outs, the Reds then strung together four more hits, chasing Cicotte en route to a 9–1 victory.

Williams lost Game Two, 4–2, even though the Sox out-hit the Reds,

5. The Mysterious Mr. Cicotte (Carney)

10–4, but back in Chicago, Dickie Kerr tossed a 3–0 shutout, to make it 2 games to 1, Reds. Cicotte started Game Four, and this time tossed a complete game five-hitter. However, he gave up two unearned runs, making both errors himself in the fifth inning. The first came on a hard hit up the middle, which Cicotte snagged, but then threw wildly to first, allowing the runner to reach second. The next batter singled sharply to left, and Joe Jackson fired his peg toward home, stopping the runner at third. But Cicotte, trying to cut off the throw, perhaps to nail the runner rounding first, deflected the ball off the diamond and a run scored. A hit made it 2–0, and that was all Reds' pitcher Jimmy Ring needed to earn the victory.

Lefty Williams lost Game Five, this time being outpitched by Hod Eller, 5–0, and the Sox were on the brink of elimination, down 4 games to 1. But Dickie Kerr came through again, winning 5–4 in ten innings. Cicotte took the hill for the third time in Game Seven and was in total control, winning 4–1. However, the Reds knocked out Lefty Williams in the first inning of Game Eight and went on to win the game, 10–5, and the series, 5–3.

Suspicions

Rumors of bribery were rampant, and there is some evidence that the White Sox management knew about the fix even before Game One. Manager Kid Gleason had confronted his team about it and threatened to bench anyone he saw not giving his best. There is also some evidence that Cicotte took some verbal heat from his manager after Game One and from Ray Schalk, his catcher, who may even have punctuated his words with a few punches. But Gleason started Cicotte three times and never hinted that he had any regrets about doing so. And there is anecdotal evidence that Schalk later went on record saying Cicotte pitched to win.

After the series, Cicotte went home, and the next spring, he signed a contract for 1920, paying him $10,000, which doubled his salary. He then won 21 games while losing just 10, as the Sox found themselves in a hot pennant race with Cleveland. Three other Sox pitchers—Williams, Kerr, and a healthy Red Faber—also had 20 or more victories.

But a Cook County grand jury, convened in September of 1920,

Mysteries from Baseball's Past

announced that it would look into the rumors of bribery in the last World Series. Owner Charles Comiskey had withheld the checks of eight players mixed up in the rumors and had offered a reward for hard evidence, but none was found. Suddenly those eight names were made public, probably by Comiskey's nemesis, American League president Ban Johnson. And Cicotte's name was among them.

Johnson proceeded to turn up the heat, claiming that he thought that the White Sox were playing as if they wanted Cleveland to win the 1920 pennant, possibly so they could make more postseason dollars by competing in the lucrative City Series with the Cubs *and* collecting second-place money. Rumors had Johnson out to wreck the Sox because they were Comiskey's team. But Johnson was a longtime opponent of gambling in baseball, and he may simply have told the grand jury what he knew—and he knew about the withheld checks from the previous fall because several players had complained to him about it.

Then, on September 27, a Philadelphia resident, Billy Maharg, said in an interview that the Sox had been offered $100,000 to throw the Series. That allegation made national headlines and the fallout was immediate.

The next day, Cicotte voluntarily went to his team and then to the grand jury. After signing a waiver of immunity, he met with the grand jury and confirmed that the fix was in and that he himself had received $10,000 before the first game. This admission made front-page headlines across the country on September 28 and 29.

The scandalous news swept the nation, and many accounts added sensational details to what had been leaked from the grand jury proceedings: Cicotte had served up easy-to-hit fastballs; he had made those Game Four errors on purpose; he was said to have had seven accomplices, maybe more; and the whole series was crooked. *Say it ain't so!*

Joe Jackson followed Cicotte to the courthouse, after which the press reported that Jackson also confessed to tossing games: he struck out in the clutch or just poked at the ball, and he let up in the field. *Guilty!*

Historians Harold Seymour and Dorothy Seymour Mills theorize that "Jackson and Felsch in their confessions almost seemed to protest too much about their crookedness. Their claims could be construed as worried attempts to convince the gamblers that they had conscientiously tried to lose, as they were expected to."[10] *See, they intended to throw the Series!*

As a result of the grand jury investigations, seven Chicago players

5. The Mysterious Mr. Cicotte (Carney)

were indicted and suspended, and the Sox's pennant chances ended with three games left to play. They won just one, and the AL flag went to Cleveland. While baseball fans were shaken badly by the scandal, they were also distracted by a slugger in New York, Babe Ruth, who smashed 54 home runs, a new record. Soon, they were watching the 1920 World Series and talking about an unassisted triple play, a grand slam, and a homer by a pitcher — all in one game! The event that would eventually go down in history as the Black Sox scandal and as baseball's darkest hour received mere minutes of coverage in the contemporary press accounts.

When Joe Jackson heard how the press handled his grand jury appearance, he protested immediately. He said that he had not thrown a game or confessed to tossing any. In fact, the transcript of Jackson's testimony agrees that he said he played to win. Moreover, the grand jury foreman stated under oath that the grand jury heard Jackson give the same testimony.[11] But it was too late: "Say it ain't so, Joe" became the iconic image for this crime. And first impressions were to become lasting ones.

On Trial Forever[12]

That was the case with Eddie Cicotte, too. At the 1921 trial, which acquitted all the ballplayers of conspiracy charges (they had violated no Illinois laws by taking bribes[13]), Cicotte's grand jury testimony was read into the record. But only a few papers bothered to point out Cicotte's defense: that he pitched and played the whole 1919 Series to win.

While testifying to the grand jury, Cicotte named all the players later banished. (He thought Jackson was involved because Lefty Williams said that he "represented" Jackson in the plotting, but Williams later said that he did so without Jackson's knowledge or permission.)[14] He said the idea of the fix had originated in a conversation he had with Chick Gandil and Fred McMullin, in which one of those two "started by saying that we were not getting a devil of a lot of money, and that it looked as though we could make a good thing if we threw the [W]orld's [S]eries to Cincinnati."[15] When asked how much it would take for him to join in, Cicotte replied, "I would not do anything like that for less than $10,000."[16]

Cicotte recalled a pre–Series meeting in either his or Happy Felsch's room at the Warner Hotel that followed soon after, with Gandil, Felsch,

Buck Weaver, and perhaps McMullin and Williams. "I was the first one that spoke about the money end of it, and said that there was so much double[-]crossing stuff that if I went into the [S]eries to throw the games[,] I wanted the money put in my hands before we started to Cincinnati."[17] Gandil assured him that he would get his money in advance. Cicotte then left his room and visited with Red Faber and Shano Collins, while the other players exited one by one to avoid the appearance of having been in a meeting. When Cicotte later returned to his room, about 11:30 P.M., there was $10,000 under his pillow. He pocketed the cash and brought it with him to Cincinnati.[18]

The infamous Arnold "Chick" Gandil (National Baseball Hall of Fame Library, Cooperstown, New York).

After the Series, Cicotte said he took the money home to Detroit and hid it. He paid off the mortgage on his farm with $4,000; the rest went to put in new floors in the barn and house and to buy livestock and feed.[19] Cicotte claimed he did not know where the money had come from: "I never asked Gandil or McMullin.... I suppose some gamblers made some money, got ahold [sic] of it, but I didn't know what to think at the time; that was the theory because the way I looked at it[,] the ordinary man would not give up money to throw a [S]eries just to have us beaten."[20]

"Wished Someone Would Shoot Him, Says Cicotte" was the *Boston Globe* headline when Cicotte's grand jury statements were read into the record at the Black Sox trial in the summer of 1921. The subhead read: "Pitcher Says He Hit Rath, First Man Up, While Trying to Walk Him In Opener, But Tried His Best Thereafter." The Reds had won Games One and Four on their own talent and not because Cicotte had let up. A few smaller papers carried the story with similar emphasis, but most gave it little space, if it was mentioned at all. It was too late now for Cicotte to change history — the leaks from a year ago had become the version Americans would believe.[21]

5. *The Mysterious Mr. Cicotte* (Carney)

Although Cicotte admitted that he put on base the first batter he faced in Game One, Morrie Rath, he made no mention that this was a signal that the fix was in. The first pitch Cicotte threw to Rath was a called strike, but in all probability, Rath was taking all the way. Questioned before the grand jury whether he wanted Rath to get on base, Cicotte replied:

> Yes. But after he passed, after he was on there, I don't know, I guess I believe I tried too hard. I didn't care, they could have had my heart and soul out there. That is the way I felt. I felt — I didn't want to be that way after I had taken the money.[22]

Cicotte spoke at some length about the play in the fourth inning of Game One that started his undoing. "That's the play they incriminate me on, but I was absolutely honest on that play.... Everybody saw me make that play," Cicotte insisted.[23] He did not think that Swede Risberg intended to miss the runner on that play. And all of the hits that followed "was [sic] clean base hits."[24]

After the 9–1 loss, "I went up in the room. I was too ill, I had the headache after the game. I stayed in my room and was sick all night long. I couldn't hit in St Louis."[25] (The lawyers were puzzled by this phrase and Cicotte did not offer to explain it.) His roommate, Felsch, gave him some aspirin tablets. A contrite Cicotte explained, "Happy, this will never be done again."[26]

Regarding the next game that he pitched in the series, Game Four, Cicotte told the grand jury:

> I tried to make good but I made two errors. I was very anxious to get the ball and I didn't make any runs. If we could make four or five runs — I would have won that game.[27]

Asked if he had tried to make a bad throw that game, Cicotte said, "No sir, I didn't, I tried to get my man. I tried to win [Game Four]."[28]

Cicotte said in effect that he had played the Series to win. "I was going to take a chance. I wanted to win. I could [meaning would] have given [the money] back with interest, if they only let me win the game that day."[29]

Asked by someone on the grand jury how he could win with seven players on his own team against him, Cicotte said, "They never talked to me at all. If they talked to me, I was deaf ears. I was a man of another country."[30]

Judge Charles McDonald, who was in charge of the grand jury, recalled Cicotte walking into his chambers that day:

> Of his own free will he told of the deals with the gamblers. I warned him he did not have to testify, that he couldn't be compelled to give evidence against himself. He said he wanted to tell the truth.[31]

McDonald then added this about Cicotte:

> He started the first game, he told me, with the intention of walking the first man. Instead[,] he hit him with a pitched ball. After that[,] he said his conscience hurt him and he realized that he was doing wrong. He regretted his action, but did not return the money.[32]

Cicotte repeated that version of events at the time he was deposed for a later trial when Jackson sued the Sox for back pay in 1924. But again, the press paid scant attention to the players' claims, even though the grand jury transcripts backed them up.

Since the verdict of 1921, Cicotte has remained an unredeemed player in the eyes of many. Unfortunately for him, the mainstream press view of his participation in the fix — a view which Eliot Asinof supplemented through interviews with people related to the scandal and with various written sources and then vividly described in *Eight Men Out* — has continued to be the most popular one, despite the efforts of Victor Luhrs to lessen Cicotte's guilt.[33]

However, amazingly, the story is not over. New evidence that shines new light on Eddie Cicotte's plight and all the events of 1919–1924 became available to researchers in May 2009. A collection of documents, once in the office of the White Sox's lawyers, reveals a startling lode of relevant material:

- According to Cicotte, when he first told his story about the fix to team lawyer Alfred Austrian and Comiskey, he said the idea came up in a discussion on a train, *before* the Sox clinched the 1919 flag. And it came up because the players had heard that $10,000 in bribe money had been offered for the fixing of the World Series in 1918, won by the Red Sox over the Cubs.[34] There is no evidence of a previous fix, but this is not the first time that the 1918 World Series has come under suspicion.[35]

  The information about possible bribery in 1918 was *not* in Cicotte's grand jury statement, but Austrian had it in Cicotte's deposition from minutes earlier. Thus, in Cicotte's words:

5. The Mysterious Mr. Cicotte (Carney)

The way it started, we were going east on the train. The ball players were talking about somebody trying to fix the National League ball players or something like that in the World's Series of 1918. Well[,] anyway[,] there was some talk about them offering $10,000 or something to throw the Cubs in the Boston Series. There was talk that somebody offered this player $10,000 or anyway the bunch of players were offered $10,000 to throw this [S]eries. This was on the train going over. Somebody made a crack about getting money, if we got into the [S]eries, to throw the [S]eries. The boys on the [c]lub got talking over there in New York about the fellows getting too much money and such stuff as that and said that they would go ahead and go through with it if they got this money.

We never held any secret meeting[,] but we would meet one or two at a time and we all agreed that for a piece of money we would throw the World Series. I was supposed to get $10,000. Some man came to the Warner and left this money in my room. $10,000. That was supposed to be mine. There was no agreement with anybody[,] but just simply an agreement like anyone else would make. I never knew if the others got any money.[36]

- Austrian or one of his assistants apparently scribbled these notes as he listened to Cicotte; the jottings agree with the statement Cicotte gave to the grand jury (see above):
  Pitched first game
  tried to walk Rath — hit him
  Risberg stumbled
  Pitched 2nd game
  ~~Would have won anyway if he could~~ [For some reason, the words have a line drawn through them, but why?]
  Could not sleep
  Felsch in room
  Conf. at Sinton
  Risberg[,] Felsch & Cicotte[37]

- Cicotte and the other players who had signed away their immunity before talking to the grand jury testified later that they had been misled.[38] They all claimed to have been promised that they would not be jailed, fined, or indicted.[39] They were indicted, however, and stood trial a year later. It is generally believed that team lawyer Alfred Austrian sacrificed the players to show that the White Sox were doing their part to clean up baseball.

Advised by their own lawyers, the accused Sox repudiated the 1920 statements, which was the only real evidence against them.

Although the statements were admitted, the 1921 jury still acquitted the players of conspiracy, and that seems right, because the planning was just not that organized, and it appeared that Joe Jackson attended no meetings at all.[40]

- The Sox management knew about the bribery, but must have believed that the players did not go through with it—despite the fact that they did lose the series.[41] How else to explain the re-signing of all but one of the suspected players (Chick Gandil left the team), offering them significant raises? Comiskey may have wanted dearly to retain his "dynasty," but Kid Gleason, who interacted with the players daily during the 1919 Series, had to fill out the starting lineups. His backup pitchers were weak, but it seems unlikely he would send out Cicotte if he believed that his ace was "tossing."

- In a lengthy letter dated February 26, 1929, Charles Comiskey told John Wray, the sporting editor of the *St. Louis Dispatch*, some incriminating things about Ban Johnson that relate directly or indirectly to Cicotte and his expelled teammates and, if true, raise further questions about who the guilty parties really were. Among Comiskey's assertions are:

    > ... Mr. Johnson[,] rather than assisting in any early disclosure of the scandal, hindered it. I was approached by an East St. Louis gambler shortly after the conclusion of the 1919 Series. This man claimed he was crossed by the Black Sox to the extent of $5,500 and said he would give me 100% full information against the players if I would make good his loss. I immediately sent my representatives to him with the money, but was informed that Johnson's men had already been with him, and we could get no information out of him thereafter.... This same man was in the company of Johnson at subsequent World Series games.
    >
    > In 1920, ... the Chicago American League Baseball Club ... finished second in the [l]eague [r]ace. Accordingly, under [b]aseball [r]ules, the players in the Chicago [c]lub were entitled to a percentage of the receipts of the first four games of the World Series of 1920. $4,800.00 of this amount was retained by Commissioner Landis—being the sum which would otherwise have gone to the seven Black Sox. In April, 1922, Judge Landis addressed a letter to Mr. Heydler, as [p]resident of the National League, and to Mr. Johnson, as [p]resident of the American League, stating these facts, and adding:

5. *The Mysterious Mr. Cicotte* (Carney)

Charles Comiskey, the owner of the Chicago White Sox from 1900 to 1931 (National Baseball Hall of Fame Library, Cooperstown, New York).

Mysteries from Baseball's Past

"What is your judgment as to the desirability of paying at this time this sum of $4,800 pro rata to the members who were *eligible* [Comiskey's emphasis] players of the Chicago American League [c]lub in October, 1920[?]"

This meant that Judge Landis was suggesting that this amount should go by way of extra compensation to those players of the [c]lub who were untouched by the scandal.

... [O]n the very next day[,] we find Johnson writing the following letter to Judge Landis[:]

"I have your letter of April 27, relative to the money retained from the *ineligible* [again, Comiskey's emphasis] players of Chicago American [c]lub. It is my thought they (the ineligible players) should receive at once the amount due them out of the World Series money of 1920, and would suggest that the seven players: Charles Risberg, 'Red' McMullen [sic], Joe Jackson, Oscar Felsch, George M. [sic] Weaver, George [sic] Williams and E.V. Cicotte, should [each] be mailed a check for $685.79."

Mr. Heydler, on the other hand, approved Judge Landis' suggestion. As was to be expected, Judge Landis did not pay $685.75 [sic], or any other sum, to any of the seven Black Sox as Johnson wanted him to do, and did distribute it in accordance with the purport of his letter to Johnson.

Under date of February 27, 1922, Johnson issued a bulletin in which he barred for all time from American League [p]arks, the Black Sox, and also the following:

Carl Zork [a possible fixer]

Ben Franklin [Frankel, a possible fixer]

Louis Levi [a possible fixer]

D.A. Zeisler [sic] (alias Bennett) [David Zelcer, a possible fixer]

Abe Attell [world featherweight boxing champion and a possible fixer]

[Joseph J.] "Sport" Sullivan [a possible fixer]

Judge Landis, the man who banned Eddie Cicotte from forever playing again in Organized Baseball (National Baseball Hall of Fame Library, Cooperstown, New York).

5. *The Mysterious Mr. Cicotte* (Carney)

> Rachel Brown [Arnold Rothstein's bookkeeper]
> Hal Chase [a former major leaguer and a possible fixer]
> Lee Magee [a former major leaguer and a possible fixer]
> Arnold Rothstein [leader of organized crime and a possible fixer]
>
> It is startling to note that among these names we do not find [Bill] Burns and [Billy] Maharg, the go-betweens between the gamblers and the guilty 1919 World Series players.
>
> Not only did Mr. Johnson not bar those two individuals[,] but the records of the American League show that as long as he was [p]resident of the American League and down to the time he left it in 1927, Mr. Johnson issued annual passes to Burns and Maharg.
>
> It is also a matter of common knowledge that for several years after the disclosure of Burns' connection with the crooked series, Johnson took a hunting trip with this same Burns, the self-confessed fixer of the Series, at the latter's place in Mexico. I am also reliably informed that Johnson has from time to time supplied Burns with money since the trial. The public can draw its own conclusion as to what interest the two men have in common, or what hold Burns has on Johnson.[42]

Eddie Cicotte said in a 1956 interview that he had made a mistake, and he had paid for it. The players had "done wrong and we deserved to get punished. But not a life sentence. That was too rough. I could have earned a living coaching later[,] but they wouldn't let me. I wasn't paid so bad."[43]

Cicotte had tried his best to make up for his mistake by leading a quiet, productive life, devoted to his family. In 1969, Eliot Asinof heard that Cicotte was ill and was finally willing to talk, so he attempted to visit him in Detroit, where the pitcher had spent most of his life. But it was too late.

We can only guess at what Cicotte might have said to Asinof. Would he have corrected the information in *Eight Men Out* so that today the 1988 movie version might begin with a chat about a fix in 1918? Would he have pleaded with Asinof to let the world know that he had pitched to win? Or would he simply have said, "There was no shine ball, you know."

Notes

1. "Eddie Cicotte's Shiner to Be as Effective as Ever," *The Sporting News*, May 2, 1918, 3.

Mysteries from Baseball's Past

2. "The Personnel of the American League Champion Team," *The Reach Official American League Base Ball Guide* (Philadelphia: A.J. Reach, 1920), 80.
3. Westbrook Pegler, "Cicotte Calls Life Sentence Too Rough," *Charleston* [West Virginia] *Gazette*, September 24, 1956.
4. Eliot Asinof, *Eight Men Out* (New York: Henry Holt, 1963), 21–22.
5. Cicotte's contract apparently was sold at an auction and is not accessible, but the Transaction Cards at the National Baseball Hall of Fame Library in Cooperstown, New York, have accurate league records for all the White Sox players for 1915 to 1921.
6. Bill James, *The Baseball Book 1991* (New York: Villard Books, 1991), 381.
7. Ibid.
8. Editors' Note: It is not clear as to where the author found this information. According to Peter Alter, the curator of the Chicago History Museum, "There is no testimony by Felsch in the Black Sox scandal papers [located at the Chicago History Museum].... It is possible that the Felsch testimony comes from the back pay [sic] case papers that are not at CHM, but held privately [by Thomas G. Cannon] in Milwaukee." E-mail message from Peter Alter to Floyd Sullivan, October 5, 2009.
9. Editors' Note: Again according Peter Alter, "The [Chicago History] Museum did buy Asinof's papers as they relate to *Eight Men Out*, but they are not yet available to researchers. Gene [Carney] did not look at them. I have read the notes of Asinof's interview with Felsch, and it contains no hush money reference. Those notes are less than one page type-written [sic].... [M]ight it be ... possible that the information regarding the Felsch interview was gathered the time Gene met with Mr. Asinof?" E-mail message from Peter Alter to Floyd Sullivan, October 5, 2009.
10. Harold Seymour and Dorothy Seymour Mills, *Baseball: The Golden Age* (New York: Oxford University Press, 1971), 333.
11. *Joe Jackson vs. Chicago White Sox*, Milwaukee, January-February 1924, transcript page 652, trial transcript and related documents courtesy of Thomas G. Cannon.
12. Editors' Note: This section contains a modified version of part of Gene Carney's article, "New Light on an Old Scandal," which was published in *The Baseball Research Journal* 35 (2007): 74–81, and appears here by permission of the Society for American Baseball Research. However, whenever possible, the quotations are taken from materials found in Black Sox Scandal Records, Box 1, Folder 2, Grand Jury, 1920, Chicago History Museum, Chicago. This information was provided by Floyd and Lucy Sullivan, and the editors are eternally grateful to them for their assistance.
13. In the wake of the Black Sox scandal a number of states, including Illinois, pressed for new legislation outlawing sports bribery; there was also a push for federal laws to curb gambling and the rewarding of "fixed" athletes.
14. Black Sox Scandal Records, Box 1, Folder 2, Grand Jury, 1920, "Synopsis of Testimony of Edward V. Cicotte, Given Before the Grand Jury of Cook County on September 28, 1920," Chicago History Museum, Chicago. Exactly what was promised Cicotte in return for his testimony remains another unsolved mystery.
15. Ibid., 1.
16. Ibid.
17. Ibid., 1–2.
18. Ibid., 2.
19. Ibid.
20. Ibid.
21. See the *Boston Globe*, July 27, 1921, and other papers for excerpts. Cicotte's grand jury testimony was in the news again in 1924, but it never saw the light of day in 1920.
22. Editors' Note: According to the author, the source for this information is *Joe Jack-*

5. The Mysterious Mr. Cicotte (Carney)

son vs. Chicago White Sox, January-February 1924, trial transcript and related documents, courtesy of Thomas G. Cannon. A published version can be found in Carney, 80.
  23. Carney, 80.
  24. Ibid.
  25. Ibid.
  26. Ibid.
  27. Ibid., 81.
  28. Ibid.
  29. Ibid.
  30. Ibid.
  31. James Doherty, "Judge M'Donald Recalls Events of Long Career," *Chicago Daily Tribune*, December 17, 1944.
  32. "Confessions Enter Trial of White Sox," *New York Times*, July 26, 1921.
  33. As Mike Shannon wrote on page 157 of his *Diamond Classics: Essays on 100 of the Best Baseball Books Ever Published* (Jefferson, NC: McFarland, 1989), "[Eliot Asinof's] reconstruction of the entire affair ... is so detailed and persuasive that *Eight Men Out: The Black Sox and the 1919 World Series* (New York: Holt, Rinehart and Winston, 1963) has become by far the most widely accepted version of the story." And that "it is also highly likely that *Eight Men Out* is as close to the truth as we will ever get...." But cf. Victor Luhrs, *The Great Baseball Mystery: The 1919 World Series* (South Brunswick, NJ: A.S. Barnes, 1966).
  34. Black Sox Scandal Records, Box 1, Folder 2, Grand Jury, 1920, Cicotte Deposition, Chicago History Museum, Chicago.
  35. See Bill Veeck with Ed Linn, *The Hustler's Handbook* (New York: G.P. Putnam's Sons, 1965), 296.
  36. Black Sox Scandal Records, Box 1, Folder 2, Grand Jury, 1920, Cicotte Deposition, 1–2, Chicago History Museum, Chicago.
  37. Black Sox Scandal Records, Box 1, Folder 8, Page of Notes, Chicago History Museum, Chicago.
  38. Black Sox Scandal Records, Box 1, Folder 2, Waivers of Immunity, September 29, 1920, Chicago History Museum, Chicago.
  39. Black Sox Scandal Records, Box 1, Folder 4, Trial Transcript, Testimony of Edward V. Cicotte, 26g, 28g, 46g–48g; Testimony of Joe Jackson, 4, 8, 28, 34, 37, 41, 43; and Testimony of Claude Williams, 63, 65, Chicago History Museum, Chicago.
  40. Despite what Cicotte said, Jackson was not placed at any meeting by his other teammates or by Bill Burns and Billy Maharg, two possible fixers who testified at the Black Sox trial.
  41. Black Sox Scandal Records, Box 1, Folder 1, Letter from J.R. Hunter to Charles Comiskey, January 29, 1924, Chicago History Museum, Chicago. However, see the fifth full paragraph on the second page of the letter.
  42. Black Sox Scandal Records, Box 1, Folder 11, Letter from Charles Comiskey to John Wray, February 26, 2009, Chicago History Museum, Chicago.
  43. Pegler.

6

The O'Connell-Dolan Affair: Scandal or Hoax?*

Daniel E. Ginsburg

Virtually every baseball game-fixing scandal is shrouded in mystery. Exactly what happened? Who were the forces behind the scenes? And what were the motivations—purely greed or something deeper?

Yet, if all these scandals are mysterious, none is harder to understand—or more strange—then the O'Connell-Dolan affair of 1924. Was it really an attempt to fix a pennant race, or a joke? Was Jimmy O'Connell, the prime figure, a villain or merely a pawn? Who knew about it? And who was involved?

Let us start by setting the scene. The 1924 season was one of those great years in which both leagues featured exciting multiteam pennant races. In the American League, the Yankees were attempting to win their fourth straight pennant, but were receiving stiff competition from the Washington Senators and the Detroit Tigers. In the National League, the New York Giants were also attempting a four-peat, trying to hold off the Pittsburgh Pirates and the Brooklyn Dodgers.

Going into the season's final series, Washington was taking control of the AL, and the Giants appeared about to do the same in the NL. New York enjoyed a one-and-a-half game lead over Brooklyn as the team prepared for its season-ending series at home against the seventh-place Philadelphia Phillies, while the Dodgers hosted the last-place Boston Braves. New York's magic number was down to two.

*Editors' Note: This chapter is a modified version of "The O'Connell-Dolan Affair," which was published in The Fix Is In: A History of Baseball Gambling and Game Fixing Scandals by Daniel E. Ginsburg (McFarland, 1995; paperback 2004). It appears here by permission of the publisher. © 1995 Daniel E. Ginsburg.

6. The O'Connell-Dolan Affair (Ginsburg)

James Joseph "Jimmy" O'Connell (1901–1976), a gifted, yet gullible, player (National Baseball Hall of Fame Library, Cooperstown, New York).

Mysteries from Baseball's Past

The Giants had a very strong ball club. Led by manager John McGraw, the team featured eight future Hall of Famers, most notably outfielder Ross Youngs, who hit .355 that year, second baseman Frank Frisch, who hit .328, and first baseman George Kelly, who hit .324, as well as McGraw himself. Also on the team was young outfielder Jimmy O'Connell, who hit .317 in his second season, and veteran coach Albert "Cozy" Dolan.

Born in Sacramento, California, in 1901, Jimmy O'Connell was considered a young player with outstanding potential. After he enjoyed a strong 1921 season with the San Francisco Seals of the Pacific Coast League, the Giants paid $75,000, a huge sum at the time, for his services, outbidding several other clubs.[1] McGraw left O'Connell with the Seals in 1922 to gain more experience and then brought him to the Giants.

In addition to his reputation as a gifted player (the immortal Ty Cobb stated that "O'Connell has perfect form and it cannot be improved upon"[2]), O'Connell had the reputation of being somewhat simple and gullible. For example, after his college manager told him "you don't show enough fight," O'Connell reportedly went out and offered to fight every member of the opposing team.[3]

On September 27, the Giants and Phillies prepared for the opening game of their series. During batting practice, O'Connell walked over to Philadelphia shortstop Heinie Sand, whom O'Connell knew well from their days together in the Coast League. According to O'Connell's later statements, the conversation went like this:

> "How do you feel about the game?" I asked him. "We don't feel," replied Heinie — "we're going to beat you." Then I said to him: "I'll give you $500 if you don't bear down too hard." He just answered "nothing doing." Then I walked back to the bench and told Dolan what Sand had said.[4]

The conversation left Sand in a quandary. His first inclination was to forget that it ever took place, but he remembered the expulsion from baseball of Joe Gedeon and Jean Dubuc for not revealing what they knew in the aftermath of the 1919 Black Sox scandal, so he reported what had happened to Art Fletcher, the Philadelphia manager. Fletcher congratulated Sand on his forthrightness, promising to get to the bottom of the incident.

As it turned out, the pennant race ended that day. The Giants defeated the Phillies by a score of 5–1, while Brooklyn lost to Boston. The Giants

6. *The O'Connell-Dolan Affair* (Ginsburg)

had won a record fourth straight pennant and prepared to face Washington in the World Series.

The O'Connell-Dolan scandal, however, was just beginning. Fletcher telephoned the National League president, John Heydler, the night of the game, saying, "I've got something important to tell you, but I do not wish to discuss it on the telephone. Where can I meet you?"⁵

The two met for breakfast in New York the next morning. Fletcher brought along Sand and had him repeat his story. Realizing that he was sitting on a powder keg, Heydler immediately telephoned Commissioner Kenesaw Mountain Landis at his office in Chicago. Judge Landis, as he was called because he had been a federal judge, was preparing to go to Washington for the opening of the World Series, but instead he immediately got on a train and headed for New York.

After meeting with Heydler, Landis summoned Sand. Upon hearing Sand's story, Landis began to probe for something deeper, questioning Sand to learn if other players had been approached, but Sand had no further knowledge. Landis then informed Giant owner Charles Stoneham and manager McGraw of the state of affairs, before summoning O'Connell.

The stenographer who Landis hired to record the proceedings was late, so no transcript exists of O'Connell's initial testimony. O'Connell, however, was more than willing to talk to the press after the hearing, so we have a pretty good idea of what took place. The accused outfielder readily admitted making the bribe offer to Sand. He claimed he was merely following orders. According to O'Connell:

> They picked me ... because they knew I had sort of a friendship with Sand" [*sic*]. It is true that I had known Sand since we were in the bushes together, but I never would have approached him with such a proposition had I not been told to do so.
>
> Cozy Dolan made the proposition to me. That was on Saturday morning before the game. He said the whole team would chip in to make up the $500. Frankie Frisch, Pep Young [*sic*], and George Kelly, all knew about it. When I told Pep what Dolan had said about the money, Young [*sic*] said: "Go for it." Then I told Frisch, and Frank told me to "give him (Sand) anything he wants."
>
> I asked Kelly what he thought of it, too, and he seemed to know what was coming off. He knew about it, for I could tell he had been let in on it by Dolan by the way he talked.⁶

James Alberts, better known as Cozy Dolan (1889–1958): Was he playing a practical joke on O'Connell or attempting to affect the outcome of a game? (National Baseball Hall of Fame Library, Cooperstown, New York).

O'Connell's revelations were startling. Dolan was a close associate of McGraw's, serving as the manager's eyes and ears with the players. Frisch, Youngs, and Kelly were three of the game's brightest stars.

Landis then summoned Cozy Dolan. Dolan, whose real name was

6. *The O'Connell-Dolan Affair* (Ginsburg)

James Alberts, had a long career as an infielder with a number of major and minor league teams before joining the Cubs as a coach in 1920 and moving to the Giants in 1921. He was considered an amusing character, always ready with a joke or a prank.

However, unfortunately for Landis, Dolan proved to be a very exasperating witness. The judge was a forthright man and liked people to come to the point. But Dolan was incredibly evasive, responding "I don't remember" to virtually all the judge's questions. When Landis pointed out that the incidents had happened only three days earlier and that surely Dolan must remember something that important, Dolan continued to respond with the same line.[7]

Frisch, Youngs, and Kelly took a much different tact. All three strongly denied any involvement in or knowledge of the plot. One interesting response came from Frisch, who stated, "On a pennant contender, you always hear a lot of stuff like that, a lot of kidding and some things. That is all I ever hear."[8]

Because O'Connell admitted making the bribe offer, he was placed on baseball's permanently ineligible list, ending his promising career. Dolan was also placed on the ineligible list, though in his case, it was for two other reasons: he had provided extremely evasive answers, and he had been implicated by O'Connell as the leader of the plot. However, since Frisch, Youngs, and Kelly strongly denied any involvement in or knowledge of what had occurred, it was O'Connell's word against theirs, and Landis cleared the three stars.

On October 1, Landis announced the expulsions of O'Connell and Dolan. He released the basic details of the scandal to the press, but not the transcripts of the testimony. According to Landis, the case was closed.

Closing the case, though, was not so easy. Coming on the eve of the World Series, the news created a sensation, and the press was in a frenzy. Who else was involved? Were Frisch, Youngs, and Kelly lying? Did the scandal go deeper in the Giants' organization? Was Stoneham involved? And what about McGraw?

American League president Ban Johnson, a longtime Landis foe, suggested that because of the bribe, Brooklyn should replace New York in the World Series, or the Series should be cancelled. Pittsburgh owner Barney Dreyfuss, whose team finished only three games behind the Giants, joined Johnson in calling for the cancellation of the Series. Dreyfuss pointed out that if the Sand offer was just the tip of the iceberg, it might well be that his club had been denied the pennant by this illicit activity.

Nevertheless, the World Series went on as planned and proved to be an exciting one. Washington beat New York in seven games, including a dramatic Game Seven.

But the press and public speculation on the scandal refused to subside. Rumors began to crop up. A letter published in a New York paper claimed that gamblers had wagered $100,000 on a New York pennant, and that they had passed on $5,000 to a Giant player who agreed to use the money to bribe opponents. In another published story, Pirate pitcher Emil Yde allegedly reported that players other than Sand had been approached in an effort to fix games. Yde later denied the story, saying he was misquoted.[9]

Pat Ragan, a coach with the Phillies, claimed the whole incident was a joke. Ragan stated:

> O'Connell is just a kid and was a sort of butt for all the jokes of the Giants and they shot plenty at him. He took everything seriously. Sand of the Phillies is much the same kind of a fellow. He has no sense of humor.
>
> The Giants were joking in their club house before that game of Sept. 27 and some one suggested that it would be awful to get eliminated from the series by a team so lowly as the Phils. "Why not buy 'em off?" some one chirped up. "It wouldn't cost much. They hadn't ought to be as expensive as the White Sox were in 1919. Why you ought to be able to buy the whole team for $500."
>
> "Cozy" Dolan thought it was a good joke. So did the rest — all except O'Connell, who took the whole thing seriously. Then Dolan suggested that O'Connell approach Sand because he had played in the Pacific Coast League.
>
> The incident was closed as far as Frisch, Kelly[,] and others were concerned. They had forgotten it. Little did they suspect that O'Connell would go to Sand, but he did.
>
> The next thing they knew, O'Connell and Dolan were summoned, and then everybody got frightened, fearful the practical joke would be misunderstood.[10]

However, everyone involved denied Ragan's claim that the matter was a joke. In the meantime, O'Connell continued to insist that he was merely acting on orders from his teammates. "They're making a goat out of me. I've been a damn fool," he said.[11]

Meanwhile, Dolan's memory suddenly improved, and he loudly proclaimed his innocence. Dolan explained, "When I replied to the Judge's

6. The O'Connell-Dolan Affair (Ginsburg)

Don Carlos "Pat" Ragan, who believed that the "bribery" incident was much ado about nothing (National Baseball Hall of Fame Library, Cooperstown, New York).

questions, and said: 'I don't remember,' I really meant to say, 'No,' ... I always use that expression."[12] Dolan then went on the offensive, hiring famous criminal lawyer William J. Fallon to represent him in a $100,000 lawsuit for libel against Landis, Heydler, and Johnson. Fallon is best known as gambler Arnold Rothstein's personal attorney.

The announcement of the lawsuit brought forth fresh speculation. Who was paying Dolan's legal bills? It was later revealed that McGraw had introduced Fallon to Dolan, and apparently the Giants were footing Fallon's bills. McGraw attempted to justify this by explaining that Dolan was a longtime loyal employee, but Landis was outraged, and the Giants withdrew their support. The lawsuit soon died away, though there was an investigation launched by Assistant United States Attorney George Brothers.

During the months following the World Series, the press clamored for full disclosure, demanding that Landis release the transcripts of the hearing on the scandal. Landis refused at first, but finally relented, and in January 1925, the transcripts were released, minus the testimony of O'Connell due to the lack of a stenographer as stated earlier.[13] Also, the U.S. Attorney's investigation was soon dropped. While some in the press continued to claim that there was a cover-up, the release of the transcripts and the dropping of the investigation served to diffuse the scandal, and the publicity soon died away.

So what is the true story behind the O'Connell-Dolan scandal? Unfortunately, we will probably never know.

One of the difficulties with this case is the lack of a reason for a fix of any kind. Why make the bribe when the Giants were virtually assured of the pennant?

John "Heinie" Sand: Why did O'Connell approach him? (National Baseball Hall of Fame Library, Cooperstown, New York).

6. The O'Connell-Dolan Affair (Ginsburg)

And why pick out only Sand, the shortstop? While the shortstop is certainly an important player, Sand was hardly a star, and it is doubtful that he could have fixed the game on his own even if he had been so inclined.

Frank Lane, the editor of *Baseball Magazine*, called the whole incident "a piece of sheer imbecility."[14] John McGraw stated, "I cannot understand why these two men did what they did ... when the chances were 100 to 1 that New York would win the pennant. The only explanation I can give is they are a couple of saps. If you search the country over[,] you probably couldn't find two bigger ones."[15]

Perhaps the best analysis of the whole affair was provided by Lane in *Baseball Magazine* shortly after the events occurred. Lane examined four theories: (1) the whole thing was an aborted joke as Ragan claimed, but once it went to Landis, everyone was afraid to admit the truth; (2) Cozy Dolan was in league with gamblers and coerced O'Connell to do his dirty work; (3) O'Connell's story was essentially correct, and many Giant players, as well as possibly the management, were involved; or (4) the whole plot was Dolan's idea, and he alone was responsible for recruiting O'Connell to attempt the fix.[16]

Of these four theories, the first and third seem most likely. Let us examine each possibility.

Given O'Connell's personality and the atmosphere of major league clubhouses during that era, Ragan's joke claim seems to make sense. We know that O'Connell was naïve, that Dolan was known for comedy and practical jokes, and that players in those days liked to tease more gullible types. It is true that everyone denied that there was a joke, but given that the Black Sox scandal and Landis' record of taking strong action against anyone involved in game fixing was fresh in the players' minds, the denials are logical. Even Dolan's evasion — not wanting to tell an outright lie by denying the charge but also being afraid to admit it was a joke — fits this theory.

And if there really was a conspiracy, O'Connell's story is the most logical — the star players and perhaps management (McGraw) were involved. It may have been a spur of the moment idea, with everyone pitching in to fund the bribe. However, this seems a bit less likely given the poorly conceived nature of the plan.

It is hard to believe this enterprise was a well-organized plot by a gambling syndicate. Gamblers generally approached players directly about

117

fixes. Going through someone like Dolan and having a bribe attempted in such an amateurish fashion seems highly unlikely, as does the concept that Dolan and O'Connell conceived and funded the plan. While $500 was not a fortune even then, it was a significant amount, especially given that these were not highly paid stars.

So it seems most likely that the whole incident began as a joke. But if it was a joke, it ended sadly for O'Connell and Dolan. Both were permanently banned and remain on the ineligible list to this day. O'Connell continued to play for a while, appearing in the outlaw Copper Frontier League for a team in Bayard, New Mexico. This league featured a number of disgraced players, including Hal Chase, Chick Gandil, Swede Risberg, Lefty Williams, and Tom Seaton, all of whom were involved in baseball gambling scandals. O'Connell eventually fell on hard times and worked as a longshoreman in California before finding a job at Richland Oil Company in Bakersfield, where he died in 1976.

Dolan surfaced from time to time after the scandal. He was McGraw's partner in real estate speculation in Florida in the 1920s and later turned up in Cincinnati as a second-line comedian. He then moved to Chicago, opening a Prohibition Era nightclub, and eventually died in the Windy City in 1958.

The other key principle in the case, Heinie Sand, was ridiculed by many fans as a "squealer."[17] He remained with the Phillies through 1928 and died in San Francisco in 1958, just a month before Cozy Dolan.

The three Giant players accused by O'Connell continued their march to the Hall of Fame. Youngs' career and life were cut short by Bright's disease, which brought about his death in 1927 at the age of 30, but both Frisch and Kelly enjoyed outstanding careers and long lives.

Thus, we are left to reflect on the O'Connell-Dolan scandal. Perhaps it was a malignant plot to fix the pennant race. Perhaps it was a failed practical joke. Whatever the case, it was certainly a tragedy for Jimmy O'Connell and Cozy Dolan.

NOTES

1. Gene Karst and Martin Jones Jr., *Who's Who in Professional Baseball* (New Rochelle, NY: Arlington House, 1973), 713.

2. Abe Kemp, "Tricks of a Boy That Prove Jimmy O'Connell Has the Pep," *The Sporting News*, January 12, 1922, 3.

6. The O'Connell-Dolan Affair (Ginsburg)

3. Ibid.
4. "Bribery Scandal Involving New York Giants Proves Cheaters Cannot Escape Detection," *The Sporting News*, October 9, 1924, 2.
5. J.G. Taylor Spink, *Judge Landis and Twenty-Five Years of Baseball* (New York: Thomas Y. Crowell, 1947), 130.
6. "Bribery Scandal Involving New York Giants Proves Cheaters Cannot Escape Detection," 2.
7. "Verbatim Testimony in Dolan and O'Connell Bribe Hearing," *New York World*, January 11, 1925.
8. Ibid.
9. "Emil Yde Denies Scandal Interview," *New York World*, October 18, 1924.
10. "Baseball Scandal Result of Big Practical Joke," *New York World*, October 9, 1924.
11. "Bribery Scandal Involving New York Giants Proves Cheaters Cannot Escape Detection," 2.
12. Spink, 138–139.
13. "Commissioner Has No Record of Confession by O'Connell," *The Sporting News*, January 29, 1925, 1.
14. F.C. Lane, "A Review of the Recent Scandal," *Baseball Magazine* 34, no. 1 (December 1924): 300.
15. "Bribery Scandal Involving New York Giants Proves Cheaters Cannot Escape Detection," 2.
16. Lane, 300.
17. Lowell Blaisdell, "Mystery and Tragedy: The O'Connell-Dolan Scandal," *Baseball Research Journal* 11 (1982), found at http://www.brj.sabrwebs.com.

7

Unraveling the Cobb-Speaker Scandal*

Timothy M. Gay

Judge Kenesaw Mountain Landis looked like something out of the Old Testament—or at least the Old Testament as produced and directed by Cecil B. DeMille. With his silver mane and stern visage, the pictures of Commissioner Landis throwing out a first ball—his body painfully erect, his right arm cocked at a fierce angle—made him appear like Moses about to smite one of the Philistines.[1]

It was this biblical image that got Landis the job in the first place. The club owners picked him to be the first commissioner of Organized Baseball not because they wanted him to exercise power, but because they wanted him to *look like* he was exercising power.

In 1920, Landis was installed in the commissionership because he had a reputation—much of it undeserved—as a tough and uncompromising judge. Five years earlier, he had issued a surprisingly strong ruling that spanked the upstart Federal League in its suit against the National and American leagues. And the owners never forgot the judge whose selective interpretation of antitrust law had gilded their pocketbooks.

If Byron Bancroft Johnson, the majordomo of the American League, resembled a biblical character, it was probably Nebuchadnezzar, the Babylonian strongman who built a great empire but was eventually punished for his pride. Before proclaiming his upstart circuit to be a major league

---

*Editors' Note: This chapter is a modified version of "Scandal," which was published in Tris Speaker: The Rough-and-Tumble Life of a Baseball Legend *by Timothy M. Gay. It appears here by permission of the University of Nebraska Press.* © *2005 by the Board of Regents of the University of Nebraska.*

7. Unraveling the Cobb-Speaker Scandal (Gay)

Judge Landis, about to smite the Philistines (National Baseball Hall of Fame Library, Cooperstown, New York).

in 1901, Johnson had inveighed against the evils of "syndicate baseball" as a columnist for the *Cincinnati Commercial Gazette*. Once he got his American League rolling, however, he made the monopolists of the National League look two-bit. Johnson became a one-man syndicate, ruling the AL with an iron fist.

Landis and Johnson, not surprisingly, never got along. Johnson hated sharing power, so whenever possible, he went out of his way to undercut the judge.

Ironically, it was the enmity between the commissioner and the American League president — not the merits of the case — that ultimately allowed two of baseball's biggest names, Ty Cobb and Tris Speaker, to escape punishment in a cheating affair almost as scandalous as the Black Sox fix of the 1919 World Series. Had Johnson and Landis cooperated in the investigation of Cobb and Speaker — instead of using the controversy as an excuse to skewer each other — the Georgia Peach and the Gray Eagle might have joined their pal Shoeless Joe Jackson in baseball's Hall of Shame.

Byron Bancroft "Ban" Johnson, the founder and president of the American League and the sworn enemy of Judge Landis (National Baseball Hall of Fame Library, Cooperstown, New York).

* * * *

We will never know precisely what transpired in the Cobb-Speaker debacle anymore than we know exactly what happened in the Black Sox affair or the Teapot Dome scandal. Any examination of the Cobb-Speaker case, though, yields one inescapable conclusion: Baseball was almost as dysfunctional and ethically challenged in the 1920s as it was before the Black Sox scandal.

Here are the few known facts about the Cobb-Speaker affair:

- In the spring of 1926, Dutch Leonard, a former pitcher for the Boston Red Sox and Detroit Tigers, produced letters sent to him

7. Unraveling the Cobb-Speaker Scandal (Gay)

from one-time teammates Joe Wood and Ty Cobb. Written seven years earlier, the letters implicated all three men and, by inference, Tris Speaker in a betting scheme that had taken place during the last weekend of the 1919 regular season.

- Leonard's allegations were first brought to the attention of Ban Johnson and other AL team executives during the early weeks of the 1926 season. The Detroit left-hander apparently made it clear that he felt betrayed by both Cobb and Speaker. Leonard later told Damon Runyon that in 1925, Cobb, the Tigers' player-manager, had used him so much that his arm was almost wrecked.
- Cobb had placed Leonard on waivers in early 1926 despite the pitcher's 11–4 mark for the Tigers the year before. Though he had begged player-manager Speaker of the Cleveland Indians for a job, Leonard was not picked up for a nominal waiver fee by his former teammate. He was then forced to sign on with a Pacific Coast League team for less money.

Those parts of the story are not in dispute — but virtually everything else about the controversy is. Leonard maintained that on the afternoon of September 24, 1919, the Tigers' Leonard and Cobb and the Indians' Wood and Speaker all met underneath the stands at Navin Field in Detroit. As related in Robert Smith's *Baseball in the Afternoon*, "According to Leonard, he and Cobb had expressed their strong desire for the Detroit club to finish third — there being no fourth-place money at that time. And a victory over Cleveland — which had already clinched second place [behind the White Sox] — would insure their finishing in the money. Tris Speaker, according to Leonard, then assured Cobb he 'needn't worry about [the next] game' because 'you'll win tomorrow.'"[2]

Leonard went further to say that since all four players knew how the next day's game would turn out, they decided to put down some action. Cobb dispatched a clubhouse attendant named Fred West to find a bookie. Leonard originally claimed that he had placed a $1500 wager, with his three co-conspirators in for a grand each, though at other times he said that Cobb had plunked down two grand.

And sure enough, the Tigers won the following day's game, 9–5. Detroit took a commanding lead early in the contest and cruised to victory.

Mysteries from Baseball's Past

In addition, Leonard claimed that after the fix had occurred, he had received letters in the fall of 1919 from first Wood, then Cobb, both lamenting that their arrangement had not yielded the dough that they had hoped. Wood's letter, as reprinted in the December 22, 1926, issue of the *New York Times*, said:

> Dear Friend Dutch:
> Enclosed please find certified check for sixteen hundred and thirty dollars ($1,630.00).
> The only bet West could get down was $600 against $420 (10 to 7). Cobb did not get up a cent. He told us that and I believed him. Could have put up some at 5 to 2 on Detroit, but did not, as that would make us put up $1,000 to win $400.
> We won the $420. I gave West $30, leaving $390, or $130 for each of us. Would not have cashed your check at all, but West thought he could get it up at 10 to 7, and I was going to put it all up at those odds. We would have won $1,750 for the $2,500 if we could have placed it.
> If we ever have another chance like this[,] we will know enough to try to get down early.
> Let me hear from you, Dutch.
> With all good wishes to Mrs. Leonard and yourself, I am,
> JOE WOOD[3]

Cobb's letter to Leonard pursued an oddly plaintive track. Its relevant paragraphs are:

> Wood and myself were considerably disappointed in our business proposition, as we had $2,000 to put into it and the other side quoted us $1,400, and when we finally secured that much money[,] it was about 2 o'clock and they refused to deal with us, as they had men in Chicago to take up the matter with and they had no time, so we completely fell down and of course we felt badly over it.
> Everything was open to Wood and he can tell you about it when we get together. It was quite a responsibility and I don't care for it again, I can assure you.[4]

It is noteworthy that both Wood and Cobb felt compelled to pursue aspects of a cover-up in their letters. Wood throws in the gratuitous phrase "and I believed him," referring to Cobb's claim that he could not get the money down. Meanwhile, Cobb, in a defensive posture, makes sure that Leonard knows that Wood was privy to all the machinations between the parties.

Was part of Leonard's pique that he had been cut out of a bonanza

7. Unraveling the Cobb-Speaker Scandal (Gay)

that Wood, Cobb, and Speaker had enjoyed all those years before? Perhaps Leonard felt that the very men who turned their backs on him in his hour of need had also denied him a big wad of bills.

The evidence against Wood, Cobb, and Speaker was strong but not necessarily damning. Neither letter specifically mentioned rigging a baseball game. Taken together, though, they certainly raised a stink. By the end of 1926, Wood had been the baseball coach at Yale University for four years. However, Cobb and Speaker were living legends, still heavily engaged in the majors.

* * * *

Ban Johnson was contacted by Leonard in the early spring of 1926, but refused to sit down with him. The AL czar first got wind of Leonard's charges from several club officials who had seen the letters. Even before he met with Leonard, Johnson rushed off to Cleveland to give Speaker a heads-up. How Speaker may have reacted to Johnson's startling news is not known. The Gray Eagle avoided the subject like the plague in the years to come.

Johnson then took a train to Detroit to meet with his loyal lieutenant, Tiger owner Frank Navin. Navin told Johnson that Leonard had already been to see him, threatening to sell the letters to a Detroit newspaper. Only then did Johnson design to meet with Cobb and Speaker's accuser to review the evidence. After consulting with American League counsel Henry Killilea, Johnson decided to buy Leonard off. This, in turn, led to Leonard surrendering the letters to Johnson for $20,000, the amount he claimed the Tigers owed him.[5]

At some point that season, Johnson hired investigators to spy on the two stars' gambling habits. The private eyes reported that Cobb's gambling was innocuous, but that Speaker liked to bet on practically everything. Speaker routinely lost a bundle at the track,[6] they told Johnson. And it was not the first time that the AL leader had sicced a gumshoe on Cleveland's player-manager, as will be seen later.[7]

By early summer 1926, at least a dozen baseball men knew of the charges against Cobb and Speaker; amazingly, however, the story never broke. Johnson kept mum until September 9, when he convened a closed-door meeting of the AL ownership. After Johnson briefed them on Leonard's allegations, the owners voted to turn the evidence over to Landis,

125

which Johnson was apparently loath to do. So, without a word leaking to the press, Johnson quietly met in mid–October with Cobb and Speaker.

It is not known what kind of deliberation may have taken place or whether Johnson put other options on the table. Neither player at that point was in the company of a lawyer. A not unreasonable conclusion is that Johnson reached a *quid pro quo* with the two legends: resign and retire from the game, and baseball will keep the real reason under wraps. Johnson later said that his motivation was to spare the players and their families humiliating publicity. And based on the timing of their respective retirement announcements, the two principals must have agreed to put some daylight between their departures in a futile effort to mislead the press.

On November 3, 1926, the sporting world awoke to the startling news that Ty Cobb was retiring, and things turned ugly in a hurry. In handing Cobb his irrevocable release, owner Navin cited Cobb's role in the "demoralization" of the Tigers.[8] Cobb returned the fire, blaming Navin's meddling for the team's recent woes. Later, Johnson would tell newsmen that the Tigers dismissed Cobb out of fear that Leonard could sue the club — and win.

However, there were no public recriminations when equally shocking news came out of Cleveland only 26 days later. The "venerable Speaker," as he was called in the next day's *Washington Post*, announced that he was leaving the Indians to pursue opportunities in the business world.[9]

When asked if he would be joining one of the syndicates seeking to acquire the Indians, Speaker replied, "No. I am taking a vacation from baseball that I expect will last the remainder of my life."[10]

Speaker retiring as a player would not have been all that surprising — he was, after all, 38 and had lost a step or two. But resigning as manager? The skipper who had recently guided Cleveland to a remarkable second-place finish just three games behind the mighty Yankees? Abandoning his life's passion to go work for something called the Geometric Stamping Co.? It did not add up, especially coming on the heels of Cobb's departure, and left the baseball world stunned. As the Seymours wrote in their book, *Baseball: The Golden Age*, "[A]ll of a sudden, within the space of a month, the two renowned stars had quit. What lay back of it? Rumors spread, and sportswriters pestered baseball officials for more information."[11]

7. Unraveling the Cobb-Speaker Scandal (Gay)

* * * *

Something closer to the truth finally surfaced several days before Christmas. Despite the owners' clear directive in early September, it had taken Johnson weeks to hand over Leonard's evidence to the commissioner, who, as might be expected, was incensed that Johnson had kept him in the dark and cut his office out of the decision making.

Once he examined Leonard's letters, Landis vowed to get to the bottom of the mess. After sitting down with Cobb, Speaker, Wood, and West, and listening to Cobb and Speaker's argument that all the information involving the case be given to the press, the commissioner went public on December 21, breaking the gentlemen's agreement that Johnson had reached with Cobb and Speaker. Johnson was infuriated.

The story was hyped on front pages across the country. "Baseball Scandal Up Again, with Cobb and Speaker Named" was how the *New York Times* played it on page one.[12]

In releasing the text of Leonard's letters to the *Times*, Landis informed the press that the reason the truth had been withheld until this point was because "none of the men involved is now associated with baseball,"[13] which, though technically correct, did little to stop one writer for the *Times* from responding, "Baseball is again on trial if for no other reason than the peculiar concealment of the Leonard charges for seven years."[14] Little did the writer know how prophetic his words would be.

* * * *

Baseball was indeed on trial, but Landis and Johnson were suppressing as much of the truth as they could. Then, a separate scandal erupted just as Landis had begun zeroing in on Cobb and Speaker. It involved baseball's most disreputable characters: two members of the old Black Sox. Swede Risberg, the embittered former White Sox shortstop, publicly charged in December of 1926 that late in the 1917 regular season, the White Sox had persuaded the Tigers to dump a slate of games so that Chicago could beat out Boston for the pennant. The grateful White Sox, Risberg claimed, then took up a collection of $45 per man and paid Detroit's pitchers a bonus for their troubles.

Why had Risberg suddenly come forward after nearly a decade? "They pushed Ty Cobb and Tris Speaker out on a piker bet. I think it's only fair that the 'white lilies' get the same treatment,"[15] Risberg told the press.

Moreover, his old Black Sox crony, Chick Gandil, embraced Risberg's claims and hinted that he could spill the beans on even more dirt.

On January 1, 1927, just 10 days after Landis had exposed Leonard's allegations against Cobb and Speaker, the commissioner sat down with Risberg in Chicago and questioned him for two hours. Landis never let on, but he was familiar with the substance of the Risberg-Gandil charges. Some four years before, another august member of the Black Sox, outfielder Oscar "Happy" Felsch, had made similar claims in his lawsuit against club owner Charles Comiskey. And even before Felsch's legal action, Landis had discussed the Detroit-Chicago "arrangement" with White Sox catcher Ray Schalk.

Landis decided to hold hearings in Chicago on January 5 and 6 to give former members of the Tigers and White Sox a forum to share what they knew. However, that provided Tiger owner Navin and White Sox owner Comiskey with nearly a week to concoct a strategy. Yes, the White Sox had given Tiger players some money collected from a pool back then, but it had not been a "bribe" to lose to Chicago, Navin and Comiskey argued. It had been a "reward" for Detroit beating the Red Sox three straight. Even White Sox second baseman Eddie Collins, formerly believed incorruptible, admitted to having provided some money toward the Tiger kitty.

Landis listened to the recollections of some 40 players on events that occurred nearly a decade before. Gandil backed up most of Risberg's story but was curiously reticent in certain areas. Ty Cobb also testified on the first day, flatly stating that "[t]here has never been any ball game that I ever played in that I know of that was ever fixed."[16]

Most of the other witnesses stuck to the Navin-Comiskey modus operandi and pooh-poohed Risberg's and Gandil's testimony, claiming that the White Sox pool was just a harmless little "thank-you fund" to the Tiger pitchers and catcher Oscar Stanage.

Ten days after the hearings ended, Landis released his findings. The commissioner accepted the notion that the pool was a "gift fund," calling it "reprehensible and censurable," but not criminal. Risberg went back home to Minnesota, an even more embittered man. Oddly though, Risberg's buddy Gandil never did trumpet the charges that supposedly would blow the lid off of baseball.

7. Unraveling the Cobb-Speaker Scandal (Gay)

* * * *

After the delightful divertissement, the commissioner had to refocus his energies on his still-incomplete investigation of Cobb and Speaker. "Won't these God damn things that happened before I came into baseball ever stop coming up?"[17] Landis supposedly barked in frustration that winter.

A month earlier, the commissioner had vowed to dig up the truth when he aired Leonard's charges against Cobb and Speaker. But now Landis turned skittish — and it is not hard to understand why. Given the circus-like atmosphere of the Risberg hearings, the last thing baseball could afford at the moment was prolonged public scrutiny of two icons. Uncovering and punishing "guilt" was no longer the judge's goal.

It probably dawned on the commissioner that airing more of the game's dirty laundry might not be in the enlightened self-interest of one Kenesaw Mountain Landis. The judge had just had his contract extended for another seven-year term, his salary rising some 30 percent to $65,000 — handsome pay in the 1920s.

There were four other factors working against a genuine probe of the Cobb-Speaker mess. First, Leonard refused to show up at a hearing to confront his alleged co-conspirators in person. Leonard, with good reason, feared for his life. The pathologically violent Cobb was eminently capable of harming him. Just after the commissioner heard about the allegations, Landis did go out to California to meet in private with Leonard. But having pocketed $20,000 in blood money from Ban Johnson, Leonard would not leave his Fresno farm to make his charges stick.

Second, Cobb and Speaker had wised up and hired capable counsel. William H. Boyd, a Cleveland-based attorney recommended by pals in the corporate community, represented Speaker. Cobb's legal team consisted of the formidable pair of Edward S. Burke, who had helped Cobb and the Tigers out of legal jams in the past, and James O. Murfin, one of Michigan's most respected trial lawyers. The attorneys demanded that Landis rescind the Johnson "order" that had pushed Cobb and Speaker into retirement.

If Smoky Joe Wood's recollections to Lawrence Ritter are accurate, the two stars and their attorneys played hardball with the commissioner. "See, they got together with an attorney in Detroit, my friend Spoke, and they got a bunch of stuff together and typewritten and deposited it in a bank vault in Cleveland, and if they would have chased Cobb and Speaker out of baseball, it would have all come out."[18]

Mysteries from Baseball's Past

Wood later regretted having been so candid with Ritter and asked him to destroy the tape and transcript of the interview. Because of this, Ritter kept Wood's incriminating comments out of *The Glory of Their Times*, but he never excised the transcript. So, along with Ritter's subsequent interview of Wood two years later, the 1963 transcript is on file in the Ritter archives at the University of Notre Dame.

Third, Cobb, no fool, spent that January playing political cards, enlisting the help of Georgia's two United States Senators. By mid–January, the two accused superstars had received expressions of support from fans across the country. Landis was caught between a rock and a hard place. He knew that if he pressed the charges, Cobb and Speaker would not have hesitated to tear the game apart.

And finally, and perhaps most importantly, it occurred to the commissioner that he could use the imbroglio to bludgeon Ban Johnson, his archrival. How? By discrediting Johnson's original handling of the situation and blowing apart the clandestine deal that the AL president had reached with the two stars. Any thought that Landis had of going easy on Johnson ended with two events later that same month.

On January 17, Johnson angered Landis by holding a press conference in which he blistered the commissioner's decision to go public with Leonard's charges. "The only thing I could see behind [Landis' action] was a desire for personal publicity," Johnson charged.[19] Johnson also confided to newsmen that he loved Cobb and did not think the Georgian was corrupt. "We let him go," Johnson volunteered, "because he had written a peculiar letter about a betting deal that he couldn't explain and because I felt that he violated a position of trust."[20]

Speaker, on the other hand, was "a different type of fellow," Johnson said. "For want of a better word I'd call Tris cute. He knows why he was forced out of the managership of the Cleveland club. If he wants me to tell him[,] I'll meet him in a court of law and tell the facts under oath."[21]

As early as 1925, the league had hired "professional men" to trail Speaker and certain members of the Indians. Johnson claimed to know all the particulars: who had action on the ponies, who bet on baseball, and which bookies they used. However, Johnson's barrage against Speaker failed to mention that there was nothing illegal about a ballplayer going to the racetrack. Nor, believe it or not, was there a rule on baseball's books back

7. Unraveling the Cobb-Speaker Scandal (Gay)

then — nearly a decade after the Black Sox scandal — that expressly forbade gambling on games.

A week later, Landis got his revenge. At an emergency closed-door meeting with AL owners on January 24, Landis demanded to know who was leaking information to the press that suggested there was other incriminating evidence about Cobb and Speaker. Stories in various newspapers that week had suggested that the AL owners had, in effect, blacklisted the pair. Landis knew going into the meeting that Johnson had planted the stories and wanted to embarrass him in front of his peers.

When Johnson sheepishly conceded that Landis had in his possession all the evidence against Cobb and Speaker, the owners, fed up with Johnson's erratic behavior, unanimously imposed a leave of absence.

On January 27, Landis distributed to newsmen copies of a statement that quashed Johnson's deal and "exonerated" the two stars. "These players have not been, nor are they now, found guilty of fixing a ball game. By no decent system of justice could such a finding be made."[22]

Landis' words clearly bore the imprint of the two stars' lawyers. Indeed, Cobb's *My Life in Baseball* claims the language in the commissioner's finding was dictated by Cobb and Speaker's legal team.

The statement went on to restore Cobb and Speaker to the active roster of their former teams. However, Landis' move had been carefully choreographed with all parties.

That same day, telegrams were sent to Cobb and Speaker from the owners of their former clubs, granting them their unconditional releases and freeing them to sign with other American League clubs. The teams to which Cobb and Speaker had devoted 33 years of their lives, winning a combined four pennants and 13 batting championships, wanted nothing to do with their tainted player-managers. It probably was not a moral decision. Navin and Edith Dunn, the owner of the Cleveland Indians, no doubt had grown weary of their superstars' egos and big salaries.

Left unwritten and unspoken was Landis' prohibition against Cobb and Speaker ever serving as managers or coaches. The commissioner was sufficiently concerned about the ethical bearings of the two stars that he did not want either one of them calling shots in a dugout. In Landis' considered judgment, dugout responsibilities would have made them too tempting a target for gamblers. So the word quietly went out to owners in both leagues. And Landis' ban stuck. Neither man ever managed again.

Mysteries from Baseball's Past

The lions in winter: Tyrus Raymond "Ty" Cobb (1886–1961) and Tristram E. "Tris" Speaker (1888–1958). The two superstars finished their major league careers with Connie Mack's Philadelphia Athletics (National Baseball Hall of Fame Library, Cooperstown, New York).

In 1928 when Speaker retired for good, the Pirates queried the commissioner's office about the prospect of bringing Speaker to Pittsburgh as a full-time coach. The Bucs were given an emphatic "no." Other clubs interested in hiring Speaker as manager in the '30s were given the same brushback. It would be 20 years before the Indians were permitted to bring Speaker back as a part-time spring training coach and advisor. But even then, in the late '40s and '50s, he never served as a full-time uniformed coach in the dugout.

Landis managed to get in one last dig against Ban Johnson before the Cobb-Speaker affair ended by insisting that both Cobb and Speaker stay in the American League. In doing so, he ensured that Johnson's original decree would be completely eviscerated.

The Cobb-Speaker debacle did produce one constructive result: Landis demanded that major league baseball adopt a rule prohibiting players from betting in any form on baseball games.

7. Unraveling the Cobb-Speaker Scandal (Gay)

But Landis came out of the affair only slightly less tarnished than Johnson. An essay on the judge's role in the scandal written by Deadball Era scholar Greg Beston is accurately entitled "Forced to Back Down." According to Beston, when Landis first got wind of the Leonard charges, he tried to reprise his avenging angel role in the Black Sox scandal, attempting to "steal the spotlight" from Johnson. However, as Beston shows, "In the end though, the judge had no other choice but to back down, thus destroying the myth that the commissioner of baseball had supreme power over the [n]ational [p]astime."[23] Robert Smith believed that Cobb and Speaker benefited from Landis' "unwillingness to dig much more deeply than a finger's length into any major baseball scandal."[24]

Years later, Fred Lieb wrote that he "understood and accepted" the judge's decision.[25] "I felt, as I think Landis did, that to expel these superstars of baseball on less than conclusive evidence might have given professional baseball a blow from which it could not recover."[26] Modern scholar Glenn Stout recently compared Landis' ambivalence to a seamstress pulling a single thread, then discovering to her horror that she is soon tearing the fabric of the whole garment. Landis did not want to rip up baseball any more than he already had. So he stopped tugging at the Cobb-Speaker thread and put his needle away.

* * * *

All these years later, the questions about the Cobb-Speaker-Wood-Leonard ruckus remain vexing. If they were innocent, why did Cobb and Speaker go along with Johnson's original ultimatum that they quit the game? Why not hire lawyers from the get-go and fight it? Why not at least publicly proclaim their outrage and their determination to clear their good names and not wait for the inevitable revelations to leak out to the press? And why were their actions in 1919 so brazen? Was cheating so routine back then that ballplayers could machinate under the stands and then exchange incriminating letters without giving it a second thought?

Ultimately, Landis did not want the truth about the scandal to come out any more than Johnson did. Instead of mounting a concerted effort to cleanse the game of cheating, Landis and Johnson conducted a charade. They cynically used the "investigations" to settle old scores and bully one another. What Cobb, Speaker, Wood, and Leonard did that late September afternoon in 1919 was tawdry. What Landis and Johnson and practically

Mysteries from Baseball's Past

every owner in the game did throughout the 1910s and 1920s was far tawdrier.

With very little thanks to the game's leadership, the role of gambling in baseball began to abate at least somewhat as the 1930s approached. But as the execrable behavior of Pete Rose demonstrates, it has never been completely wrung out of the dugout.

* * * *

The truth is that had the Cobb-Speaker-Wood-Leonard story broken when it occurred — in the fall of 1919 — it would have dwarfed what happened in the World Series a few weeks later. The Georgia Peach and the Gray Eagle were much bigger names than Swede and Chick. And because of their perceived roles as pillars of the game, they were bigger names than Shoeless Joe. When the whole ugly episode finally blew over in 1927, Leonard was interviewed by Damon Runyon at the ballplayer's home in California. He told the writer, "I have had my revenge."[27]

Leonard took the $20,000 he had gotten from Johnson and Navin and started a vineyard in Fresno. Over time, he became a fairly prosperous vintner. It is probably safe to conclude that Cobb and Speaker were not on his Christmas list.

The writer for the *New York Times* was right: Baseball was indeed on trial in the 1920s. Had a real verdict ever

Hubert "Dutch" Leonard: Troublemaker or man of integrity? (National Baseball Hall of Fame Library, Cooperstown, New York).

7. Unraveling the Cobb-Speaker Scandal (Gay)

been rendered, the game would never have been declared innocent. Baseball's Moses — like his biblical counterpart — did not smite the Philistines.

NOTES

1. Editors' Note: Although there is no evidence that Moses ever smote a Philistine, the appearance of Kenesaw Mountain Landis, photographed throwing out the first ball at a game, conjures the image of Moses doing so.
2. Robert Smith, *Baseball in the Afternoon: Tales from a Bygone Era* (New York: Simon & Schuster, 1993), 233.
3. "Baseball Scandal Up Again, with Cobb and Speaker Named," *New York Times*, December 22, 1926.
4. Ibid.
5. Charles C. Alexander, *Ty Cobb* (New York: Oxford University Press, 1984), 187.
6. Ibid., 190, and Charles C. Alexander, "Triple Play: Cleveland's Hall of Fame Triumvirate," *Timeline* 9, no. 2 (April-May 1992): 16.
7. "Johnson Accepts Landis Challenge," *New York Times*, January 18, 1927.
8. Alexander, *Ty Cobb*, 190.
9. "Tris Speaker Resigns as Cleveland Club Manager," *Washington Post*, November 30, 1926.
10. "Tris Quits, M'Callister in Line," *Cleveland Plain Dealer*, November 30, 1926.
11. Harold Seymour and Dorothy Seymour Mills, *Baseball: The Golden Age* (New York: Oxford University Press, 1971), 382.
12. "Baseball Scandal Up Again, with Cobb and Speaker Named."
13. Seymour, 383.
14. "The Baseball Scandal," *New York Times*, December 23, 1926.
15. Seymour, 384.
16. "29 Baseball Men Confront Risberg, Deny His Charges," *New York Times*, January 6, 1927.
17. Seymour, 385.
18. Joe Wood, interview with Lawrence Ritter, Ritter Papers, University of Notre Dame, Notre Dame, Indiana, 1963.
19. "Johnson Accepts Landis Challenge."
20. Alexander, *Ty Cobb*, 190.
21. "Johnson Accepts Landis Challenge."
22. Alexander, *Ty Cobb*, 194.
23. Greg Beston, "Forced to Back Down," paper submitted to the Society for American Baseball Research, 1996, 23.
24. Smith, 232.
25. Fred Lieb, *Baseball as I Have Known It* (New York: Grosset & Dunlap, 1977), 62.
26. Ibid., 62–63.
27. Alexander, *Ty Cobb*, 189.

8

Satch vs. Josh: The Showdown in Shadow Ball

David C. Ogden

Tennis had Jimmy Connors and John McEnroe. Boxing had Muhammad Ali and Joe Frazier. Basketball had Larry Bird and Magic Johnson. Each sport has had its legendary battles between its titans, but no battle is perhaps more legendary than the one in the Negro Leagues between Satchel Paige and Josh Gibson.

Satchel Paige, the wayfaring fireballer, built his reputation as a menace on the mound and as one of Negro League baseball's marquee drawing cards. Josh Gibson, the boyish-looking catcher, had established himself as one of black baseball's greatest power threats and as one of its most prodigious home run hitters. As Mark Ribowsky has written:

> When the two men were teamed to form the battery of the Pittsburgh Crawfords in the thirties, the mad rush of publicity they set off carried the black game through the Depression. Out on the barnstorming circuit, the marquees promised that Paige would strike out the first nine men who stood in against him and that Gibson would hit three home runs.[1]

As opponents years later, Paige and Gibson became the primary subjects of one of the best known, and perhaps embellished, showdowns in Negro League history. The legend of black baseball's most celebrated pitcher striking out black baseball's most celebrated hitter in a Negro League World Series game and with the bases loaded stands with other epic pitcher-batter confrontations in the major leagues. Its stature has grown among the lore of black baseball, as interest in Negro League history has grown, but the story would not be as compelling if the two primary characters were not already legends in and of themselves.

8. Satch vs. Josh (Ogden)

Having begun his professional career in 1926 with the Chattanooga Black Lookouts,[2] Satchel Paige supposedly developed an array of pitches, with names like the four-day creeper, the hesitation pitch, the jump ball, and the midnight rider.[3] During his 22 seasons in black baseball, he also developed a reputation for theatrics on the mound. For example, in a game against a semipro team in Denver, Paige responded to a racial slur by one of the opposing players by having his infielders and outfielders abandon their positions before he proceeded to strike out the side.[4] Furthermore, he demonstrated his dominance of major league players during games against Dizzy Dean's barnstorming all-star team. And despite his propensity for ignoring contracts to play for a higher bidder, a 42-year-old Paige joined the Cleveland Indians in 1948, becoming the oldest rookie in major league history and helping the Indians to capture the pennant. He would later pitch for the St. Louis Browns and the Kansas City Athletics during his six-year major league career, and although he is the only Hall of Fame pitcher with a losing record in the majors (28 wins and 31 losses), he amassed 2,000 wins (by his own estimate) during his days in black baseball.[5]

Leroy Robert "Satchel" Paige (1906–1982), pitcher extraordinaire and gate attraction (National Baseball Hall of Fame Library, Cooperstown, New York).

The year following Paige's Hall of Fame induction, Josh Gibson was given the same honor. But while Paige's longevity would be a hallmark of his career, Gibson's career ended prematurely.

Joshua "Josh" Gibson (1911–1947), the Babe Ruth of black baseball (National Baseball Hall of Fame Library, Cooperstown, New York).

8. Satch vs. Josh (Ogden)

Gibson carried numerous labels during his playing days, many of which were linked to the baseball legend usually considered to have been Gibson's white counterpart: George Herman Ruth. The Black Babe Ruth and the Bronze Bambino were among those labels, and the tales surrounding Gibson's on-field exploits lived up to those tags. Playing for the Crawfords and the Homestead Grays as well as teams outside of the United States, Gibson's mammoth home runs became mythical. In 1937, he supposedly knocked a ball out of Yankee Stadium,[6] and during a game at Forbes Field in Pittsburgh, he purportedly hit a ball so far that it did not come down until the next day when it landed in Philadelphia.

Unfortunately, Gibson's yearly home run totals, while closer to the truth, are based on conjecture and cannot be verified because of the lack of official Negro League records. Historian Robert Peterson claims that Gibson hit 75 homers in 1931,[7] and some historians estimate that Gibson hit almost 1,000 homers during his career.[8] But it was a career cut short. Of all the players in black baseball, Gibson may be the most tragic figure, having battled alcoholism and drug abuse the last several years of his life and dying on January 20, 1947, almost one month after his 35th birthday.

The Legend of Satch vs. Josh

As legends go, the story has different versions, depending on the source, but there is agreement among the accounts on the following details: the showdown happened in 1942; Paige pitched for the Kansas City Monarchs and Gibson caught for the Homestead Grays; and Paige intentionally loaded the bases to face Gibson. Perhaps the most popular retelling of the legend can be found in Ken Burns' documentary, *Baseball*, and the companion book, *Baseball: An Illustrated History*, which is based on the documentary's film script written by Geoffrey Ward and Burns.[9] As with other retellings, Ward and Burns' version depends on the firsthand narrative of Monarchs' first baseman and Paige confidante, Buck O'Neil.

O'Neil places the famous Paige-Gibson confrontation during the second game of the 1942 Negro League World Series, according to the retelling by baseball historian Mark Ribowsky.[10] As O'Neil relates the story in Ward and Burns' book, the Monarchs were leading with Paige on the mound and two outs in the ninth. Paige allowed a triple and then called O'Neil over from his position at first base for a conference on the mound. O'Neil relates the conversation:

> I said, "What are you fixing to do?" He said, "I'm gonna walk Howard Easterling. I'm gonna walk Buck Leonard. I'm gonna pitch to Josh Gibson." I said, "Man, don't be facetious." He said, "That's what I'm gonna do."[11]

O'Neil then said that he invited the Monarchs' manager Frank Duncan to join the meeting, probably to try to talk Paige out of doing what he proposed to do. However, Paige was unswayed and proceeded to walk Easterling and Leonard.

> ... [N]ow, when he was walking Buck, Josh was in the [batter's] circle, and he's talking to Josh all the time, said, "Josh, do you remember the day when we were playing on the same team, and I told you that one day we were going to meet and we were going to see who was the best?" He said, "Yeah, I know what you're talking about, Satchel." Said, "All right." Said, "Now is the time to prove this thing."[12]

O'Neil claims that when Gibson stepped to the plate, Paige called for a time-out and summoned the Monarchs' trainer, Frank "Jewbaby" Floyd, to the mound. Floyd, wearing a doctor's smock, brought with him a bicarbonate of soda that Paige gulped down before belching. Then, according to O'Neil, the crowd of 40,000 rose to their feet and Paige told Gibson that the first two pitches would be fastballs and that they would be in the strike zone. O'Neil went on to say that Paige proceeded to throw the first two pitches, both fastballs, for strikes, after which the lanky right-hander continued his bantering:

> He said, "Now, Josh, I've got you. Two strikes and no balls. You know, in this situation, I'm supposed to knock you down. You know, brush you back." He said, "But, unh, unh. I'm not gonna throw any smoke at your yoke. I'm gonna throw a pea at your knee!" Boom! Strike three. And, when he struck him out, you know, Satchel must be six-five, Satchel stretched out, looked like he was seven feet tall. And he walked off the field and walked by me and said, "You know what? Nobody hits Satchel."[13]

While the gist of the story remains the same for all versions, there are variations of it. For example, Negro League historian Donn Rogosin claims the incident did not happen during the 1942 World Series, but rather during a "regular season" Monarch-Gray game on July 21, 1942. Rogosin's retelling has Paige facing Gibson in the seventh inning with two outs after the pitcher had purposefully walked two batters to load the bases. But the

8. *Satch vs. Josh* (Ogden)

results were the same as those in O'Neil's narrative in Ward and Burns' book.[14]

The presence or absence of Jewbaby Floyd is another difference between versions of the story. Floyd has a prominent role in the accounts offered by Ward and Burns and by David Sterry and Arielle Eckstut in their profile of Paige.[15] In the latter, Floyd's trip to the mound becomes a central theme. Paige's consumption of the tonic that Floyd brings to the mound is a comedic high point in the circus that Paige is supposedly attempting to create from the battle with Gibson.

> As the crowd went crazy, Satchel (renowned for his gastrointestinal difficulties) grabbed his belly, dropped his glove, and motioned for the trainer, Jewbaby Floyd, to come out and minister to his aching guts. Jewbaby walked to the mound with a big glass of bubbling bicarbonate of soda that Paige slowly drank, as the tension built and built. He waited a moment, concentrated, and a hush fell over the fans. Suddenly, Satchel let out a huge belch that echoed throughout the stadium. The crowd erupted and Satch grinned ear to ear.[16]

Frank "Jewbaby" Floyd, the trainer for the Kansas City Monarchs (NoirTech Collection and Archives).

Ribowsky and Rogosin, however, do not mention that part of the story or Floyd. Instead, their focus is on the meeting at the mound between O'Neil and Paige and especially on Paige's chatter while he was striking out Gibson. O'Neil's recollection of that chatter in Ribowsky's book also varies somewhat from what he told Ward and Burns. In Ribowsky's version, O'Neil embellishes the crowd's reaction after Paige walks Easterling and Leonard and recalls Paige's comments to Gibson after the first two strikes:

> Now everybody's standin' and goin' crazy. And Satch looks in at Josh and says, "Okay, now I got you oh and two, and in this league I'm supposed to knock you down. But I'm not gonna throw smoke at yo' yolk — I'm gonna throw a pea at yo' knee"— and, *boom*, strike three; Josh didn't move the bat. And Satch walks off the mound and the crowd is yellin' and screamin' and he walks by me and he says real slow, "You know what, Buck? Nobody hits Satchel's fastball."[17]

Press Coverage of Satch vs. Josh

The only other first-hand accounts of the second game of the 1942 Negro League World Series and of the July 21, 1942, game (when Rogosin claimed the incident happened) are those found in the three local newspapers of the city where the game took place: the *Pittsburgh Press*, the *Pittsburgh Post-Gazette*, and the *Pittsburgh Courier*. Based on those newspaper articles, O'Neil's story cannot be substantiated. Paige may have loaded the bases to get to Gibson in another game, but it was not during the 1942 Negro League World Series or during the game on July 21.

Gibson and Paige did indeed face each other in both the July 21 game and the 1942 World Series, but the situations were different than that described by O'Neil. According to an article in the July 22, 1942, issue of the *Pittsburgh Post-Gazette*, Paige faced Gibson in the bottom of the ninth inning of the July 21 game at Forbes Field. But the game was tied at 4-4.

As *Post-Gazette* writer Jack Sell reported:

> The Grays had a good chance in the last of the ninth when Whatley singled with one gone and was sacrificed to second. However, Paige intentionally walked Easterling to get at Josh Gibson, the vaunted slugger of the Homesteaders, and the big catcher flied weakly to left to end the frame.[18]

The Grays won the game, 5-4, in 11 innings and handed Paige the loss. The coverage of the game in the *Pittsburgh Press* on July 22, 1942,

8. Satch vs. Josh (Ogden)

varied little from that in the *Post-Gazette*.[19] But perhaps the first hint that the story might take on more epic proportions was Chester L. Washington's column almost two weeks later in Pittsburgh's African American newspaper, the *Courier*. Washington embraced the showmanship of Paige during that game, despite Paige being the losing pitcher:

> The fact that the Homestead Grays finally won the extra[-]inning contest was inconsequential. Paige grabbed the spotlight from the first pitch he tossed across the diamond ... and held it until the final putout.... And to top the evening off, he held the mighty jolter, Joshua Gibson, hitless, fanning him at one particular time when the chips were really down and after he had walked Easterling, another good hitter, to get to Josh. Few fans expected the "Suitcase" sensation to go the distance. But there he was still in there through the ninth and into the extra innings, still pitching his heart out.[20]

Almost two months later in the Negro League World Series, Paige again faced Gibson. Here, Paige entered the September 10 game in the bottom of the sixth inning to relieve starter Hilton Smith, as stated in the September 11 issue of the *Pittsburgh Press*:

> Paige whiffed Leonard and Bankhead, the first two to face him in the sixth, and then caught Ray Brown's puny pop-up. In the seventh, singles by Lefty Partlow, Vic Harris[,] and Easterling filled the bases. Mr. Paige then toyed with Gibson and struck out the big catcher for another thrilling performance.[21]

The *Post-Gazette*'s coverage of that game — a game that the Monarchs won, 8-4 — did not stray from the facts presented by the *Press*, but the former did add a few superlatives to the action:

> The most dramatic moment for the fans came prior to the closing outburst of slugging. In the last of the seventh[,] the Grays, trailing by 2-0, loaded the sacks against Leroy (Satchell [*sic*]) Paige, greatest colored hurler in the game. Next at bat was burly Josh Gibson, the Babe Ruth of the colored ranks. While Homestead fans groaned, Josh fouled off the first two tosses weakly, then fanned on the third.[22]

The July 21 and September 10 games were not the only two contests in which Paige and Gibson squared off. Paige faced Gibson in one of the 1942 East-West Games (the Negro League all-star games), according to Ribowsky's biography of Gibson.[23] In that game, Paige intentionally walked Gibson. But their first meeting as opponents occurred earlier that summer,

Mysteries from Baseball's Past

Ribowsky said, during a June 18 game between the Monarchs and the Grays at Griffith Stadium in Washington, D.C. The *Pittsburgh Courier* confirms that June matchup between Gibson and Paige. In its June 27, 1942, issue, the *Courier* reported that Paige was "brilliant" and "put on a great show, unapproached by any other hurler anywhere and anytime.... He fanned the heavy-hitting Josh Gibson twice, Buck Leonard, great first baseman; Bankhead, Easterling, Benjamin[,] and Chester Williams, [*sic*] were handled like babies."[24]

Despite Ribowsky's claims that the June 1942 game was the first time Paige and Gibson faced each other, the *Pittsburgh Courier* presents evidence that Gibson may have batted against Paige years earlier. In its August 8, 1931, issue, the *Courier* reports on a Crawford-Gray game at McKeesport, Pennsylvania, in which Paige pitched for the Crawfords and Gibson caught for the Homesteaders. The story does not mention Gibson, though he is listed in the box score as batting in the cleanup spot and going hitless. Because Gibson was in his second season with the Grays and had not attained the stature that he would come to enjoy years later, the focus of the *Courier* story was on Paige, who was getting increasing attention in the Pittsburgh newspapers. The *Courier* noted that the highlight of the game, which the Crawfords won, 10-7, was "the masterful and sensational pitching of Paige."[25] Since Paige entered the game in the fourth inning to relieve Harry Kincannon and since the score was tied, 7-7, it is more than likely that he faced Gibson. But the story does not mention any at-bat by Gibson.

How to Explain the Legend

Overall, the evidence suggests that Paige and Gibson faced each other as opponents on several occasions. While Buck O'Neil's story cannot simply be brushed aside and labeled as a legend, the various versions of the Paige-Gibson meetings on the diamond by Pittsburgh newspapers do not substantiate the story. Why O'Neil's narrative of the 1942 Negro League World Series game differs from the press accounts remains a mystery. But Chester Washington's column in the *Courier* on August 1, 1942, might provide a clue. Washington's contention that Paige struck Gibson out in that fateful at-bat of the extra-inning game (although his own newspaper's coverage

8. Satch vs. Josh (Ogden)

of the game differed from his claim) might have planted the seed for what would later become O'Neil's recollection.

If Washington's column served as fertile soil for the story's germination, O'Neil appears to have added to its development through his supposed involvement in the incident and through the widespread dissemination of the tale, particularly via Ken Burns' baseball documentary. Over time, stories such as O'Neil's become part of the cultural sediment, and when those stories reach that stage, they usually turn into legends, making it difficult to separate fact from fiction. Legends, unlike myths, are grounded in truth and are often based on or rooted in historical events. And attempting to separate fact from fiction in legends can be an exercise in futility. Baseball scholar Lowell Blaisdell reminds baseball historians "that there is so often a vagueness of origins that it becomes almost impossible to track down the original source, and thus make an assessment of the relationship between the originating event and the tale in its full-blown form."[26]

Part of the process by which stories develop into legends may be due to what Barbie Zelizer calls "collective memory," in which stories are modified over time and details are adopted from various sources to conform to cultural norms and to bolster cultural identity.[27] Accuracy may be sacrificed, Zelizer says, in the service of aspects of the story that confirm cultural identity and solidarity. As author Fred Davis notes, "[T]he remembered past like all other products of human consciousness is something that must constantly be filtered, selected, arranged, constructed, and reconstructed from collective experience."[28]

Despite the lack of corroboration from Pittsburgh newspapers, it is not safe to say that O'Neil's story is more fiction than fact. It is possible that the Paige-Gibson confrontation, as told by O'Neil, did occur in a "regular season" game that received little or no coverage by the press and was linked at some point with the 1942 World Series. It seems more likely, however, that the story is a hybrid of the July 21 and September 10 games in 1942 and was coaxed along by *Courier* columnist Chester Washington. Other details were added through the years and the "final" versions gained popularity with their retelling by one of the Negro Leagues' most cherished veterans, Buck O'Neil.

Whatever or whoever the story's progenitor was, O'Neil gave the story authenticity through his stature as one of baseball's elder statesmen and by his self-professed role in the event. With O'Neil's death in 2006, the

Mysteries from Baseball's Past

John "Buck" O'Neil, the longtime first baseman of the Kansas City Monarchs and Satchel Paige's friend. Did he spin a yarn about the legendary encounter between Paige and Josh Gibson? (National Baseball Hall of Fame Library, Cooperstown, New York).

legend seems frozen in time and makes its disputation that much more difficult. The particulars of the tale may never be verified and the entire incident serves as a prime example of the difficulty of separating fact from fiction in stories involving Negro League players and their on-field feats.

Deconstructing Negro League legends does not cheapen the significance of that lore nor diminish its contributions to the richness of Negro League history. O'Neil's story about Satch and Josh in its various forms is, if nothing else, a study in the process of legend-making and underscores the importance of legends in the maintenance of collective memory, both socially and culturally. As a cultural vestige, the legend personifies the depth of talent and the defiant competitive spirit that drove black baseball. O'Neil's narrative, whether accurate or not, serves as a cultural artifact to remind the public of the greatness of the Negro Leagues and of its players who were not allowed to showcase their talents on baseball's grandest stage, the major leagues. Because blacks were excluded from the major leagues,

8. Satch vs. Josh (Ogden)

the play of the Negro Leaguers created its own complex mythology, which helped to define African American culture and continues to do so today.

Notes

1. Mark Ribowsky, *The Power and the Darkness: The Life of Josh Gibson in the Shadows of the Game* (New York: Simon & Schuster, 1996), 13.
2. Paige pitched for the semiprofessional Mobile Tigers in 1924 and 1925.
3. Geoffrey C. Ward and Ken Burns, *Baseball: An Illustrated History* (New York: Alfred A. Knopf, 1994), 203.
4. David Sterry and Arielle Eckstut, *Satchel Sez* (New York: Three Rivers Press, 2001), 65.
5. Ward and Burns, 206.
6. Ribowsky, *The Power and the Darkness*, 184.
7. Robert Peterson, *Only the Ball Was White: A History of Legendary Black Players and All-Black Professional Teams* (New York: McGraw-Hill, 1970), 164.
8. Ward and Burns, 199.
9. Ibid., 245–248.
10. Mark Ribowsky, *A Complete History of the Negro Leagues: 1884 to 1955* (New York: Birch Lane Press, 1995), 260–261.
11. Ward and Burns, 248.
12. Ibid.
13. Ibid. The Paige-Gibson showdown in the second game of the 1942 Negro League World Series did not get nearly as much public attention as the fourth game of the series did. The Grays won that game, 4–1, after losing the first three to the Monarchs, but the team used "ringers" to win it, according to accounts in two issues of the *Pittsburgh Courier* ("Monarchs Protest: Charged Grays Used 'Ringers' in Fourth World Series Game," September 26, 1942, and "KC 'Welched' on Player Deal—Grays," October 10, 1942). The injury-riddled Grays signed four players for that game: Leon Day, Len Pearson, and Ed Stone from the Newark Eagles, and Bus Clarkson of the Philadelphia Stars. The Monarchs protested, but the Grays' secretary, John Clark, claimed that the Monarchs knew of and agreed to allow the additions. However, Clark's claim was not enough, and the Grays had to forfeit the game and lost the series.
14. Donn Rogosin, *Invisible Men: Life in Baseball's Negro Leagues* (New York: Atheneum, 1983), 97–99.
15. Sterry and Eckstut, 66–67.
16. Ibid.
17. Ribowsky, *A Complete History of the Negro Leagues*, 261.
18. Jack Sell, "Grays Defeat Paige in 11 Innings, 5–4," *Pittsburgh Post-Gazette*, July 22, 1942.
19. Paul Kurtz, "Grays' Late Rally Shades Monarchs," *Pittsburgh Press*, July 22, 1942.
20. Chester Washington, "Sez 'Ches,'" *Pittsburgh Courier*, August 1, 1942.
21. "Grays Laced by Monarchs," *Pittsburgh Press*, September 11, 1942.
22. Jack Sell, "Late Spurt by Monarchs Beats Grays," *Pittsburgh Post-Gazette*, September 11, 1942.
23. Ribowsky, *The Power and the Darkness*, 241–242.
24. "Two Runs in Tenth Win for Grays as Paige, Partlow Star," *Pittsburgh Courier*, June 27, 1942.

Mysteries from Baseball's Past

25. "Grays Bow in 10–7 Thriller," *Pittsburgh Courier*, August 8, 1931.

26. Lowell D. Blaisdell, "Legends as an Expression of Baseball Memory," *Journal of Sport History* 19, no. 3 (Winter 1992): 230.

27. Barbie Zelizer, "Reading the Past Against the Grain: The Shape of Memory Studies," *Critical Studies in Mass Communication* 12, no. 2 (1995): 214–239.

28. Fred Davis, *Yearning for Yesterday: A Sociology of Nostalgia*. (New York: The Free Press, 1979), 115–116.

9

The Brooklyn Dodgers, the Move to Los Angeles, and the Search for Villains: Was Walter O'Malley a Bum, a Victim, or Something Else?

ROBERT TRUMPBOUR

In 1983, two legendary New York writers with strong ties to Brooklyn, Pete Hamill and Jack Newfield, met at the Lion's Head Bar in Manhattan. On that fateful night, they agreed to simultaneously compile lists of the 10 worst human beings of the 20th century on their respective bar napkins, which they subsequently decided to compare.[1] Hitler, Stalin, and Dodger team owner Walter O'Malley topped both of their lists, in this precise order, suggesting that O'Malley's decision to move the Dodgers from Brooklyn to California in October 1957 might have been the kind of mortal sin that no sane Brooklyn native would ever forgive.

When Peter O'Malley, Walter's son, planned a return visit to his boyhood Brooklyn neighborhood in March 2009 to address the Brooklyn Historical Society, the local newspaper's story promoting the event described his father in its lead paragraph as "perhaps the most reviled man in the history of the Western Hemisphere." The web version of this story included a photograph of the elder O'Malley with bright red devil's horns irreverently inked onto his image.[2]

That two of New York City's most seasoned and knowledgeable reporters and a Brooklyn-based publisher would continue to vilify Walter O'Malley many decades after the Dodgers moved to Los Angeles ought to offer compelling evidence that O'Malley had more than earned his long-tarnished reputation among New Yorkers. Or does it? A close examination of various documents related to the Dodgers' departure shows that the event is actually a multilayered mystery, shrouded in myth, intrigue, and passion, and that assessing blame for what happened is far from an open-and-shut case. As Leonard Koppett has written, "[A] simple story, however inaccurate or misleading, is preferred to a complicated explanation, however true. Perhaps it's a general human characteristic. But it certainly applies to baseball."[3] And it definitely applies to the reasons behind the Dodgers leaving Brooklyn, raising the question of who and/or what really caused the Dodgers to move to Los Angeles.

The Dodgers, Community, and Team Movement

Carl Prince, in his *Brooklyn Dodgers: the Bums, the Borough, and the Best of Baseball*, offers a vivid description of how the Dodgers were woven into the fabric of the community, with players living among the residents and partaking in various community rituals. It was common to see the players on mass transit, for example, when heading to the ballpark. As such, the team's departure was painful, shocking, and confronted by many in Brooklyn as one might approach the death of a close friend. According to Prince, "the Dodgers' presence helped maintain an uneasy truce among ethnic groups" as the borough's demographics were rapidly changing.[4] Prince asserts that the team was a major force in binding a community that was undergoing dramatic postwar changes, perhaps making the loss of the team substantially more profound than the loss of sports teams in various other urban environments.[5]

For example, when the Braves left Boston for Wisconsin and subsequently departed from Milwaukee to Atlanta, the tension level was high, and local baseball fans were angry, but the team departures were not nearly as traumatic as Brooklyn's loss of the Dodgers, and the change was greeted with eventual acceptance by a large percentage of the involved communities.[6] The outpouring of anger within Brooklyn, what was once a tight-knit community with a long-standing passion for baseball in the nation's largest city, may have been understandable when one looks through the cultural prism portrayed by Prince. It was the desire to bring closure to

9. The Brooklyn Dodgers, the Move to Los Angeles (Trumpbour)

the unfolding emotional pain by identifying a real-world scapegoat or culprit for the team's relocation, who in this case, became Walter O'Malley. But did O'Malley deserve the ongoing vilification that has lasted more than 50 years and is likely to last several decades longer?

Because it was O'Malley's choice to transplant his Dodgers to Los Angeles, New Yorkers are not entirely wrong blaming him for the team's departure. Moreover, that he acquired great profits after settling in a city that was a media rival to New York City did little to endear him to those he abandoned on the East Coast.

However, O'Malley and the Dodgers were part of a much larger mosaic, one that meant that staying in Brooklyn without some level of backing from local political leaders would have been extremely difficult. The decision to move the Dodgers, though ultimately O'Malley's, was prompted by a combination of factors that were exceedingly complex. The inability to get a new ballpark built is a common assertion used to defend O'Malley's decision. Nevertheless, changing demographics at both the national and local level and a rapidly evolving sports landscape were other issues that complicated the Dodgers' likelihood of remaining in Brooklyn beyond 1957.

O'Malley, the Dodgers, and the Early Push for a New Ballpark

Unlike today's team owners who frequently shake down communities to acquire hundreds of millions of dollars in stadium subsidies from local taxpayers, O'Malley was willing to purchase land and fund the construction of his own privately owned ballpark, one that would replace an aging and structurally inadequate Ebbets Field. But his desire to achieve that goal never took hold in New York. If it had, baseball history might have moved in a very different direction, though major league baseball would have eventually unfolded on the West Coast in one form or another.

O'Malley left a career in bankruptcy law in 1943 to become vice president and general counsel of the Dodgers. After numerous shrewd investments, he jumped in as a minority owner of the team in 1944. One of his fellow minority owners, Andrew Schmitz, explained that in buying their shares of the team, "we feel that we are keeping that much more of the ownership in Brooklyn where it belongs."[7] Over time, O'Malley increased his investment in the team, eventually gaining a majority stake.

Although the Dodgers did not move westward until after the 1957 season, O'Malley regarded the stadium as such a sufficiently important element in achieving profitability that he confronted the issue more than a decade before committing to the West Coast. The plan for stadium construction in Los Angeles is frequently cited as a reason for the move by those who blame O'Malley for the team's departure, but the team owner devoted substantial time and attention to getting a new ballpark constructed in Brooklyn long before making a commitment to California.

Shortly after the conclusion of the 1946 season, O'Malley solicited the advice of engineer and stadium designer Emil Praeger for "enlarging or replacing our present stadium."[8] After almost 18 months, news emerged that the team owner had received plans from well-known architect Norman Bel Geddes "for a streamlined Ebbets Field to be erected on the present site."[9] Citing a total cost that would exceed $6 million, O'Malley told reporters that a decision to build a new stadium "was not substantially correct."[10] He explained, "We appreciate that the Brooklyn fans are entitled to more seats and in a modern stadium[,] but it just does not seem possible in the near future."[11]

In 1948, two days after O'Malley publicly pushed back rumors that a new ballpark plan might be in the works, Praeger sent a report to O'Malley that was focused on options that would "locate a suitable site for a new stadium in the downtown section of the [b]orough of Brooklyn."[12] The stadium matter was presented to the citizens of Brooklyn early in O'Malley's tenure as owner, but his public pronouncements were in contrast to his behind-the-scenes machinations, perhaps setting the stage for his portrayal later on as duplicitous and scheming. Among the considerations cited by Praeger in his early analysis of the ballpark issue was access to "rapid transit facilities."[13]

Mass-transit access would always be a factor in a New York–based ballpark, but by the 1950s, the transit landscape had changed. Connecting a new stadium design closely to rapid transit worked against O'Malley in a number of ways. First, Robert Moses, as head of the Triborough Bridge and Tunnel Authority, was attached to increased automobile use as a means of building his powerful empire, as much of his transit construction was funded by bridge and tunnel tolls that mass-transit patrons would be able

9. The Brooklyn Dodgers, the Move to Los Angeles (Trumpbour)

to circumvent. Any plan for a new ballpark had to be cognizant of the revenue picture as it would affect Moses and his administrative domain.

Second, O'Malley's customer base was rapidly moving to the suburbs in Long Island and elsewhere in the New York metropolitan area, and, as such, future plans had to be more wedded to increased parking options for suburban patrons. Finally, O'Malley, clearly a profit seeker, perceived parking revenues to be something that he could never get while at Ebbets Field. Fewer than 900 parking spaces surrounded the ballpark, with some estimates pegged at 700, so the facility's automobile accommodations were antiquated when compared to more modern places with a vast sea of parking accommodations such as County Stadium in Milwaukee, Wisconsin, a new ballpark that was unveiled to patrons in 1953. Whether O'Malley's venture was municipally controlled or privately built, and no matter which location was chosen, it had to have improved parking facilities because of the emergence of an automobile culture and the revenue implications that increased parking facilities would bring.

O'Malley was among the first of the team owners to envision the value of a modern ballpark that was serviced by vast paved parking. He looked at the Milwaukee stadium as one that was worth emulating, even if he did not buy into the municipal ownership model that was used to construct this modern facility. Although no team had yet committed to Milwaukee's County Stadium when ground was broken in 1951, O'Malley was contemplating dramatic construction plans of his own as this new ballpark was being assembled on the fringe of a Midwest urban center.

Parking was just one aspect of Ebetts Field that proved to be problematic. Despite the grandeur of the park's entryway rotunda, the Dodgers' home was an anachronism that would need substantial and costly renovation or, more likely in a postwar era where modernity was a much more coveted outcome, complete replacement with a brand new state-of-the-art facility. Ebbets Field may have been cutting edge when formally christened in 1913, but by the 1950s, it was cramped, creaky, and inadequate. When O'Malley pestered city officials to help him acquire land to get a new ballpark built, his motives may have been mercenary, but the need to replace Ebbets Field was utilitarian. Baseball historian Peter Ellsworth has described the park as structurally unsound. He has further explained that "by the 1940s the plumbing was so bad that the walkways often smelled of urine."[14] Ongoing maintenance costs for the ballpark were substantially

Ebbets Field, the home of the Brooklyn Dodgers from 1913 to 1957 (National Baseball Hall of Fame Library, Cooperstown, New York).

higher than those of competing teams and O'Malley knew this. Annually, such costs were $236,981 for the Dodgers, while teams in Philadelphia, Chicago, Pittsburgh, and St. Louis devoted less than half that amount to the same thing.[15] In sum, the Dodgers had an inferior ballpark with little opportunity for parking revenues, and they were paying more than their rivals to maintain it.

No privately funded major league ballpark had been built since the construction of Yankee Stadium in 1923, but the Dodger owner, swimming against the tide, forged ahead with plans to construct a modern sports palace of his own. A utopian blueprint for a cutting-edge new stadium was released to the media on March 5, 1952. The plan, once again spearheaded by Norman Bel Geddes, proposed a facility with "a retractable roof; foam rubber seats, heated in cold weather; a 7,000-car garage...;

9. The Brooklyn Dodgers, the Move to Los Angeles (Trumpbour)

automatic hot dog vending machines everywhere...; and a synthetic substance to replace grass on the entire field and which can be painted any color."[16] One report suggested the grandiose plans were probably "far in the future," but O'Malley started to push others to buy into his vision.[17]

On June 17, 1952, O'Malley personally lobbied Frank Schroth, publisher of the influential *Brooklyn Eagle*, asking him to support "a modern athletic stadium seating approximately 52,000 people."[18] O'Malley's letter to Schroth argued that this facility "would be nearer Wall Street and Rockefeller Centre [sic] than the Polo Grounds, Yankee Stadium or Ebbets Field."[19] The Dodger owner gushed that such a facility, with a moveable roof, "would provide convention facilities unequalled elsewhere."[20]

Once Milwaukee's new facility was unveiled and the Braves began to use this ballpark, O'Malley quickly focused on the advantages that this particular publicly funded facility had over his. The rationale for isolating the Milwaukee ballpark as a tangible case study for moving ballpark construction forward was compelling. In 1947, the Dodgers set a National League attendance record, drawing 1,807,000 patrons, but by 1954, the Dodgers' attendance had dipped to 1,022,581, their lowest turnstile record of the postwar era. Before the Braves moved from Boston, their attendance was so weak that they would be outdrawn by many of today's minor league teams. However, the Milwaukee Braves broke the Dodgers' 1947 league attendance record in 1953 and 1954, during their first two years of operation in Wisconsin.[21]

Simply put, the Dodgers were losing patrons at a rapid pace, while the Braves were gaining customers. Unless something changed, the Brooklyn team would have fewer resources for player development, scouting, and salaries, even with the advantage of being in the lucrative New York market. The team might be able to maintain a strong roster for a while, based on its prior acquisition of talent, but over time, the Dodgers might struggle to remain competitive as the team aged while potentially losing profitable revenue streams that were so consistently important to O'Malley.

On June 18, 1953, mere months after the Braves began playing in Milwaukee, O'Malley pushed George McLaughlin, who was a key member of the Triborough Bridge and Tunnel Authority, the president of the Brooklyn Trust Company, and one of his allies, to work with him to set up a meeting with Robert Moses and others to consider ballpark construction in Brooklyn's Fort Greene section, a move that would require abandoning fledgling plans to build housing. His goal was to lock in a ballpark site before the plans for new apartments moved too far along to turn back. O'Malley asserted that "there are only a limited number of places, one perhaps[,] but maybe two, where a new ball park and parking garage could be built and be successful. Apartments, however, can be located in any one of many areas in Brooklyn."[22]

In his letter to McLaughlin, O'Malley narrowly focused on the parking issue, comparing his meager allocation of 850 parking spaces "in the odd and scattered parking lots"[23] surrounding his ballpark to the abundance of 8,752 spots available to Milwaukee's baseball patrons at that time.[24] In pleading his case to McLaughlin, he further emphasized that "Ebbets Field was built in the trolley car era. There are no trolleys to speak of today[,] but there are automobiles and intelligently planned parkways."[25]

O'Malley Versus Moses: Self-Interest Collides with Bureaucratic Power

O'Malley's goal was not to have land given to him for his ballpark construction, as is often the case in stadium building today, but rather to have the city assist him in purchasing land at a reasonable cost through the use of eminent domain. By the 1950s, the complexities related to construction were such that without a mechanism to make a large swath of land available at a fair-market price, O'Malley's ability to get a ballpark built would be impossible. Robert Moses controlled the process for taking over land through the use of eminent domain by virtue of his role as the head of the mayor's Committee on Slum Clearance, but each time O'Malley introduced a potential stadium option, his proposal was rebuffed by Moses.

Moses argued that legal constraints prevented him from using eminent domain for a project of this nature, but he had vast latitude in determining what constituted a "public purpose," the legal term used as a threshold for takeover. Historian Robert Caro explains that Title I of the Housing Act of 1949 gave the government so much discretion over the application of eminent domain that it "could now condemn land and turn it over to individuals — for them to build on it projects agreeable to government."[26]

9. The Brooklyn Dodgers, the Move to Los Angeles (Trumpbour)

This legislation was so sweeping that urban expert Charles Abrams stated that "under present redevelopment laws, Macy's could condemn Gimbels [a department store rival] — if Robert Moses gave the word...."[27] Peter Ellsworth asserted that if Moses "wanted to tear down homes to make room for an office building, he did it. No one stopped him — not presidents, governors, or mayors."[28] Caro noted that Moses evicted many thousands of individuals and businesses to build a broad range of projects, and he was fond of saying, "Once you get that first stake driven..., no one could stop you."[29]

Moses could have acted unilaterally to help the Dodgers stay in Brooklyn, but he refused to do so and took steps that repeatedly obstructed O'Malley's goals. Moses' grand vision was to build a new stadium in the Flushing Meadows section of Queens as part of a larger city-administered public park. It was a plan that Moses believed would make the city a more attractive recreational hub for suburban residents, many of whom were moving from Brooklyn and other parts of the city to the nearby Long Island communities east of the city. The plan also put the stadium near a mass-transit hub so that a Moses-controlled authority could set policy for the expansive parking lots that might facilitate commuting into Manhattan. Under this plan, Moses could charge suburban residents to park and take a train into the city during the day, a time when games were not scheduled, giving him a profitable ongoing revenue stream that would be denied to O'Malley. Such a plan would make mass transit financially beneficial for Moses, an important factor since he did not have jurisdiction over the New York City

Robert Moses, the power broker, pictured here at the age of 46 in 1934 (Library of Congress, Prints & Photographs Division, NYWT&S Collection, [LC-USZ62-136065]).

mass-transit system but had broad authority over the city's housing and roadways.

O'Malley took tangible steps to coax the city to assist him, but these steps did not seem to matter. On October 28, 1953, he worked with Robert Moses to clarify that he did not want government subsidies of any kind and was willing to work through any legal issues in as reasonable manner as was possible. Cognizant of Moses' focus on automobiles and roadways, O'Malley stated, "I want a new baseball stadium. You want a parking garage to ease a public problem. It is my hope that we can combine the two needs, using public authority to assemble the plot and private money to finance it."[30] Moses curtly responded, "[N]either the [c]ity nor any existing public agency has any power or right to acquire by eminent domain property for the purposes you outline.... [I]t is obvious that the garage is financially incidental to the stadium and that the real purpose is to build a new Dodger Stadium."[31] He then told O'Malley he would need "special legislation" to establish a stadium as a "public purpose" in order to even begin the process of stadium land acquisition by a public entity.[32] And he further stated that O'Malley was free to purchase land on the open market and that public officials might help with street widening and other "general neighborhood improvement" should he be successful.[33]

Without public assistance to acquire land, O'Malley would struggle to find anything substantial enough on which to build a ballpark, particularly in an area as densely populated as Brooklyn. Perhaps as a result of this, he sent a terse letter to Moses in December 1953 which included a report "on major league baseball opportunities in Los Angeles."[34] He closed the letter with a request to meet after the holidays to talk about "my problem"[35] and then worked with Emil Praeger on a stadium design and site, soliciting another meeting with Moses in April 1954 to develop a land acquisition strategy.[36] But instead of arranging a meeting with O'Malley, Moses passed the request to George Spargo, general manager of the Triborough Bridge and Tunnel Authority, who told O'Malley that he should first meet with Brooklyn borough president John Cashmore "before wasting any more time on it."[37]

Despite the stormy environment, O'Malley forged forward, soliciting a plan from Emil Praeger and then arranging a meeting with Moses. His hope was to combine the ballpark with public parking and rail access. In a letter to Moses, he tried to be sensitive to his adversary's concerns about

9. The Brooklyn Dodgers, the Move to Los Angeles (Trumpbour)

parking, stating, "This use would be available to the public. It is expected that it would be used mostly Monday through Friday during ordinary business hours. We would play our games at night at a time when other cars presumably would not require it."[38] He also laid out a strategy to involve the Long Island Railroad and the subway system in the overall plans.[39]

However, Moses was never excited about O'Malley's vision, and without his support, the baseball team owner was locked into an inferior and crumbling ballpark unless the Dodgers moved elsewhere or developed a strategy to circumvent Moses' authority. If New York mayor Robert Wagner had been a more influential figure, the situation might have played out differently, but with land decisions either fully in the hands of Moses or diffusely spread among the membership of the Board of Estimate, O'Malley needed Moses much more than Moses needed O'Malley.

Unfortunately, though, for O'Malley, as early as June 22, 1953, George McLaughlin told him bluntly that he did not believe Moses could be convinced to support O'Malley's plans, and that "I don't think you would find members of the Board of Estimate sympathetic to using any [g]overnment grant for the construction of a ballpark at this time."[40] Although O'Malley did not want government funds, but rather the use of eminent domain to allow him to acquire land at fair market value, McLaughlin's observations delivered a very sobering message: O'Malley would not be able to count on Moses in any way, and the Board of Estimate, the best chance to bypass Moses, was not likely to be sympathetic either. On the same day, O'Malley received confirmation of his feelings when Moses sent him a letter arguing that "our Slum Clearance Committee cannot be used to encourage speculation in baseball enterprises."[41]

By the summer of 1955, the unwillingness of Moses to work with the Dodgers in any meaningful manner escalated when the building magnate chastised O'Malley in very blunt terms. Moses scolded, "I don't see how you can have the nerve to indicate that you have not received proper support from public officials involved."[42] He further asserted that "if the Board of Estimate on the advice of the [b]orough [p]resident of Brooklyn wants to put through a reasonably sensible plan for highway, railroad terminal, traffic, street, market[,] and related conventional public improvements, and incidentally wants to provide a new Dodgers Field at Flatbush and Atlantic [a]venues, you can be sure that my boys will fully respect the wishes of the [b]oard and do everything possible to help."[43]

To achieve what Moses was suggesting, O'Malley would have had to navigate a complex political process that would have required getting the Brooklyn borough president to agree to coordinate intricate aspects of the plan that had nothing to do with the ballpark construction, the project that O'Malley was working to facilitate. John Cashmore, in turn, would have had to complete pieces of a job, typically spearheaded by Moses, in a political environment where O'Malley would have surely suspected that Moses was working behind the scenes to circumvent his efforts. At the same time, if Cashmore had followed through as was suggested, he may have had to face the political wrath of Moses, and his borough could have been forced to suffer the consequences if the power broker was angered at how this was handled.

Simply put, if O'Malley pushed a detailed proposal forward with Cashmore that included all the elements Moses cited, O'Malley could have been chastised for overstepping his bounds, and was likely to have been reined in by Moses, while Cashmore could have jeopardized housing and road-related construction in his borough that was under the direction and supervision of Moses. However, if O'Malley did not try to prod Cashmore and go through the Board of Estimate, he could be blamed for not being sufficiently proactive and thorough in his approach. Moses had, in effect, created a catch-22 for O'Malley, and O'Malley had to know this.

O'Malley Takes the Gloves Off

After struggling to achieve what he had desired but getting nowhere during the first seven and a half months of 1955, O'Malley had hoped to use the success of a top-tier Dodger team that eventually earned a World Series victory in October 1955 to get more positive action. He may have believed a winning team and an excited fan base might finally prod politicians to work with him if he could somehow raise public consciousness about his plight, but O'Malley was in a difficult box. Knowing he faced stiff political obstacles and sensing that an incremental strategy would not coax the most powerful New York politicians out of lethargy or opposition, he tested the waters with a more combative approach.

On August 17, 1955, a mere two days after receiving a verbal dressing-down by the mighty Moses, O'Malley issued a press release that

9. The Brooklyn Dodgers, the Move to Los Angeles (Trumpbour)

announced a decision to schedule seven Dodger games in nearby Jersey City, New Jersey, during the 1956 season.[44] He did this as a way to shake up things and to let both the citizens and the politicians know that he meant business. For a few days of the year, New York and Brooklyn would lose baseball-related revenue, something the Dodger owner hoped would bring New York political officials to the bargaining table. Instead, the New York press painted O'Malley as a fool or a scoundrel, with one fan calling the move "a dirty trick."[45]

O'Malley then alternated between a threat offensive and a charm offensive, in a Jekyll and Hyde strategy that telegraphed his desperation. He prophetically told New Yorkers in a front-page *New York Times* article that he feared without support for a new ballpark, New York could become a one-team city, with both National League teams leaving the area.[46] He said, "This problem is bigger than the Dodgers alone.... It is serious, Mr. Mayor, very serious."[47]

Moses taunted O'Malley both for appealing to the mayor and for suggesting a team shift might be possible, aggressively stating, "What you're saying is that, unless a way is found to make a home for the Dodgers in this location, you'll pick up your marbles and take them away."[48] After Moses recited a number of reasons why O'Malley's goals could not be achieved, the Dodger-owner countered, "Other cities can't understand why we can't do it when they can. We have to start trying to find out how it can be done, not why it can't be done."[49]

Following a direct appeal to New York's mayor, theoretically Robert Moses' boss, and a public slap at Moses' inability to get things done, O'Malley attempted to arrange a personal meeting with Moses using attendance at a Brooklyn Dodger game with his choice of game and guest list as a carrot. He assured the Gotham power broker that this would be a low pressure get-together, one that would include "[n]o business," but that could include dinner at the Brooklyn Club.[50] Moses replied promptly, indicating he was too busy, but suggesting he might attend a future game,[51] even though he was not fond of baseball and he regarded the Brooklyn fans as low class and pedestrian. Further attempts to cajole Moses to attend a game fell on deaf ears.

Los Angeles Jumps in the Mix

Nevertheless, the seeds of New York's political stall tactics were being noticed in Los Angeles, and several prominent Californians became more overt in plans to lure a major league team, particularly the Dodgers, to their city. On August 22, 1955, the same day O'Malley extended a ballpark invitation to Moses, Walter Peterson, the Los Angeles city clerk, contacted O'Malley to let him know that the city had passed a motion to invite the owners of both the New York Giants and Brooklyn Dodgers "for a serious conference and a 'look-see' at our facilities."[52] If that was not possible, public officials would reach out to consult with team representatives in September, the next time they had a meeting scheduled in New York.[53] The letter to O'Malley was on stationery from Los Angeles mayor Norris Poulson's office, suggesting that the desire to get together with the Dodger president had broad political support, something O'Malley was unable to gain in New York.

O'Malley did not respond to the invitation, so on September 1, 1955, Rosalind Wyman, a Los Angeles city councilwoman who campaigned to bring major league baseball to the city, contacted him. She offered to meet with him, along with another city council colleague, while in New York on other business.[54] Despite being savaged or ignored by New York political leaders, O'Malley curtly responded that "perhaps there might be an occasion when a meeting would be appropriate," but because the Los Angeles area had minor league representation "we would not want to be a party to any publicity which might be construed to be detrimental to their franchises."[55] However, at the top of the letter, O'Malley scribbled that he wanted his correspondence to be inserted in the "new stadium" file, an indication that a Los Angeles move that may have been a distant consideration was now on the radar screen as a possibility.[56]

Eleven days later, Vincent Flaherty, a columnist with the *Los Angeles Examiner*, wrote to O'Malley, asking him to "give Los Angeles serious thought."[57] According to Flaherty, if he did not, "[he] will regret it some day [sic] when major league baseball comes here and you find Los Angeles the richest baseball town in history."[58] On September 20, 1955, Red Patterson, the Dodgers' assistant general manager, indicated that "Walter will be only too glad to discuss the L.A. situation with you, off the record," an indication that O'Malley's resolve to stay in New York may have been softening, though Patterson went further to say, "but as of now[,] we've got something started in Brooklyn which we plan to see right down to a conclusion."[59]

The Battle for a Brooklyn Ballpark Intensifies

In November 1955, John Cashmore worked toward that conclusion by preparing a $100,000 survey that could have led to putting a ballpark in Brooklyn. With predictable caution, Cashmore minimized the stadium as a part of the project and emphasized the railroad upgrades, traffic, and nonbaseball commercial aspects of the project, presumably to avoid antagonizing Moses. O'Malley praised the mayor, Moses, and Cashmore for their role in supporting the survey, and optimistically concluded that "[w]ith Mayor Wagner, Commissioner Moses[,] and Borough President Cashmore working together as a team, I am sure that significant results can be expected for Brooklyn."[60]

To avoid losing leverage with city officials, in December 1955, O'Malley worked to solidify his temporary seven-game arrangement with Jersey City, signing a three-year agreement with New Jersey authorities. This was a shot across the bow to New York officials, an attempt to demonstrate the seriousness of the issue, though O'Malley disingenuously denied that his goal in doing this was to push city officials to take action on his ballpark plans.[61] However, even after hearing the denial, *New York Times* columnist Arthur Daley argued that the move sent a clear signal that "[t]he man ain't foolin.' He means business."[62] But later in that same column, Daley encouraged calm, suggesting that despite the message these moves sent, "there is no immediate cause for concern."[63]

As 1956 began, O'Malley was realistic, but tried to remain upbeat about getting a ballpark built in Brooklyn. When courted again by *Los Angeles Examiner* columnist Vincent Flaherty, O'Malley asserted, "It is my sincere belief that the Dodgers belong in Brooklyn. If the Dodgers are forced to move[,] it will not be because I have failed to do everything within my power to bring our problem to the attention of the proper authorities and the fans."[64]

With preliminary feasibility studies concluding, Cashmore continued to act cautiously, indicating that further examination would be needed to provide "a comparison with other uses which would accrue to the benefit of this area and the borough."[65] A day after Cashmore's assertion appeared in New York newspapers, Moses sent O'Malley a letter which he had authored that was given to the city editor of the *New York Herald Tribune*, stressing that "Title I of the National Housing Act cannot be used for a Dodger Field as such."[66] He cautioned O'Malley in the letter, rhetorically asking, "Why stir up the animals? Something constructive will no doubt be worked out with or without the Dodgers."[67]

Nonetheless, O'Malley plowed forward, demonstrating a willingness to allocate $4 million of team funds to the ballpark project if the move to sell bonds for the larger community renewal project was approved.[68] Surprisingly, while Moses talked down the possibility of stadium building in personal contact with O'Malley, he went on record as a supporter of a state-level strategy to issue $30 million in bonds for the large public works project, though he was generally silent about the Dodgers' ballpark as a part of this larger plan. O'Malley stated he would prefer something "less grandiose" than what was being suggested, but he praised the formation of an authority for "blazing the trail whereby the [s]tate [l]egislature would have the power to get land — that is something a ball team can't do."[69]

Columnist Arthur Daley joked that fellow writers were satirizing the Dodgers' situation by singing "give me a home with a translucent dome," a reference to a covered stadium concept that O'Malley worked diligently to bring to fruition, with particular help from famed visionary and architect R. Buckminster Fuller.[70] Moses remained somewhat quiet on the ballpark front, but publicly urged caution, indicating that there was a good chance the entire project could fall through.[71]

O'Malley tried to cultivate a positive working relationship with Moses, knowing that the forceful construction czar had the connections and contacts that could enable him to torpedo the Dodgers' plans. The team owner invited Moses and Moses' assistant, George Spargo, to attend opening day festivities, and followed that invitation up with a cheery letter about ballpark construction in other cities.[72] Perhaps irritated by what O'Malley wrote, Moses matter-of-factly declined his invitation, though in his reply, he said that Spargo would attend. He then closed his response by explaining that O'Malley's analysis of the Milwaukee stadium project's parking situation was flawed, a backhanded slap as he moved away from any attempt to assist O'Malley and his goals.[73]

9. The Brooklyn Dodgers, the Move to Los Angeles (Trumpbour)

A July report from consultants in charge of the general survey for the proposed Brooklyn site delivered particularly bad news to O'Malley. The report stated that properties valued at more than $109 million would be removed from the tax rolls in order to vacate the development area. This outcome was estimated to cost the city $5 million per year if the project moved forward. Expanding the acreage substantially to provide a larger "public purpose," as insisted upon by Moses, created a poison pill dimension to this project.

Though no follow-up report was prepared to explain the economic impact that new development on that same land might have over a longer period, Moses' insistence that the project serve a public purpose would likely ensure that some of the acreage dedicated to the project would be city owned and not subject to taxation. The presumed revenue loss would give Moses substantial ammunition to oppose the plan and allow him to appear responsible for doing so. It also eroded support from O'Malley's other political option, the Board of Estimate, which was comprised of members from each of the city's five boroughs. The prospect of raising taxes outside of Brooklyn, even if temporary, to compensate for revenue losses caused by a project that would primarily benefit Brooklyn, made progress difficult.

By the fall of 1956, the New York political process was so convoluted that O'Malley seemed to be leaning in the direction of moving the team, though no public declarations suggested such an outcome. As October closed, O'Malley sold Ebbets Field to a real estate developer in a deal that included an option for a five-year leaseback agreement, if desired.[74] Marvin Krattner, the buyer, announced long-range plans to create a mixed-use real estate design that would consist of the construction of housing, retail units, and recreational areas, but for now, O'Malley could continue to use the ballpark if needed.[75]

In early December, Moses wrote to O'Malley that he "reluctantly aided and abetted the cause of Atlantic Avenue public improvements[,] and incidentally, the [s]ports [s]tadium to the best of my ability."[76] Now likely more aware than ever that Moses was not on his side, O'Malley contacted John Cashmore and suggested patience with the project. However, to gain leverage that almost certainly would have filtered back to Moses, O'Malley told the Brooklyn borough president that "if things do not seem to be working out[,] we will have to be practical and reluctantly go elsewhere."[77] Despite that veiled threat, as the year came to a close, Moses offered ominous signs that the ballpark portion of the project was likely to fall through. In a Christmas Eve story, he indicated that the ballpark portion of the plan deserved a chance to prove itself, but he suggested that the ability to sell bonds for that portion of the project was in doubt.[78]

As New Year's Eve approached, it became apparent that the plan to build a new ballpark would not receive the necessary funding and had little chance of broader approval in any political venue. The New York Board of Estimate trimmed funding for the economic and engineering aspects of the stadium project by more than 90 percent, with the lion's share of overall planning funds allocated to school-related projects. This pullback effectively killed the opportunity to make a case for a successful bond issue. O'Malley cautioned that only a short time remained before he would have to "commit the Dodgers elsewhere," and he lamented that he had taken steps to raise $4 million to fund a new ballpark only to see "that this program is the subject of sabotage."[79]

It was not until April 1957 that Moses placed an offer on the table to work with O'Malley to build a municipally owned ballpark in Flushing Meadows in Queens rather than Brooklyn, though there were political difficulties to realizing that vision — something Moses chose to minimize in making his pitch.[80] That plan had problems, but alternatives that were bandied about at this late stage were either blocked by Moses or so sufficiently flawed that they would not succeed. If the Queens site was not acceptable, Moses proposed giving O'Malley access to land in a run-down section of Brooklyn that might be tougher to work with than remaining in Ebbets Field. O'Malley countered with a proposal to build on public parkland in a better area, an idea that was quickly rejected by Moses.[81] As a result, a far-from-certain Queens stadium plan was all O'Malley had left if he wanted to remain near Brooklyn and within New York City. Unfortunately, the transportation in and out of Brooklyn to Moses' proposed site was inadequate at that time, an issue that could keep some Dodger fans away from the turnstiles unless things changed.

With all that had transpired, O'Malley was so skeptical of the intentions of the New York City political leaders that he needed clear evidence that a plan of this nature could succeed or he would be forced to head to Los Angeles. From Moses' perspective, the Dodgers were not a priority, though he did want to build a grand new ballpark and make it part of a larger public parks project. If the Dodgers were eliminated from the city landscape and a new expansion team was inserted in their place, which could occur by virtue of the size and scope of the New York market, Moses' ambitious vision for a ballpark and much larger recreational area in Queens might be easier to implement.

Demographics, Culture, and Politics: Los Angeles Versus Brooklyn

Even with the availability of bargain-priced land in California and a rapidly expanding demographic that promised an exceedingly lucrative arrangement for O'Malley, the Dodger owner reacted reluctantly to overtures to move to Los Angeles. When Rosalind Wyman, a long-time proponent of bringing a major league baseball team to the West Coast, attempted to pin down O'Malley, asking bluntly if he would come to Los Angeles if the city council voted to make stadium land in Chavez Ravine available to him, she was unable to get a clear and firm commitment.

If occurring early in the process, this lack of commitment would have been understandable, but this conversation took place as a six-hour council meeting transpired with O'Malley facing a one-day deadline to inform the major leagues if a move was to be approved.

According to Wyman, O'Malley's precise words to her were "I am a New Yorker. If I can get the best deal in New York, I will stay in New York."[82] He thanked the city councilwoman and apologized for the difficulty of the council's decision, but he made no clear-cut promise to move when a Los Angeles city council vote could have undermined him if he was not more accommodating. Although O'Malley had been thoroughly convinced he could not count on New York politicians to help him, he struggled emotionally to finalize his divorce from Brooklyn, which would occur a day later.

The Los Angeles city council agreed to terms that would provide an exchange of O'Malley's less desirable minor league ballpark in Fort Worth, Texas, for land which included 300 acres of property in Chavez Ravine and a commitment of $4.75 million for building access roads and for preparing the hilly terrain for ballpark construction. Wyman confessed later that she did not share the outcome of her one-on-one conversation with O'Malley with fellow council members, indicating that "[w]e had wobbly people."[83] If she had relayed this information to her colleagues, she firmly believed "we would have lost."[84]

There was still some chance, though slim, that O'Malley may have backed out of a deal with Los Angeles, even at this late stage in the negotiations, if New York City officials had formally approved a clear and attractive plan to help him build a ballpark by October 7, 1957, either in Brooklyn or in Queens. But by then, O'Malley had grown so skeptical of New York officials that he did not trust their ability to commit to his team's interests. As such, any agreement would have to have been in writing and approvals by all necessary individuals and organizations would have to have been in place. That would not occur and was not a reasonable expectation in light of the various personalities involved.

When a plan to do survey work on a stadium emerged in March 1957, O'Malley told Frank Schroth, then working for the *New York Daily News*, that "I am so convinced that they [New York politicians] have made my decision for me that I would really not want to see any more money wasted for another survey."[85] In short, by March 1957, the power dynamic had changed to such an extent that from this point onward, New York politicians had to convince O'Malley they were fully committed to his vision and could get a new ballpark built in order to forestall a move.

What unfolded from that time was simply inadequate in the eyes of O'Malley in light of all that had transpired earlier. Even though Robert Moses, New York's strongest political voice, publicly backed ballpark construction in Queens, no formal agreement was in place and the ability to get the New York Board of Estimate to approve a plan that would move the Dodgers to Queens was complicated by vehement opposition from John Cashmore. It was certain that the Brooklyn borough president would be expected to undermine the approval process, and Moses had repeatedly demonstrated that he was not an ally of O'Malley. The Dodger owner had little reason to trust Moses and would have been foolish to do so. O'Malley's inability to work with Moses in any meaningful way after numerous attempts to reach out to him under a variety of circumstances had to raise a red flag and put him in a much stronger position to move his team from Brooklyn.

Beyond that, despite O'Malley's oft-repeated desire to stay in Brooklyn, the demographic changes conspired against an inner-city ballpark

9. The Brooklyn Dodgers, the Move to Los Angeles (Trumpbour)

anywhere within the New York metropolitan area. The postwar flight of middle-class whites to suburban Long Island and New Jersey gradually changed the complexion of the urban northeast. The allure of a newly constructed home on a plot of suburban land, often funded by low-interest government financing, proved to be too attractive for many World War II veterans intent on raising their families in bright, clean communities with rows and rows of brand new housing stock. Thus, from 1950 to 1960, Brooklyn's population diminished by over 100,000 people, with the minority population nearly doubling during that same period.[86]

Although Brooklyn remained largely white, a generally poorer Hispanic and African American population gradually began to fill the void created by "white flight" to the suburbs, with much of this change made possible by Robert Moses' commitment to public housing and highway building. Even though O'Malley's team was famous for introducing integration to baseball, the influx of minority citizens created an ironic set of circumstances. Some suburban white patrons were less likely to visit their old urban environment, including the ballpark, because of where they now lived, while much of the newly situated minority population was too immersed in eking out a living to routinely visit the ballpark. With O'Malley exceedingly aware of attendance disparities that gave the Milwaukee Braves a profound advantage over his team, he had to feel uneasy about his future in the New York market even if a present-day analysis of profit potential in the sporting landscape would make a Milwaukee–New York comparison appear to be absurd.

The allure of pay-per-view TV in 1957 added yet another wrinkle to the picture. While in Brooklyn, O'Malley was among the most successful owners with television revenue, but all these broadcasts were on free television channels. As the Giants and Dodgers were contemplating a shift, Skaitron, a proposed pay-per-view company that never became fully operational, touted the prospect of a payout of $2 million per year to each team in exchange for the broadcast rights to games in California.[87] That figure, if achieved, would more than double O'Malley's television broadcast revenue, making a move to California even more attractive to his bottom line.

Meanwhile, in Los Angeles, government investment in the defense industry along the Pacific coast during World War II fostered an environment that attracted industry and a high-salaried workforce. Industrial and defense spending continued as the Korean War and the Cold War escalated. By 1958, 90% of all California-based defense appropriations had been earmarked for three southern counties, with Los Angeles as a leader.[88] Five hundred people had moved into Los Angeles each day between 1945 and 1955, an influx of 1,725,000 over this 10-year period, eventually eclipsing Chicago as the nation's second largest population center.[89]

Robert Moses attempted to counter these complex demographic and financial forces by pushing O'Malley to move into a Queens ballpark that would be municipally owned. To do so, the Dodgers faced two obstacles, one political and the other practical. In order to make the Queens proposal work, O'Malley would need the support of John Cashmore, who was not only the president of the borough of Brooklyn, but also an important member of the New York Board of Estimate. The board's approval was required for things to move forward, and Cashmore was likely to slow down and obstruct the approval process. If he truly wanted this proposal to work, Moses would have to convince O'Malley to willingly forgo dramatic parking revenues or offer a creative strategy that would give the team owner some portion of the parking profits to offset what would be certain parking-related revenue in Los Angeles. However, Moses, hardly a fan of O'Malley, never approached the Dodger owner with even a rudimentary plan to address the parking revenue issue in a way that would lure O'Malley to accept this idea. Furthermore, Moses did his best to paint O'Malley as a villain in his public outreach.

O'Malley's concept of a new privately funded ballpark that was woven into the community was in some ways visionary, but in other ways a throwback to a bygone era that doomed his ability to gain political traction. He worked feverishly to get Robert Moses on his side, but time after time, he achieved no success. For his own reasons, Moses was wedded to an emerging model of stadium building that would include direct government involvement and oversight, something O'Malley resisted.

New York mayor Robert Wagner may have offered commitments to resolving the problem in various communications with those involved, but his public proclamations were more political posturing than a genuine promise to act. Wagner was not one to confront difficult issues, so he was more likely to let the process play itself out than to propose a solution. Because of this, Robert Moses enjoyed wide latitude to interpret and enforce city policy during the Wagner administration. According to Moses,

9. The Brooklyn Dodgers, the Move to Los Angeles (Trumpbour)

Wagner was a "sweep-it-under-the-rug guy.... If there's a problem, don't look at it and it will go away. If the phone rings, don't answer and it'll stop ringing. Don't answer mail and it will answer itself."[90]

O'Malley's decision in the late 1940s to keep his vision for stadium construction close to the vest perhaps convinced some that his subsequent efforts years later were a ruse intended to limit fallout for the decision to move his team to Los Angeles. However, O'Malley's willingness to jeopardize the Los Angeles move in his conversation with Rosalind Wyman on October 7, 1957, as a deadline loomed for a decision on what would transpire for the 1958 season, suggests that the Dodger owner might have been convinced to stay in New York, but New York politicians were simply not as committed to retaining the Dodgers as top officials in Los Angeles were to luring them away from their original home.

Before Charles Ebbets began to construct Ebbets Field, he was able to create a shadow company that allowed him to gradually buy up enough land for his legendary ballpark without getting shaken down by a land owner who might have had him over a barrel. But by the time O'Malley took over the team, such a strategy was not feasible. Media coverage was too efficient and public records were more readily available, so O'Malley would need the support of legislators to acquire the many individual parcels of land required to make a project this complex work. His commitment to private construction, something he was able to execute successfully in Los Angeles, was anachronistic, no matter how visionary the ballpark design strategy may have been.

The new model for ballpark construction was more in keeping with what Robert Moses envisioned: a municipally owned stadium. But after being whipsawed by New York officials every time he proposed something novel, O'Malley could not be convinced to trust the same individuals to build a ballpark that would house his team and to serve as his landlords on terms that he could accept.

Pulling the Trigger, Power Limits, and Blame

O'Malley will continue to be blamed by New Yorkers for moving the Dodgers from Brooklyn to Los Angeles, and that blame is likely to remain for decades. But as the facts are teased out, he is not the only culprit in this story. Robert Moses, the headstrong power broker, Robert Wagner, a confrontation-avoiding politician, and a long line of New York's political and business leaders smugly believed they could push O'Malley around without consequence. Over time, however, O'Malley grew tired of trying to make things work in Brooklyn and began to look forward to resettling in Los Angeles.

The evidence reveals that O'Malley was willing to contemplate staying in New York through 1956, but by 1957, his attitude about the New York political process was sufficiently tinged with skepticism that a decision to remain in Brooklyn was unlikely. He worked exceedingly hard to put the pieces in place to orchestrate what would later unfold as a move to Los Angeles after the 1957 season was over. On January 17, 1957, O'Malley wrote New York City councilman Joseph Sharkey that "[i]t appears pretty definite that the stadium project is dying a slow death, the result of malnutrition.... The trouble is that when I make my decision to move the franchise[,] it will then be too late to reactivate our original plans to keep the Dodgers in Brooklyn."[91] As 1957 unfolded, O'Malley acquired rights to the National League's minor league affiliate in Los Angeles in a franchise swap with his Fort Worth, Texas, property. He also bought a team plane and actively visited with Los Angeles officials.

The highly methodical and clearly calculating nature of the steps that were taken to set the stage for a move to Los Angeles make it easy to unilaterally blame the Dodger magnate for the team's departure. However, O'Malley maintained slim, though fleeting, hope that even in 1957 things might work out for him in Brooklyn, but by then, he seemed more accepting of heading down a path that would move the team to Los Angeles. He could have sold the team to someone who would have kept the franchise in metropolitan New York, but if he wanted to retain control of the Dodgers, remaining in the New York area became an increasingly problematic outcome.

Critics of O'Malley maintain that he was a ruthless mercenary who cared more about money than anything else. Evidence of his desire to maximize team profits is abundant, and perhaps this is the best argument for blaming O'Malley for abandoning Brooklyn for Los Angeles. His hardline positions in ballplayer salary negotiations were legendary, as were some of the tactics he used to improve his bottom line. His team routinely scheduled doubleheaders on Memorial Day and July 4, both holiday periods

9. The Brooklyn Dodgers, the Move to Los Angeles (Trumpbour)

when fan enthusiasm and gate attendance would be high. However, instead of charging a single admission for a doubleheader, as was typical practice in the major leagues at that time, O'Malley's team scheduled afternoon and night contests that allowed for double charging his fans, a move that forced the team's most loyal followers to buy two tickets for same-day ballgames. When Lawrence Murphy, a Brooklyn legislator, attempted to ban the practice, offering a bill in the New York State Assembly to do so, O'Malley told reporters, "If such a law were constitutional[,] it would abolish all theatre and circus matinees."[92]

O'Malley's dogged pursuit of profit may have made him easier to peg as the villain when the Dodgers abandoned Brooklyn, but his imperious demeanor, close-to-the-vest approach to business decisions, and his overall appearance further enhanced the public's ability to demonize him. His tendency to deny the obvious — for example, the linkage between the Jersey City games starting in 1956 with his desire to prod New York's political officials — allowed him to be easily portrayed as duplicitous. His wool suits, horn-rimmed glasses, and pudgy-cheeked face, when linked to his ongoing profit-oriented machinations, created the impression of a real-life Machiavelli, straight from casting central, with parallels to Scrooge or Henry Potter, the calculating, mercenary character played by Lionel Barrymore in Frank Capra's film classic, *It's a Wonderful Life*.

However, O'Malley's clout within metropolitan New York was exceedingly limited, so when he stepped up to the table to bargain with Robert Moses and Robert Wagner, O'Malley was either steamrolled or ignored. But when he went to Los Angeles, the local dignitaries rolled out the red carpet and treated him with abundant respect. And although he was emotionally attached to stay-

Walter Francis O'Malley (1903–1979): Villain or victim? (National Baseball Hall of Fame Library, Cooperstown, New York).

ing in Brooklyn, the ongoing rejection that he faced while in New York set the stage for a cross-country relocation of the Dodgers.

Author and Columbia University professor Michael Shapiro asserts that O'Malley was "not nearly as powerful as he would have liked to be, a man without the muscle and influence to get what he wanted. So he had to scheme, playing people and cities off each other because otherwise he would have ended up the loser, the owner of a team that fewer and fewer people were willing to go out of their way to see."[93] Despite possessing business acumen that allowed him to outflank some rivals, O'Malley had limitations which prevented him from creatively maneuvering around the dramatic minefields of New York City politics. Neil Sullivan, a public administration scholar, asserts that "O'Malley was more a reactor to events around him than an instigator."[94]

But when it came to getting a new stadium, O'Malley pushed himself to be much more than a reactor. He took numerous steps that could have allowed the team to remain in Brooklyn, though after repeated frustration, he subsequently worked out a deal in California that he could not obtain in New York. This was due largely to the difference between the people in authority in the two cities. New York politicians who were in a position to placate O'Malley chose to erect barriers, in part, to achieve their own agendas. On the other coast, political leaders in Los Angeles were excited about stepping out of the shadows of the minor leagues to become recognized as a major league city, and to accomplish this goal, they bent over backwards to lure O'Malley.

O'Malley worked with numerous architects, contractors, and designers to assemble ballpark construction plans that would capture the imagination of New York area politicians and residents, but city leaders did little to facilitate his goals, and in many instances worked behind the scenes to undermine his plans. This lack of action is in sharp contrast to the elaborate courting and enticements that are extended to team owners today.

Conclusion: O'Malley, the Media, and the Message

With such strong evidence that O'Malley's chances in New York were severely damaged by a complex and unpredictable political process, one key mystery might be how did the Dodger owner get painted so clearly as

9. The Brooklyn Dodgers, the Move to Los Angeles (Trumpbour)

a villain? Part of that has to do with O'Malley's persona, part of that has to do with the circumstances surrounding the departure, and part of it has to do with how the media coverage of O'Malley's efforts unfolded within the New York media itself.

Moses, never a fan of team sports, finally realized by 1957 that a move by O'Malley and the Dodgers could cost him dearly in the form of political capital. As such, he pushed his public relations machine into high gear, and the New York press, which up to then had been almost universally supportive of the legendary power broker, acted as a conveyer belt, setting the stage for the vilification of the Dodger owner when the inevitable did unfold.

On July 22, 1957, New York–based *Sports Illustrated* provided a ready forum for Moses in the form of a seven-page article that he authored, which outlined his plans for a new ballpark in Queens. Moses opened the article arguing that baseball's problems have been confronted by "quack remedies from assorted tribal doctors, medicine and confidence men, shills, barkers, swamis[,] and self-anointed pundits, addressing themselves to an increasingly bewildered and disgusted public."[95] Subsequently, he mocked O'Malley directly and personally for routinely giving a "speech indicating that he would die for dear old Brooklyn."[96] Moses stated he had "heard this speech over and over again *ad nauseam*. From time to time[,] Walter has embroidered it with shamrocks, harps[,] and wolfhounds and has added the bouquet of liqueur Irish whiskey."[97] He argued that O'Malley's "nervy and Napoleonic" demands included turning land "over to him."[98]

Moses went further to argue that "[f]rom my seat in the bleachers[,] it looks as if the Dodgers at least are already on the way"[99] out of town, while explaining that a five-year window to build a ballpark at O'Malley's proposed Atlantic Avenue site could not work because of "delay and loss of time and for many other reasons."[100] But the New York construction czar failed to explain his role in creating barriers, arguing instead that "it is absolutely impossible to build any kind of a stadium at this location and have it ready before 1962,"[101] while also outlining his proposal for a new ballpark in Queens that he called "eminently sensible."[102] His plan, he concluded, was worth trying in order to "dissipate the smog of controversy and the atmosphere of evasion, haggling[,] and penny[-] pinching which overhangs the scene."[103] The article, which included graphic images of the ballpark location, painted O'Malley in a highly negative light on a national scale. Moreover, the subsequent construction of a ballpark on the same proposed location less than a decade later was likely to have further undermined O'Malley's credibility.

Moses expected and tended to receive generally positive press coverage within the New York metropolitan area, something that O'Malley struggled to obtain. When a federal official attempted to rein in Robert Moses in July 1957, ironically for his overly aggressive use of eminent domain, the *New York Times* editors crafted a highly supportive editorial that praised "Moses for getting things done."[104] The piece indicated that President Franklin Delano Roosevelt was unsuccessful in his attempts to control Moses, further asserting

> that New York City is not going to drop Bob Moses as a public servant as long as he is willing to keep working for the city.... You don't bench a Babe Ruth because he strikes out once and a while. You consider the home runs and the batting average.... The [f]ederal [g]overnment is not going to change Mr. Moses. It had better try to get along with him, for that is the way we will travel farthest fastest for the public good.[105]

With support this compelling and dramatic, it was unlikely that O'Malley could take on Moses and beat him in a public relations game that would require the popular press as a forum. As such, the media landscape helped assign blame in very clear ways, more directly and overtly demonizing O'Malley when the team moved to Los Angeles instead of looking for alternative narratives that might be more complex. Although the positive image Moses crafted was tarnished years later, attacking the integrity or ability of Robert Moses in the 1950s was bound to be a losing battle.

Demographic factors, a changing media landscape, advances in the aviation industry that made coast-to-coast transportation feasible, and the burgeoning promise of Southern California's fast-growing economy became increasingly tempting to O'Malley at a time when prominent New York officials treated him with smug disdain or neglect. Once Horace Stoneham, owner of the New York Giants, committed to moving to the West Coast rather than Minneapolis, as was widely speculated, a second team would have to be repositioned in California or the West Coast experiment would have met with only limited success.

As such, it should be no mystery as to why O'Malley took his team and moved it 3,000 miles after the 1957 season concluded. Both West

9. The Brooklyn Dodgers, the Move to Los Angeles (Trumpbour)

Coast cities worked in tandem to attract teams, with San Francisco mayor George Christopher telling Los Angeles mayor Norris Poulson in a March 2, 1957, telegram, "We consider this practically a joint venture and know that if you are successful[,] San Francisco also will eventually receive major league baseball."[106]

In May 1957, Walter O'Malley joined influential Los Angeles County supervisor Kenneth Hahn on a helicopter ride.[107] This junket opened O'Malley's eyes to the opportunities that would await him in California. After dealing with numerous failed attempts to cajole reluctant public officials in New York, he was exposed to an impressive aerial view that revealed how a series of freshly built freeways might be tied into a privately funded state-of-the-art ballpark that could be surrounded by parking and placed within close proximity to a burgeoning population base. During that ride, Hahn suggested that O'Malley excitedly indicated "[t]his is the place," a statement that suggests the Dodger owner was unlikely to turn the clock back after May 1957 as long as Los Angeles city officials followed through on their promise to swap land in Chavez Ravine for an old minor league ballpark.[108]

Careful examination of the facts leading up to the Dodgers' move westward reveals a significantly complex tale, one that portrays the Dodger owner as a somewhat sympathetic figure rather than a villain. Residents of Brooklyn may not like that characterization, but the facts show that if O'Malley had been helped by New York politicians in his land acquisition strategy before 1957, he likely would have remained in Brooklyn. However, by the time 1957 unfolded, O'Malley had been exposed to such a long pattern of obstructionism that convincing him to turn back the clock and stay in Brooklyn would have required more civility and a more serious commitment on the part of New York's political leaders than they were prepared to provide.

In 1952, O'Malley told *Brooklyn Eagle* publisher Frank Schroth, "I wish this were Bob Moses' [i]dea and not mine[,] as he has the know[-]how and zeal to see it through."[109] O'Malley's words were prophetic. Moses had the capacity to get a new ballpark built, but he lacked the resolve to do so unless construction took place on his terms. He could have acquired the land O'Malley needed and no one would have stopped him. But Moses chose not to work with O'Malley.

The legendary power broker had no desire to help the Dodgers or O'Malley, and by the time Moses laid out his plans for a new ballpark in

Mysteries from Baseball's Past

Queens, it is probable that O'Malley was convinced that he could not get a fair deal from anyone who was even remotely affiliated with Moses, and he was already emotionally wedded to the idea of settling in Los Angeles. In May 1957, he was exposed to what he might gain in Los Angeles, and what was being offered was highly appealing.

If Moses had pushed hard to work with O'Malley early in the planning process, the outcome would have been radically different. However, to keep the Dodgers in Brooklyn by 1957, Moses would have had to have

Dodger Stadium, the home of the Los Angeles Dodgers since 1962 (National Baseball Hall of Fame Library, Cooperstown, New York).

9. The Brooklyn Dodgers, the Move to Los Angeles (Trumpbour)

acted in a conciliatory manner by making an attractive offer that would have satisfied the Dodger owner and by sharing power with someone whom he regarded as a lesser talent. But it was not in Moses' nature to share power, and it certainly was not in his nature to be conciliatory. As such, O'Malley had little choice but to head to California or someplace else in 1958 if his goal was to have control of his team and, over time, the ballpark which he had hoped to build.

The departure of the Dodgers would not be such a mystery if the New York media were not so consistently supportive of Robert Moses throughout the 1950s and so intensely determined to portray Walter O'Malley as a villain. In what was clearly an unintended consequence, New York's response to the Dodgers' departure endeared O'Malley to the citizens of southern California, much to the chagrin and distaste of New Yorkers. Although his move was a bumpy ride in the first few years, with high attendance but unexpected difficulties, including a referendum and lawsuit threats on the stadium-construction front, the Dodgers became a beloved fixture in Los Angeles.

Professional baseball eventually returned to Brooklyn many decades later. The Cyclones, an affiliate of the New York Mets, are a minor league team that plays its games in a Brooklyn-based, taxpayer-funded ballpark that was vigorously supported by New York politicians and built without delay and obstruction. And in a fitting endnote, the stadium that Moses designed and constructed after the Dodgers left town suffered much criticism and was replaced in 2009 by a new ballpark that looks very much like Ebbets Field. In contrast, the facility that was subsequently built in Los Angeles by O'Malley remains a California landmark to this day.

Notes

1. Matt Schudel, "Muckraking N.Y. Reporter Jack Newfield Dies at 66," *Washington Post*, December 23, 2004.

2. Mike McLaughlin, "Sympathy for THIS Devil? For O'Malley? Neva!" *Brooklyn Paper*, March 12, 2009. For the web version, see http://www.brooklynpaper.com/stories/32/10/32_10_mm_dodger_event.html.

3. Leonard Koppett, *Koppett's Concise History of Major League Baseball* (Philadelphia: Temple University Press, 1998), 136.

4. Carl E. Prince, *Brooklyn's Dodgers: The Bums, the Borough, and the Best of Baseball, 1947–1957* (New York: Oxford University Press, 1996), 103.

5. Ibid.

6. Some Boston Brave fans passionately vowed to boycott Milwaukee beer when the Braves left Boston. For an example of the anger that resulted when the Braves moved from Boston to Milwaukee and subsequently from Milwaukee to Atlanta, see Glen Gendzel, "Competitive Boosterism: How Milwaukee Lost the Braves," *The Business History Review* 69, no. 4 (Winter 1995): 559.

7. "Rickey Purchases Share in Dodgers," *New York Times*, November 2, 1944.

8. Letter from Walter O'Malley to Emil Prager [sic], Long Island City, New York, October 14, 1946. Walter O'Malley: The Official Website, Historic Documents, http://www.walteromalley.com.

9. "Dodgers Deny Field Plan," *New York Times*, March 16, 1948.

10. Ibid.

11. Ibid.

12. Letter from Emil Praeger to Walter O'Malley, March 18, 1948. Walter O'Malley: The Official Website, Historic Documents, http://www.walteromalley.com.

13. Ibid.

14. Peter Ellsworth, "The Brooklyn Dodgers Move to Los Angeles: Was Walter O'Malley Solely Responsible?" *Nine: A Journal of Baseball History and Culture* 14, no. 1 (2005): 20–21.

15. Letter from Walter O'Malley to Jim Thomson, Vice President, Allied Maintenance Company, New York, New York, April 12, 1955. Walter O'Malley: The Official Website, Historic Documents, http://www.walteromalley.com.

16. "New Ebbets Field to Have Hot Dogs and Hot Seats," *New York Times*, March 6, 1952.

17. Ibid.

18. Letter from Walter O'Malley to Frank Schroth, Brooklyn, New York, June 17, 1952. Walter O'Malley: The Official Website, Historic Documents, http://www.walteromalley.com.

19. Ibid.

20. Ibid.

21. John Drebinger, "Dodgers Consider Going to Coast for Spring Exhibitions in 1956," *New York Times*, November 20, 1954.

22. Letter from Walter O'Malley to George McLaughlin, Brooklyn, New York, June 18, 1953. Walter O'Malley: The Official Website, Historic Documents, http://www.walteromalley.com.

23. Ibid.

24. Ibid. O'Malley's citing of the precise number of parking spaces available in Milwaukee offers strong evidence of how important he perceived this feature as a future revenue enhancement for his team.

25. Ibid.

26. Robert A. Caro, *The Power Broker: Robert Moses and the Fall of New York* (New York: Alfred A. Knopf, 1974), 777.

27. Ibid.

28. Ellsworth, 28.

29. Caro, 779.

30. Letter from Walter O'Malley to Robert Moses, New York, New York, October 28, 1953. Walter O'Malley: The Official Website, Historic Documents, http://www.walteromalley.com.

31. Letter from Robert Moses to Walter O'Malley, Brooklyn, New York, November 2, 1953. Walter O'Malley: The Official Website, Historic Documents, http://www.walteromalley.com.

9. The Brooklyn Dodgers, the Move to Los Angeles (Trumpbour)

32. Ibid.
33. Ibid.
34. Letter from Walter O'Malley to Robert Moses, New York, New York, December 17, 1953. Walter O'Malley: The Official Website, Historic Documents, http://www.walteromalley.com.
35. Ibid.
36. Letter from Walter O'Malley to Robert Moses, New York, New York, April 1, 1954. Walter O'Malley: The Official Website, Historic Documents, http://www.walteromalley.com.
37. Letter from George Spargo to Walter O'Malley, Brooklyn, New York, April 7, 1954. Walter O'Malley: The Official Website, Historic Documents, http://www.walteromalley.com.
38. Letter from Walter O'Malley to Robert Moses, New York, New York, August 17, 1954. Walter O'Malley: The Official Website, Historic Documents, http://www.walteromalley.com.
39. Ibid.
40. Letter from George McLaughlin to Walter O'Malley, Brooklyn, New York, June 22, 1953. Walter O'Malley: The Official Website, Historic Documents, http://www.walteromalley.com.
41. Letter from Robert Moses to Walter O'Malley, Brooklyn, New York, June 22, 1953. Walter O'Malley: The Official Website, Historic Documents, http://www.walteromalley.com.
42. Letter from Robert Moses to Walter O'Malley, Brooklyn, New York, August 15, 1955. Walter O'Malley: The Official Website, Historic Documents, http://www.walteromalley.com.
43. Ibid. In the letter, Moses also suggested that O'Malley could sell the ballpark or the team as options.
44. Brooklyn National League Baseball Club, Press Release, Brooklyn, New York, August 17, 1955. Walter O'Malley: The Official Website, Historic Documents, http://www.walteromalley.com.
45. "Fans Are Frantic Over Game Shifts," *New York Times*, August 18, 1955.
46. Sydney Gruson, "O'Malley Is Fearful of a One-Team City," *New York Times*, August 20, 1955.
47. Ibid.
48. Ibid.
49. Ibid.
50. Letter from Walter O'Malley to Robert Moses, New York, New York, August 22, 1955. Walter O'Malley: The Official Website, Historic Documents, http://www.walteromalley.com.
51. Letter from Robert Moses to Walter O'Malley, Brooklyn, New York, August 25, 1955. Walter O'Malley: The Official Website, Historic Documents, http://www.walteromalley.com.
52. Letter from Walter Peterson to Walter O'Malley, Brooklyn, New York, August 22, 1955. Walter O'Malley: The Official Website, Historic Documents, http://www.walteromalley.com.
53. Ibid.
54. Letter from Rosalind Wyman to Walter O'Malley, Brooklyn, New York, September 1, 1955. Walter O'Malley: The Official Website, Historic Documents, http://www.walteromalley.com.
55. Letter from Walter O'Malley to Rosalind Wyman, Los Angeles, California, Sep-

tember 7, 1955. Walter O'Malley: The Official Website, Historic Documents, http://www.walteromalley.com.

56. Ibid.

57. Letter from Vincent Flaherty to Walter O'Malley, Brooklyn, New York, September 18, 1955. Walter O'Malley: The Official Website, Historic Documents, http://www.walteromalley.com.

58. Ibid.

59. Letter from Red Patterson to Vincent Flaherty, New York, New York, September 20, 1955. Walter O'Malley: The Official Website, Historic Documents, http://www.walteromalley.com.

60. "Study on to Find New Dodger Park," *New York Times*, November 2, 1955.

61. Roscoe McGowen, "Dodgers Will Play 7 League Games Plus Exhibition at Jersey City in 1956," *New York Times*, December 2, 1955.

62. Arthur Daley, "Sports of the Times," *New York Times*, December 4, 1955.

63. Ibid.

64. Letter from Walter O'Malley to Vincent Flaherty, Los Angeles, California, January 4, 1956. Walter O'Malley: The Official Website, Historic Documents, http://www.walteromalley.com.

65. "Cashmore Spurs New Ball Park; Mid-Brooklyn Plan Is Drafted," *New York Times*, January 12, 1956.

66. Letter from Robert Moses to City Editor, *New York Herald Tribune*, New York, New York, January 13, 1956. Walter O'Malley: The Official Website, Historic Documents, http://www.walteromalley.com.

67. Ibid.

68. Brooklyn National League Baseball Club, Minutes of a Special Meeting of Stockholders, Brooklyn, New York, January 16, 1956. Walter O'Malley: The Official Website, Historic Documents, http://www.walteromalley.com.

69. "Dodgers Endorse Sports Authority," *New York Times*, February 7, 1956.

70. Arthur Daley, "Sports of the Times," *New York Times*, February 9, 1956.

71. "2 Brooklyn Units Back Sports Plan," *New York Times*, March 9, 1956.

72. Letter from Walter O'Malley to Robert Moses, New York, New York, April 11, 1956. Walter O'Malley: The Official Website, Historic Documents, http://www.walteromalley.com.

73. Letter from Robert Moses to Walter O'Malley, Brooklyn, New York, April 12, 1956. Walter O'Malley: The Official Website, Historic Documents, http://www.walteromalley.com.

74. For a detailed description of the intricate financial issues related to O'Malley's project, see Ellsworth, 31–35.

75. Walter H. Stern, "Wide Plans Made for Ebbets Field," *New York Times*, November 4, 1956.

76. Letter from Robert Moses to Walter O'Malley, Brooklyn, New York, December 6, 1956. Walter O'Malley: The Official Website, Historic Documents, http://www.walteromalley.com.

77. Letter from Walter O'Malley to John Cashmore, Brooklyn, New York, December 7, 1956. Walter O'Malley: The Official Website, Historic Documents, http://www.walteromalley.com.

78. "Housing Favored if Sport Site Fails," *New York Times*, December 24, 1956.

79. Charles. G. Bennett, "$125,000 Allotted Brooklyn Survey," *New York Times*, December 29, 1956.

80. "Dodgers Get Plan for Site in Queens," *New York Times*, April 19, 1957.

9. The Brooklyn Dodgers, the Move to Los Angeles (Trumpbour)

81. Walter O'Malley, File Memorandum of Meeting between Robert Moses and Walter O'Malley in Babylon, New York, April 11, 1957. Walter O'Malley: The Official Website, Historic Documents, http://www.walteromalley.com.
82. Michael Shapiro, *The Last Good Season: Brooklyn, the Dodgers, and Their Final Pennant Race Together* (New York: Doubleday, 2003), 321.
83. Ibid.
84. Ibid.
85. Letter from Walter O'Malley to Frank Schroth, Brooklyn, New York, March 26. 1957. Walter O'Malley: The Official Website, Historic Documents, http://www.walteromalley.com.
86. Neil J. Sullivan, *The Dodgers Move West* (New York: Oxford University Press, 1987), 52.
87. Shapiro, 317.
88. Kevin Starr, *Golden Dreams: California in an Age of Abundance, 1950–1963* (New York: Oxford University Press, 2009), 227.
89. George Lipsitz, "Sports Stadia and Urban Development: A Tale of Three Cities," *Journal of Sport and Social Issues* 8, no. 2 (1984): 7.
90. Red Smith, "Sports of The Times," *New York Times*, August 5, 1981.
91. Letter from Walter O'Malley to Joseph T. Sharkey, New York, New York, January 17, 1957. Walter O'Malley: The Official Website, Historic Documents, http://www.walteromalley.com.
92. "Dodger Lawyer Hits Bill," *New York Times*, March 17, 1950.
93. Shapiro, 316.
94. Sullivan, 53.
95. Robert Moses, "Robert Moses on the Battle of Brooklyn," *Sports Illustrated*, July 22, 1957, 26.
96. Ibid., 27.
97. Ibid.
98. Ibid.
99. Ibid., 28.
100. Ibid., 46.
101. Ibid.
102. Ibid., 48.
103. Ibid., 49.
104. "The 'Unique' Bob Moses," *New York Times*, July 29, 1957.
105. Ibid.
106. Telegram from George Christopher to Norris Poulson, Los Angeles, California, March 2, 1957. Walter O'Malley: The Official Website, Historic Documents, http://www.walteromalley.com.
107. Letter from Kenneth Hahn to Walter O'Malley, Brooklyn, New York, May 3, 1957. Walter O'Malley: The Official Website, Historic Documents, http://www.walteromalley.com, and "Kenneth F. Hahn, 77, Is Dead; Political Giant in Los Angeles," *New York Times*, October 14, 1997.
108. Letter from Kenneth Hahn to Walter O'Malley, Los Angeles, California, September 7, 1962. Walter O'Malley: The Official Website, Historic Documents, http://www.walteromalley.com.
109. Letter from Walter O'Malley to Frank Schroth, Brooklyn, New York, June 17, 1952. Walter O'Malley: The Official Website, Historic Documents, http://www.walteromalley.com.

Editors and Contributors

Dennis H. Auger is a clinical supervisor at an outpatient substance abuse agency and a member of the Society for American Baseball Research. He has written several articles covering baseball during the 1893–1919 era.

The late **Gene Carney** was the writer and editor of *Notes from the Shadows of Cooperstown* and the leading scholar on the Black Sox scandal at the time of his death in 2009. A former member of the Society for American Baseball Research, his most famous publication is *Burying the Black Sox: How Baseball's Cover-Up of the 1919 World Series Fix Almost Succeeded* (Potomac, 2006), which received the Larry Ritter Award and was a finalist for the Dave Moore Award.

Jerrold Casway, a professor of history, is the chairperson of the Social Sciences Division at Howard Community College in Columbia, Maryland, and a member of the Society for American Baseball Research. He has written widely on early modern British history and 19th-century baseball and is the author of two award-winning books, the second being *Ed Delahanty in the Emerald Age of Baseball* (University of Notre Dame Press, 2006).

David Cicotello is a member of the Society for American Baseball Research and a contributor to its *Deadball Stars* volumes. Along with Angelo J. Louisa, he edited *Forbes Field: Essays and Memories of the Pirates' Historic Ballpark, 1909–1971* (McFarland, 2007). A student affairs administrator at Middle Tennessee State University, he lives in Murfreesboro, Tennessee.

Timothy M. Gay is a writer, historian, and member of the Society for American Baseball Research who lives in Vienna, Virginia. His articles have appeared in the *Washington Post,* the *Boston Globe,* and many other publications, and his first book, *Tris Speaker: The Rough-and-Tumble Life of a Baseball Legend* (University of Nebraska Press, 2005; paperback, Lyons, 2007), was a finalist for both the Seymour Medal and the Larry Ritter Award.

The late **Daniel E. Ginsburg** was part owner of the Class AA Norwich Navigators and the majority owner of Champagne de Meric, the only American-owned winery in Champagne. One of the founders of the Society for American Baseball Research,

Editors and Contributors

he is the author of *The Fix Is In: A History of Baseball Gambling and Game Fixing Scandals* (McFarland, 1995; paperback 2004).

Angelo J. Louisa is a researcher, writer, and community educator who lives in Omaha, Nebraska. A member of the Society for American Baseball Research, he has contributed articles to books, periodicals, and websites and is, along with David Cicotello, the editor of *Forbes Field: Essays and Memories of the Pirates' Historic Ballpark, 1909–1971* (McFarland, 2007).

David C. Ogden is an associate professor in the School of Communication at the University of Nebraska at Omaha. A specialist on the relationship between African American communities and baseball, he has published articles in various journals and is the co-editor of *Reconstructing Fame: Sport, Race, and Evolving Reputations* (University Press of Mississippi, 2008).

Floyd Sullivan is the author of *Waiting for the Cubs: The 2008 Season, a Hundred-Year Slump, and One Fan's Lifelong Vigil* (McFarland, 2010). A Chicago native, Mr. Sullivan has a degree in history from the University of Illinois at Chicago and is a member of the Society for American Baseball Research.

Robert Trumpbour, an associate professor of communications at Pennsylvania State University's Altoona College, is the author of *The New Cathedrals: Politics and Media in the History of Stadium Construction* (Syracuse University Press, 2006) and the co-editor of *The Rise of Stadiums in the Modern United States: Cathedrals of Sport* (Routledge, 2009).

Index

Numbers in **_bold italics_** indicate pages with photographs.

The ABC Monday Mystery Movie 11n9
The ABC Saturday Mystery Movie see The ABC Monday Mystery Movie
Abrams, Al 77, 79
Abrams, Charles 157
Alberts, James (Cozy Dolan) 108, 110, 111, 112, **_112_**, 113, 114, 116, 117, 118
Alexander, Charles C. 64
Alexander, Grover Cleveland "Pete" or "Alex" or "Alex the Great" 4, 76, 77, 78, 79, 80, **_80_**, 81, 82, 83, 84, 85, 86
Ali, Muhammad 136
Alter, Peter 106n8, 106n9
American Association 70
American League (AL) 2, 13, 35, 46, 97, 104, 105, 108, 121, 123, 125, 131, 132
Anghelescu, Judy 10–11n3
Asinof, Eliot 90, 93, 94, 100, 105, 106n9, 107n33
Atlanta, Georgia 150, 180n6
Atlanta Constitution 45
Atlantic Avenue 159, 165, 175
Attell, Abe 104
Auger, Dennis H. 2, 29, 185
Austrian, Alfred 100, 101

Baker Bowl 82
Baltimore Orioles 1
Bankhead, Samuel "Sam" 143, 144
Barnhart, Clyde 77, 81, 82, 83, **_83_**, 85
Barrymore, Lionel 173
Baseball 139
Baseball: A Comprehensive Bibliography 5
Baseball: The Golden Age 126
Baseball: An Illustrated History 139
Baseball and American Culture: Across the Diamond 8
Baseball Digest 34
Baseball in the Afternoon 123
Baseball Magazine 117

Baseball Mysteries 6
Baseball Writers Association of America 47
Bel Geddes, Norman 152, 154
Benevolent Order of Elks 32
Benjamin, Jerry 144
Benton, Rube 85
Bergen, Marty 2
Bermuda Triangle 9
Beston, Greg 133
Bird, Larry 136
Black Rock Station, New York 19
Black Sox *see* Chicago White Sox
Blaisdell, Lowell D. 84, 145
Boeckel, Tony 85, 86
Boston, Massachusetts 32, 36, 150, 155, 180n6
Boston Americans *see* Boston Red Sox
Boston Braves 108, 110, 150, 155, 180n6
Boston Doves *see* Boston Braves
Boston Globe 98
Boston Post 33
Boston Red Sox 29, 33–34, 41–42n4, 100, 127, 128
Bowman, John 35
Boyd, William H. 129
Brady, Thomas 44, 70
Bresnahan, Roger 58
Bridwell, Al 48
Broadway (New York City) 44, 47, 63
Brooklyn, New York 57, 63, 149, 150, 151, 152, 156, 157, 158, 161, 163, 165, 166, 167, 168, 169, 171, 172, 173, 174, 175, 177, 178, 179
Brooklyn Club 161
Brooklyn Dodgers 9, 108, 110, 113, 149, 150, 151, 152, 153, 154, 155, 157, 159, 161, 162, 163, 164, 166, 167, 168, 169, 170, 171, 172, 173, 174, 175, 177, 178, 179
Brooklyn Dodgers: The Bums, the Borough, and the Best of Baseball 150

187

Index

Brooklyn Eagle 155, 177
Brooklyn Historical Society 149
Brooklyn Trust Company 155
Brothers, George 116
Brown, Rachel 105
Brown, Ray 143
Bruce, John E. *45*
Brush, John 14, 16, 23, 27*n*25, 48, 51, 52, *52*, 53, 54, 55, 56, 58, 59, 60, 61, 62, 63, 64, 68, 69, 71, 72–73*n*30
Buffalo, New York 17, 18, 21, 23, 25, 30
Burke, Edward S. 129
Burns, Bill 105, 107*n*40
Burns, Ken 139, 141, 142, 145

Cain, George W. 67
Cain, Grace Pulliam 50
Calvary Cemetery 25
Capra, Frank 173
Carey, Max 85, 86
Carney, Gene 4, 90, 106*n*9, 185
Caro, Robert 156, 157
Cashmore, John 158, 160, 163, 164, 165, 168, 170
Casway, Jerrold 2, 13, 185
Cavanaugh, Joanne Ferguson 10–11*n*3
Caylor, Lenore 70
Caylor, O.P. 70
Chase, Hal 105, 118
Chattanooga Black Lookouts 137
Chavez Ravine 167, 177
Chicago, Illinois 33, 34, 62, 67, 68, 95, 111, 118, 124, 128, 154, 170
Chicago Automobile Club 61
Chicago City Series 96
Chicago Cubs 48, 49, 50, 79, 82, 85, 96, 100, 101, 113
Chicago Daily Tribune 45, 57, 58
Chicago Sunday Tribune 59
Chicago White Sox 1, 92, 93, 94, 95, 96, 97, 98, 100, 101, 102, 104, 106*n*13, 107*n*40, 110, 114, 117, 122, 123, 127, 128, 131, 133
Chinatown 8
Chippawa Channel 25
Christopher, George 177
Cicotello, David 2, 4, 5, 76, 185
Cicotello, Louis *6*
Cicotte, Edward Victor "Eddie" or "Knuckles" *6–7*, 90, *91*, 92, 93, 94, 95, 96, 97, 98, 99, 100, 101, 102, 104, 105, 106*n*14, 106*n*21, 107*n*40
Cincinnati, Ohio 14, 67, 69, 86, 98, 118
Cincinnati Commercial Gazette 121
Cincinnati Enquirer 45, 68, 69
Cincinnati Reds 86, 94, 95, 97, 98
Clark, John 147*n*13

Clarke, Fred 29
Clarkson, Bus 147*n*13
Cleveland, Ohio 15, 16, 21, 22, 25, 125, 126, 129
Cleveland Indians 95, 96, 97, 123, 126, 130, 132, 137
Cleveland Spiders 1
Cobb, Tyrus Raymond "Ty" or "The Georgia Peach" 2, 4, *6–7*, 29, 77, 110, 122, 123, 124, 125, 126, 127, 128, 129, 130, 131, 132, *132*, 133, 134
Cold War 170
Cole, John 17, 20, 21
Collins, Eddie 128
Collins, Jimmy 29, 30, 31, *31*
Collins, Shano 98
Columbo 11*n*9
Comiskey, Charles 61, 71*n*7, 92, 93, 96, 100, 102, *103*, 104, 128
The Complete Boston Red Sox 33
Conner, Floyd 33
Connors, Jimmy 136
Cook County, Illinois 95
Cooper, Arley Wilbur *6–7*, 76, 77, 78, *78*, 79, 80, 81, 82, 83, 84, 85, 86, 87*n*10
Copper Frontier League 118
Cornell University 34
County Stadium, Milwaukee *see* Milwaukee County Stadium
Cratty, A.R. 50, 67, 69
Crawford, Sam 29
Creamer, Joseph 50, 51, 52, 53, 54, 55, 56, 57, 58, 59, 61, 62, 63, 64, 65, 66, 72*n*27, 72–73*n*30
Criger, Lou 30
Cutshaw, George 86

Daley, Arthur 163, 164
Danna, Theresa M. 8
Dash, Mike 51, 63
Davis, Fred 145
Davis, George 15, *15*, 16, 17, 23
Day, Leon 147*n*13
Deadball Era 78, 80, 87*n*12
Deadball Stars of the National League 76, 81
Dean, Dizzy 137
Delahanty, Bridget Croke 16, 17, 21
Delahanty, Edward James "Del" or "King of Swatsville" 2, *6–7*, 13, 14, *14*, 15, 16, 17, 18, 19, 20, 21, 22, 23, 24, 25, 26, 27*n*25
Delahanty, Frank 21
Delahanty, Norine 15, 16, 25, 26
DeMille, Cecil B. 120
Detroit, Michigan 16, 17, 21, 22, 23, 98, 105, 123, 125, 129

188

Index

Detroit Tigers 108, 123, 124, 125, 126, 127, 128, 129
DeValeria, Dennis 66, 67
DeValeria, Jeanne Burke 66, 67
Devery, Bill 63
Diamonds in the Rough 35
Doak, Bill 86
Dodger Field 159, 164
Dodger Stadium 158, **178**, 179
Dodgers Field *see* Dodger Field
Dolan, Cozy *see* Alberts, James
Dolan, Harry 39
Dovey, George 61, 62, 67, 69
Doyle, Charles J. "Chilly" 79, 86
Dreyfuss, Barney 48, 64, 79, 113
Drummonville, Ontario 25
Dubuc, Jean 110
Duncan, Frank 140
Dunn, Edith 131
Durham, Israel 69

Earhart, Amelia 9
East-West Games 143
Easterling, Howard 140, 142, 143, 144
Ebbets, Charles 50, 52, 54, 55, 56, 57, 58, 60, 61, 68, 171
Ebbets Field **6-7**, 151, 152, 153, **154**, 155, 156, 165, 166, 171, 179
Eckstut, Arielle 141
Eight Men Out 90, 93, 94, 100, 105, 106n9, 107n33
Eller, Hod 95
Ellsworth, Peter 153, 157
Emslie, Bob 49
Evers, Johnny 49

Faber, Red 94, 95, 98
Fallon, William J. 65, 116
The Falls from Prospect Park **3**
Farrell, Father E.J. 37
Farrell, Frank 63
Federal League 120
Felsch, Oscar "Happy" 92, 94, 96, 97, 99, 101, 104, 106n8, 106n9, 128
Ferris, Hobe 30
Feuchtwanger, Henry 67
Field of Dreams 1
Flaherty, Vincent 162, 163
Flatbush Avenue 159
Fleming, Bruce 81, 84
Fletcher, Art 110, 111
Floyd, Frank "Jewbaby" 140, 141, **141**, 142
Flushing Meadows, New York 157, 166
Forbes Field 69, 76, 77, 81, 82, 85, 86, 139, 142

Forr, James 84
Fort Erie, Ontario 17
Fort Greene, New York 156
Fort Wayne, Indiana 32, 33, 36, 38, 40
Fort Wayne *Journal Gazette* 36, 38
Fort Worth, Texas 167, 172
Francis, Bill 72n23
Franklin, Ben 104
Fraternal Order of Eagles 32, 77
Frazier, Joe 136
Fresno, California 129, 134
Frisch, Frank 110, 111, 112, 113, 114, 118
Fuller, R. Buckminster 164

Gandil, Arnold "Chick" 97, 98, **98**, 102, 118, 128, 134
Gay, Timothy M. 4, 120, 185
Gedeon, Joe 110
Gentile, Derek 29, 33
Geometric Stamping Co. 126
Gibson, George 85
Gibson, Joshua "Josh" or "The Black Babe Ruth" or "The Bronze Bambino" **6-7**, 136, 137, **138**, 139, 140, 141, 142, 143, 144, 145, 146, 147n13
Ginsburg, Daniel E. 4, 108, 185
Gleason, Kid 93, 95, 102
The Glory of Their Times 130
Grand Island, New York 25
Grand Trunk Railway Company 20, 21
Griffith Stadium 144
Grimm, Charlie 77, 79

Hahn, Kenneth 177
Hamill, Pete 149
Hanlon, Ned 1
Haring, Father Bernard 39-40
Harmon, Julia 30, 31, 32, 33, 35, 36, 37, 39
Harris, Vic 143
Hart, James 71n7
Hayden, Jack 30
Heitz, Thomas R. 5
Herrmann, August "Garry" 23, **45**, 52, 54, 56, 57, 58, 60, 61, 67, 68, 71n7
Heydler, John 51, 52, 58, 62, 68, 73n33, 102, 104, 111, 116
Higgins, J.J. 45, 46
Higham, Richard 1
Hillerman, Tony 8
Hinchman, Bill 85
History and Records of Base Ball 29
History Channel 9
Hittner, Arthur D. 46
Hofman, Art 49
Hoie, Bob 93

189

Index

Homestead Grays 139, 140, 142, 143, 144, 147n13
Honolulu, Hawaii 67
Honus Wagner: A Biography 66
Horseshoe Falls *see* Niagara Falls
Hot Springs, Arkansas 30

Immaculate Conception Church 25
International Bridge *18*, *19*, 20, 22, 23, 27n23
It's a Wonderful Life 173

Jack the Ripper 9
Jackson, Joe "Shoeless Joe" 1, 94, 95, 96, 97, 100, 102, 104, 107n40, 122
James, Bill 29, 76
James, P.D. 8
Jansenism 39
Jersey City, New Jersey 161, 163, 173
Johnson, Byron Bancroft "Ban" 9, *45*, 58, 71n7, 96, 102, 104, 105, 113, 116, 120, 121, 122, *122*, 123, 125, 126, 127, 129, 130, 131, 132, 133, 134
Johnson, Magic 136
Johnstone, Jimmy 51, 52, 54, 55, 56, 57, 59, 73n33

Kansas City Athletics 137
Kansas City Monarchs 139, 140, 143, 144, 147n13
Keeler, Willie 29
Kelly, George 110, 111, 112, 113, 114, 118
Kennedy, John F. 9
Kerr, Dickie 94, 95
Killilea, Henry 71n7, 125
Kincannon, Harry 144
King, Lee 85
King of Swatsville *see* Delahanty, Edward James
Kingston, Samuel 18, 20, 21, 22, 23, 24
Kinsella, W.P. 1
Klem, Bill 50, 51, 52, 53, 54, 55, 56, 57, 59, 63, 64, 65, 66, 72n27, 72–73n30
Knowles, Fred 53
Koppett, Leonard 150
Korean War 170
Krattner, Marvin 165

Landis, Kenesaw Mountain 9–10, *10*, 102, 104, *104*, 111, 112, 113, 116, 117, 120, *121*, 122, 125, 127, 128, 129, 130, 131, 132, 133, 135, 135n1
Lane, Frank 117
Lardner, Ring 90
Lavender, Jimmy 85
Leach, Tommy 86

Legends as an Expression of Baseball Memory 84
Leonard, Buck 140, 142, 143, 144
Leonard, Hubert "Dutch" 122, 123, 124, 125, 126, 127, 128, 129, 130, 133, 134, *134*
Levi, Louis 104
Lieb, Fred 133
Lindenwood Cemetery 32
Lion's Head Bar 149
Little Rock, Arkansas 31, 34, 39
Logan, Thomas 60, 61, 68
Lone Star 8
Long Island, New York 153, 157, 169
Long Island Railroad 159
Los Angeles, California 9, 60, 149, 150, 151, 152, 158, 162, 166, 167, 168, 169, 170, 171, 172, 173, 174, 176, 177, 178, 179
Los Angeles County, California 170
Los Angeles Examiner 162, 163
Los Angeles Times 45, 60
Louisa, Angelo J. 2, 5, 44, 186
Louisa, Pamela 72–73n30
Louisville, Kentucky 1, 31, 61, 66, 67
Luhrs, Victor 100
Luque, Dolf 86

Machiavelli 173
Magee, Lee 105
Maharg, Billy 96, 105, 107n40
Malamud, Bernard 1
The Maltese Falcon 8
Manhattan, New York 23, 63, 149, 157
Maranville, Rabbit 77, 79
Marcaccio, Vincent 43n47, 43n51
Masterpiece 8
Masterpiece Theatre 8
Mathewson, Christy 58
McCormick, Moose 48, 49
McCue, Andy 10–11n3
McDonald, Charles 99, 100
McEnroe, John 136
McGinnity, Joe 49
McGivney, Father Michael 39
McGraw, John 9, 13, 14, 16, 17, 18, 23, 48, 51, 53, 54, 58, 59, 62, 64, *64*, 65, 71, 110, 111, 112, 113, 116, 117, 118
McGrath, Mr. 35
McLaughlan, Hugh 63
McLaughlin, George 155, 156, 159
McLaughlin, Hugh *see* McLaughlan, Hugh
McMullen, "Red" *see* McMullin, Fred
McMullin, Fred 97, 98, 104
Mercer, George 22, 27n22
Merkle, Fred 48, 49, 58, 63, 65
Michigan Central Railroad 20, 25
Michigan Central train #6 17, 18, 23

190

Index

Miller, Mike 77, 82
Milligan, Bernie 77
Milwaukee, Wisconsin 150, 155, 156, 169, 180n6
Milwaukee Braves 155, 169
Milwaukee County Stadium 153, 155, 164, 180n24
Minneapolis, Minnesota 176
Mobile, Alabama 26
Mobile Tigers 147n2
Mollwitz, Fritz 86
Moses, Robert "Bob" 152, 153, 155, 156, 157, *157*, 158, 159, 160, 161, 162, 163, 164, 165, 166, 167, 168, 169, 170, 171, 172, 173, 175, 176, 177, 178, 179
Murder on the Orient Express 8
Murder, She Wrote 11n9
Murfin, James O. 129
Murphy, Charles 53, 68, 69
Murphy, David 40
Murphy, Lawrence 173
My Life in Baseball 131
Mystery! 8

National Baseball Hall of Fame Library 76
National Commission *45*, 58, 68
National League (NL) 1, 14, 41–42n4, 46, 47, 48, 49, 51, 52, 54, 55, 56, 60, 61, 67, 68, 108, 121, 155, 161
The Natural 1
Navin, Frank 125, 126, 128, 131, 134
Navin Field 123
Navy Island, Ontario 25
The NBC Mystery Movie 11n9
The NBC Sunday Mystery Movie see *The NBC Mystery Movie*
NCIS 8
Negro Leagues 4, 136, 139, 146, 147
New Jersey 161, 163, 169
New York Athletic Club 44
New York Board of Estimate 159, 160, 165, 166, 168, 170
New York City, New York 14, 15, 17, 18, 23, 44, 46, 47, 48, 51, 56, 62, 65, 66, 97, 111, 114, 149, 151, 152, 153, 155, 157–158, 160, 161, 162, 163, 164, 165, 166, 167, 168, 169, 171, 172, 173, 174, 175, 176, 177, 179
New York Committee on Slum Clearance 156, 159
New York Cyclones 179
New York Daily News 168
New York Evening Journal 59
New York Giants 13, 14, 15, 16, 17, 23, 41–42n4, 47, 48, 49, 50, 51, 52, 58–59, 63, 65, 86, 92, 108, 110–111, 113, 114, 116, 117, 162, 169

New York Herald Tribune 164
New York Highlanders 63
New York Mets 179
New York Mutuals 1
New York Police Department 70
New York State 55
New York State Assembly 173
New York State Gambling Commission 63
New York State League 21
New York Times 45, 57, 63, 86, 124, 127, 134, 161, 176
New York Yankees 108, 126
Newfield, Jack 149
Niagara Falls 2, *3*, 13, 21, 22, 25
Niagara Falls, Ontario *see* Drummonville, Ontario
Niagara River 17, 19, 21, 24, 25
Nicoll, DeLancey 55, 57
1918 World Series 100, 101
1918 World's Series *see* 1918 World Series
1955 World Series 160
1942 Negro League World Series 139, 140, 142, 143, 144, 145, 147n13
1919 World Series 65, 90, 93, 94, 95–96, 101, 102, 105, 107n33, 122, 134
1920 World Series 97, 102, 104
1924 World Series 110–111, 113, 114

O'Connell, Frederick 33, 34, 35, 39, 40
O'Connell, James Joseph "Jimmy" *6–7*, 108, *109*, 110, 111, 112, 113, 114, 116, 117, 118
O'Day, Hank 49
Ogden, David C. 4, 136, 186
O'Malley, Peter 149
O'Malley, Walter Francis *6–7*, 149, 150, 151, 152, 153, 154, 155, 156, 157, 158, 159, 160, 161, 162, 163, 164, 165, 166, 167, 168, 169, 170, 171, 172, 173, *173*, 174, 175, 176, 177, 178, 179, 180n24
O'Neil, John "Buck" 139, 140, 141, 142, 144, 145, 146, *146*
Organized Baseball 46, 59, 62, 120
Ortman, Lulu 33, 37, 38
Owens, Clarence 68

Pacific Coast League 110, 114, 123
Paige, Leroy Robert "Satch" or "Satchel" *6–7*, 136, 137, *137*, 139, 140, 141, 142, 143, 144, 145, 146, 147n2, 147n13
Partlow, Lefty 143
Patterson, Red 162, 163
Pawtucket *Evening Times* 35
Pearson, Len 147n13
Peters, Ellis 8
Peterson, Robert 139
Peterson, Walter 162

Index

Phelon, W.A. 67
Philadelphia, Pennsylvania 80, 139, 154
Philadelphia Phillies 1, 14, 58, 65, 77, 82, 85, 108, 110, 118
Pittsburgh, Pennsylvania 46, 48, 66, 77, 84, 139, 154
Pittsburgh Courier 142, 143, 144, 147n13
Pittsburgh Crawfords 136, 139, 144
Pittsburgh Pirates 48, 69, 77, 79, 82, 83, 85, 86, 108, 132
Pittsburgh Post 86
Pittsburgh Post-Gazette 142, 143
Pittsburgh Press 142, 143
Plimpton, George 8
Polo Grounds 48, 49, 85, 86, 155
Postal, Fred 23
Potter, Henry 173
Poulson, Norris 162, 177
Praeger, Emil 152, 158
Price, Elizabeth 72n23, 72–73n30
Prince, Carl 150
Princes in the Tower 9
ProQuest 82
Psych 8
Pulliam, Harry Clay "Haberdashery Harry" 2, **6–7**, 16, 44, 45, **45**, 46, 47, 48, 49, 50, 51, 52, 53, 54, 56, 57, 58, 59, 60, 61, 62, 63, 64, 65, 66, 67, 68, 69, 70, 71

Queens, New York 157, 166, 167, 168, 170, 175, 178

Ragan, Don Carlos "Pat" 114, **115**, 117
Rariden, Bill 86
Rath, Morrie 98, 99, 101
The Reach Guide 92
Rear Window 8
Red Sox Journal 33
Redland Field 86
Reilly, Edward J. 8
Retrosheet 81, 82, 84, 88n33
Ribowsky, Mark 136, 139, 142, 143, 144
Richland Oil Company 118
Richter, Francis C. 29, 59, 67, 69
Ring, Jimmy 95
Risberg, Charles "Swede" 94, 99, 101, 104, 118, 127, 128, 129
Ritter, Lawrence 58, 129, 130
Rixey, Eppa 85
Roanoke colony 9
Robinson, John R. 16
Robison, Frank 71n7
Rogosin, Donn 140, 142
Roman Universal Inquisition 39–40
Roosevelt, Franklin Delano 176
Rose, Pete 134

Rothstein, Arnold 65, 105, 116
Roush, Edd 77
Rowdyism 46, 64
Runyon, Damon 123, 134
Russell, Mr. 67
Ruth, George Herman "Babe" 97, 139, 176
Ryan, Father F.J. 39
Ryan, Jimmy 16

St. Francis De Sales Church 30
St. Louis, Missouri 61, 67, 154
St. Louis Browns 137
St. Louis Cardinals 86
St. Louis Dispatch 102
San Francisco, California 118, 177
San Francisco Seals 110
Sand, John "Heinie" 110, 111, 114, **116**, 117, 118
Satan's Circus: Murder, Vice, Police Corruption, and New York's Trial of the Century 63
Schalk, Ray 95, 128
Schmidt, Walter 79
Schmitz, Andrew 151
Schneider, Mr. and Mrs. 36
Schroth, Frank 155, 168, 177
Schupp, Ferdie 85
Scrooge 173
Seaton, Tom 118
Sell, Jack 142
Seymour, Harold and Dorothy 34, 96, 126
Shakespeare, William 47, 90
Shannon, Mike 107n33
Shapiro, Michael 174
Sharkey, Joseph 172
Shoeless Joe 1
Shrady, George 45, 46
Skaitron 169
Skipper, John 80, 83, 84, 86
Small Ball Theory 8
Smith, Hilton 143
Smith, Myron J., Jr. 5
Smith, Robert 123, 133
Snyder, John 33, 37
Somers, Charles 71n7
Soos, Troy 1, 4
Southworth, Billy 86
Spargo, George 158, 164
Speaker, Tristram E. "Tris" or "The Gray Eagle" or "Spoke" 4, **6–7**, 29, 122, 123, 125, 126, 127, 128, 129, 130, 131, 132, **132**, 133, 134
Sporting Life 16, 29, 30, 35, 59, 60, 67, 68, 69
The Sporting News 23, 47, 60, 92
Sports Illustrated 175

Index

Squaw Island, New York 25
Stahl, Charles Sylvester "Chick" 2, **6–7**, 29, 30, **30**, 31, 32, 33, 34, 35, 36, 37, 38, 39, 40, 41
Stahl, Julia Harmon *see* Harmon, Julia
Stanage, Oscar 128
Sterry, David 141
Stevens, Harry 55, 57
Stone, Ed 147n13
Stoneham, Charles 111, 113
Stoneham, Horace 176
Stout, Glenn 33, 34, 36, 133
Stump, Al 34
Sullivan, Floyd 2, 44, 106n12, 186
Sullivan, Joseph J. "Sport" 104
Sullivan, Lucy 106n12
Sullivan, Neil 174
Sullivan, Timothy "Big Tim" 51, 52, 55, 56, 57, 58, 59, 62, **62**, 63, 65, 66, 71, 72–73n30
Sullivan, Timothy "Little Tim" 51, 52, 55, 56, 57, 58, 59, 61, 62, 63, 65, 66, 71, 72–73n30
Syracuse Stars 21, 80

Tammany Hall, New York 1, 51, 55, 56, 57, 58–59, 61, 65, 66
Taylor, John 30
Teapot Dome 122
Tebeau, Patsy 1
Thompson, Richard J. "Dick" 38, 40, **41**
Tingstad, Marlyce "Candy" 72n24, 72n26
Title I of the National Housing Act 156, 164
Tonawanda, New York 21
Toney, Fred 86
Toronto, Ontario 26
Traynor, Harold "Pie" 77, **77**, 81, 82, 83, 84, 85, 86
Triborough Bridge and Tunnel Authority 152, 155, 158
Trumpbour, Robert 4, 149, 186
Tweed, Boss 1
Tygiel, Jules 10n1

University of Notre Dame 130
Unsolved Mysteries 11n9

Van Nuys, California 77
Voigt, David Quentin 5, 34
Volstead Act 65

Wagner, Bill 85
Wagner, Honus 77
Wagner, Robert 159, 161, 163, 170, 171, 172. 173
Waitkus, Eddie 1
Waldorf-Astoria Hotel 47
Wall Street, New York City 155
Ward, Geoffrey 139, 141, 142
Warner Hotel 97, 101
Washington, Chester L. 143, 144, 145
Washington, D.C. 13, 14, 22, 23, 144
Washington Nationals 13, 14, 15, 16, 17, 23, 38, 108, 110–111, 114
Washington Post 23, 126
Washington Senators *see* Washington Nationals
Weaver, George "Buck" 98, 104
West, Fred 123, 124, 127
West Baden, Indiana 31
West Baden Springs Hotel **32**
Wiles, Tim 75n119
Williams, Chester 144
Williams, Lefty 94, 95, 97, 98, 104, 118
Wood, Smoky Joe 123, 124, 125, 127, 129, 130, 133, 134
Woodruff, Harvey 57, 58
World Series 102
World War II 169
Wray, John 102
Wrigley Field 82
Wyman, Rosalind 162, 167, 171

Yale University 125
Yankee Stadium 139, 154, 155
Yde, Emil 114
Young, Pep *see* Youngs, Ross
Youngs, Ross 110, 111, 112, 113, 118

Zeisler, D.A. *see* Zelcer, David
Zelcer, David 104
Zelizer, Barbie 145
Zork, Carl 104
Zoss, Joel 35

193

www.ingramcontent.com/pod-product-compliance
Ingram Content Group UK Ltd.
Pitfield, Milton Keynes, MK11 3LW, UK
UKHW042009140426
5217IPUK00015B/1065